Pieces of the Musical World

In *Pieces of the Musical World: Sounds and Cultures*, each "piece" is a musical sound or object that provides a springboard from which to tell a story about a particular geographic region. A collaborative venture by staff and research associates of the Department of Music at SOAS, University of London, the text provides in-depth introductions to key aspects of the cultures in which these musical "pieces" are embedded, the contexts of performance, the musicians who create or perform them, the journeys they have taken, and their evolving meanings and connotations.

Organized thematically, with an emphasis on the role of field research, each of the book's 14 chapters highlights a single musical "piece" broadly defined, spanning the range of "traditional," "popular," "classical," and "contemporary" musics, and even sounds that might be considered "not music," and in the process, explores topics of interest to the discipline of ethnomusicology, including music and environment, digital mediation, globalization and diaspora, politics, among others.

With the inclusion of primary sources and an interactive companion website that features audio and video recordings, listening guides, a glossary of musical terms, and maps, this unique and dynamic textbook creates for students a complete and enhanced experience of the musical world.

Rachel Harris is Reader in the Music of China and Central Asia at SOAS, University of London. She is the author of two books on musical life in China's Xinjiang Uyghur Autonomous Region, and leader of the research project "Sounding Islam in China."

Rowan Pease is Editorial Manager of the *China Quarterly* and was a Senior Teaching Fellow for the Department of Music, SOAS, University of London. She has published several chapters on music of the Chinese Koreans and also on the Korean Wave in China.

Pieces of the Musical World
Sounds and Cultures

Edited by
*Rachel Harris and
Rowan Pease*

SOAS, University of London

Routledge
Taylor & Francis Group

NEW YORK AND LONDON

First published 2015
by Routledge
711 Third Avenue, New York, NY 10017

and by Routledge
2 Park Square, Milton Park, Abingdon, Oxon OX14 4RN

Routledge is an imprint of the Taylor & Francis Group, an informa business

© 2015 Taylor & Francis

The right of Rachel Harris and Rowan Pease to be identified as the authors of the editorial material, and of the authors for their individual chapters, has been asserted in accordance with sections 77 and 78 of the Copyright, Designs and Patents Act 1988.

All rights reserved. No part of this book may be reprinted or reproduced or utilised in any form or by any electronic, mechanical, or other means, now known or hereafter invented, including photocopying and recording, or in any information storage or retrieval system, without permission in writing from the publishers.

Trademark notice: Product or corporate names may be trademarks or registered trademarks, and are used only for identification and explanation without intent to infringe.

Library of Congress Cataloging-in-Publication Data
Pieces of the musical world : sounds and culture / edited by Rachel
    Harris and Rowan Pease.
    pages cm
    Includes bibliographical references and index.
    1. Ethnomusicology. 2. Music—History and criticism. I. Harris,
    Rachel (Rachel A.), editor. II. Pease, Rowan, editor.
    ML3798.P54 2015
    780.9—dc23
    2015006671

ISBN: 978–0-415–72310–7 (hbk)
ISBN: 978–0-415–72311–4 (pbk)
ISBN: 978–1-315–85787–9 (ebk)

Typeset in Sabon and Helvetica
by Florence Production Ltd, Stoodleigh, Devon, UK

Senior Editor: Constance Ditzel
Senior Editorial Assistant: Elysse Preposi
Production Manager: Mhairi Bennett
Marketing Manager: Amy Langlais
Copy Editor: Helen Baxter
Proofreader: Jackie Dias
Cover Design: Jayne Varney

Printed and bound in the United States of America by Sheridan Books, Inc. (a Sheridan Group Company).

Contents

Illustrations, Music Examples, and Audio Tracks

Figures

List of Music Examples

List of Audio Tracks

www.routledge.com/cw/harris

"Aqqu." Played by Raushan Orazbaeva.
       Recorded by Kairat Zhünisov, Almaty, January 2014

"Asŭrang." Played by Kim Ch'angnyong with Kim Yisŏn.
       Recorded by Rowan Pease, Yanji City, August 1999

"Dancing Girl." Written and sung by Terry Callier. *What Color is Love*
       (Cadet Records, 1972)

"El Alto de La Paz." Produced by Mati Zundel, featuring MC Boogat.
       Amazonico Gravitante (Waxploitation/ZZK Records, 2011)

"Grande Mestre." Mestre Valmir, with Jurandir, Valmir and Cobra Mansa.
       International Capoeira Angola Foundation, Bahia, 2011

"Orin Ìbejì." Sung by Doyin 'Fáníyì. Recorded by Amanda Villepastour,
       Òṣogbo, August 1999

"Sogasugā." Sung by M.S. Subbulakshmi, with Radha Vishwanathan.
       M.S. Subbulakshmi, Vol. 1. (Saregama Records 2009 reissue)

"Soliyo." Sung by Hawa Kasse Mady Diabaté. Recorded by Lucy Duran,
       December, 2012

"Song of Akuac." Anonymous. Courtesy of Angela Impey

"Soundscapes from the Old City." Recorded by Abigail Wood in Jerusalem,
       2009 and 2010, edited by Maria del Mar Hollis Oyaga

"Subhan'Allāh." Anonymous. Recorded by Rachel Harris, August 2009

"Sudamala." Played by Segara Madu *gendér wayang* group, live in
       concert in SOAS, University of London, 19 March 2012.
       Courtesy of Nicholas Gray

"Tamuke." Played by Okuda Atsuya, *Sound of Zen*
       (Son Tech D00EM04802)

"Tezeta." Performed by Asnaqetch Werqu. *Ethiopiques, Volume 16:*
       Asnakètch Wèrqu, The Lady With the Krar (Buda Musique 2004,
       France)

Preface

What is a Musical "Piece"?

> Argentinean producer Mati Zundel began writing 'El Alto de La Paz' on his laptop while travelling through Bolivia on an extended Latin American road trip. He emailed a demo version of the track to MC Boogat in Montreal, Canada; Boogat recorded rapped vocals over the top and emailed it back to Zundel, who was now at a beach in Ecuador.

So writes Geoffrey Baker introducing his "piece" of digital cumbia. "El Alto de La Paz" is a fusion of several regional and international genres, produced on a computer. This is a piece that gets us straight into thinking about process: how music is produced, the spaces and places in which it is made, and the ways in which music-makers and musical sounds move around our contemporary world.

Pieces of the Musical World: Sounds and Cultures is not about pieces in the narrow Western art music interpretation: as compositions that exist in the form of a written score. We are not in the business of re-inscribing the centrality of "the work" in the study of music. In fact, only one of our chapters (Kiku Day on the global re-imaginings of the Japanese *shakuhachi*) includes a score. This is a book about musicking, about people making and listening to music. The 14 pieces that are the focus of the chapters of the book—digitally recorded sounds streamed into your ears via our website—are snapshots of the musical world, auditory postcards. They are pieces of oral tradition, pieces of performance, pieces of creativity that have been captured and frozen in time. They serve as a way to draw you into the extraordinary and diverse musical worlds that produced them.

Let us take an example from one of the chapters. What kind of a piece is "Soliyo"? Lucy Duran has heard hundreds of versions of this piece during her 30 years travelling around West Africa and its diaspora. You can tell it's "Soliyo" because it's short, sung without accompaniment, and it has fixed opening and closing phrases. In between these two "musical bookends," the singer inserts improvised texts that depend on where she comes from, her knowledge and skill, and whom she is singing to. "Soliyo" is a typical piece of oral tradition: a mass of variants that are constantly re-created in the act of singing to suit the moment. Pieces like this are not confined to one medium of performance. Amanda Villepastour introduces "Ìbejì," a song for twins that exists as chanted text, sung melody, or played on talking drums: pitched drums that render the speech tones and periodicity of Yorùbá speech in instrumental form.

Just as the musical score is a physical trace of musical practice, modern recording technologies, such as the CD or the cassette, also render music into a tangible object. Such musical objects may come to have lives of their own; as we learn from Angela Impey's account of a sung audio-letter, carried on a cassette to bring news to family members abroad, or from Caspar Melville's chapter on a track from his much loved, dog-eared album, *What Color is Love*. They may be purchased as commodities, or passed from hand to hand, they may be cherished, broken or discarded, recycled, or sent to a landfill site. In the internet age, such tangible objects are no longer the primary way in which we experience music; many of the musical sounds we consume are intangible and free-flowing, circulating the globe at dizzying speeds. Those of us with access to the technology (by no means the whole of humanity although access is steadily growing) now have almost unlimited access to a world of musical sounds via our laptops or mobile phones, and we can easily put our own creative practice into circulation. In the age of the remix, scratch DJs and the mash-up, musical creativity takes on new forms, which are, in fact, very similar to oral tradition, where live performance, physical recordings, and virtual sounds can be endlessly recombined.

These chapters impel us to consider how different people around the world think about, and how they define, music. "I don't understand how you can work on music. When I listen to music, it makes me sad. It's not a good thing." So says Abdulmalik, an Ethiopian in Abu Dhabi, to Ilana Webster-Kogen. For him, music brings only painful memories of his distant home. Some of the chapters focus on what are musical pieces only in the loosest sense. Rachel Harris introduces a piece of *dhikr*: a short excerpt from a long field recording of a Sufi ritual, an Arabic prayer recited rhythmically over 80 times. In many ways it is highly musical, but the women who recite it definitely do not consider it to be music. Perhaps our most radical interpretation is Abigail Wood's audio track created especially for this book: a reconstruction of the soundscape of Jerusalem's Old City put together from her many recordings made while wandering through its narrow streets. This "piece" makes us think about the boundaries we create between sound and music: can we listen musically to the melody of goats' bells, or the rhythm of chopping sugar cane in the bazaar?

What are the Aims of the Book?

The primary aim of *Pieces of the Musical World* is to uncover and open up the world through a piece of music, and to give students the analytical tools to engage in depth with new pieces of the musical world. Each piece provides a springboard from which to tell a story; it asks you to think about each piece of music as a social event in which meaning is produced. Each chapter introduces key aspects of the culture or cultures in which the piece is embedded: the contexts in which it is performed, the people who experience it as performers or dancers or listeners, the journeys it has travelled, its changing meanings, and the beliefs, aesthetics, and politics associated with it. When a West African Malian *jeli* bard encounters a free-born compatriot on a Paris street, asks Lucy Duran, why does she "sing the horses" for him? This very short piece of music, "Soliyo," holds many stories across a long period of time and a wide geographical space that stretches across West Africa and its diaspora.

This book is a collaborative venture by the staff, outstanding alumni and research associates of the Department of Music at SOAS, University of London, an institution specializing in the study of Asia and Africa, which is widely recognized as the UK's leading centre for research and teaching in ethnomusicology. It arises out of our long experience in teaching introductory courses on world music to first year UK undergraduates in a way that harnesses our own active research interests to teaching methodologies aimed at these beginning students.

Each author explains their choice of piece from a personal standpoint. Thus we encounter Rowan Pease standing at a noisy traffic junction in northeast China engaging in yelled conversation on the trail of the *t'ungso* flute; Casper Melville grounded in California after an earthquake, leafing through a box of second-hand LPs; Lucy Duran singing "Soliyo" to a guard to get across the border between Mali and Guinea without even having to pay a bribe. Our chosen musical objects are not intended objectively as "the best" or "most representative" of their kind; we do not aim to canonize particular pieces or genres. They are chosen subjectively because they gave the author an insight into musical culture. In our teaching, we find this an effective way to engage our students' interest, highlighting that music is individually as well as socially experienced. The multi-author format of this volume taps into the deep local knowledge of the contributors. Above all, these chapters are fieldwork based, sharing first-hand experience of musical happenings: the spine-tingling emotional charge of sitting in the middle of a *dhikr* ritual; a London audience going wild after a concert on the Kazakh *qobyz*. Our authors are deeply engaged with the places in which they work, and the musicians with whom they work. Often they themselves are performers, writing about their teachers, and sharing insights they obtained the hard way through learning to play the instruments: Nicholas Gray teasing out the fast and furious interlocking rhythms of Balinese *gendér wayang*; Zoë Marriage undergoing the physical training for the dance-martial art-musical form that is Brazilian capoeira.

By focusing each chapter around a single piece, we place the focus firmly on musical sound. Our students at SOAS are great musical enthusiasts; they like playing music, they like listening to new and extraordinary sounds, and they are curious about the wider world of musical production. The focus on a musical object draws them in, and makes theoretical and stylistic description instantly relevant, addressing the novice listeners' natural questions: "Why does it sound like that? How does that work?"

Where Are the Pieces From (and Where Are They Going)?

The pieces span the continents of Africa, Asia, and the Americas, as well as the range of traditional, popular, and contemporary musics, and even sounds that might be considered "not music," thus helping to collapse the boundaries between these classificatory niches. Because we do not teach Western art music at SOAS, we have not included any chapters that focus on this music culture, but its impact on local traditions through processes of modernization is often present: the piece "Aqqu" (White Swan), for example, is linked to shamanic traditions and when played is thought to summon the spirit of a swan, but today it is taught in Kazakhstan's conservatories from a score that includes directions such as *pizzicato* and *sforzando*.

This book is not designed in the form of a typical regional survey course. We are not claiming to cover the whole world in 14 short chapters. Our approach takes us away from the familiar ethnomusicological canons to address musicking that cross-cuts geographical boundaries. We highlight flows and movement that redefine boundaries and reflect the intensely mobile world in which we live. Thus we encounter an imagined Africa musically evoked in London warehouse dance parties and in Brazilian capoeira; a Western *shakuhachi* player uploading a *shakuhachi* "requiem" for the tsunami onto YouTube in a radical re-imagining of Japanese tradition. Some of the pieces come from places you may not even have heard of (East Turkestan, South Sudan); they are lined up beside places that are likely very familiar (Chicago, London), and they are treated as far as possible in the same way. Placing these global trends at the heart of the book's narrative speaks to the interests and experiences of our own students, many of whom themselves belong to diasporic communities, and who engage with a whole range of globalized forms of music-making.

How the Book is Organized

Organized into 14 chapters, the book is constructed under three broad themes, "Music and Place," "Music and Spirituality," and "Music and Movement," which link to connect to key issues in ethnomusicology, including diaspora and transnational flows, music and the environment, music, and the body.

Accessible overviews of contemporary thinking in the discipline are presented in section introductions, and highlight the ways that these theoretical approaches are taken up in the individual chapters. Location and a series of key words further identify each chapter, allowing teachers to select by sub-themes, as well as by geographical region, if desired.

Key Features

Timed Listening Guides

Although each chapter has its own distinctive voice and concerns, a level of consistency is provided by a standard format. Each piece is explained through a timed listening guide, which helps listeners to follow in real time the details of its musical structure and style, and link it directly to other aspects of the musical culture:

- Focusing on a single musical object provides a way into understanding more about wider processes of musical creativity. Richard Widdess' elegant analysis of the South Indian song "Sogasugā" reveals the ways in which singers structure their improvised performance.
- The aim of these guides is also to teach you *how* to listen; to understand how people in different parts of the world listen to musical sound in different ways. Widdess provides practical exercises to acquaint you with the principles of *rāga* and *tāla* in classical Indian music. Amanda Villepastour attunes your ears to Yorùbá drumming rhythms: they might sound like a steady 2-beat to you, but that's not how Nigerians dance to these drums. Only by watching the dancer's feet can you attempt to transcribe this piece.
- The guides are not only about musical structure, melody and rhythm, they also draw your attention to sound quality: the many different named sounds that can be produced on one pitch by the Japanese *shakuhachi*; the mix in a studio-produced soul album. In some of these guides, sound and meaning is linked with remarkable precision. Saida Daukeyeva's guide to "Aqqu" unfolds a whole story of a heroic battle in which the instrument simulates the beating of swans' wings, gunshots, even the words of the protagonists. Casper Melville's guide to "Dancing Girl" traces a journey through the history of black American music, referencing, in miniature, Afro-American musical styles from New Orleans jazz to gospel and electrified soul, providing an almost cinematic tour of black life in the American ghetto.

Text Boxes

- Technology boxes include introductions to musical instruments, but also to software packages for mixing and editing tracks, the humble cassette, and—with a nod to Foucault—even a discussion of the technologies of the body.
- Primary source boxes incorporate primary materials, such as media interviews or related objects including record sleeves, restaurants and ritual figurines, to draw students into direct engagement with the culture surrounding the musical piece.
- Biography boxes, usually featuring the creators or performers of the piece under discussion, emphasize the human dimension. Widdess, for example, introduces the south Indian singer and film star M.S. Subbulakshmi who broke through the age-old prejudices about women singing in public and achieved

huge popularity, in part through her artistry but also by carefully cultivating an image of spirituality, devotion, and domestic respectability.

Other Features

Discussion questions and activities tie each chapter together, helping students to review what they have learned, and stretching them beyond that information to other, suggested readings.

Short notation examples are in some (not all) chapters to illustrate discussions of musical style, but musical literacy is not needed to engage with the bulk of the material.

A short glossary is provided to help students quickly check unfamiliar terms.

Another crucial aspect of the project is an interactive website

www.routledge.com/cw/harris

which contains the following features:

- audio and video recordings
- timed listening guides
- a glossary of musical terms
- an annotated list of links for further listening, viewing, and reading
- chapter summaries, maps and images.

Acknowledgments

The editors would like to acknowledge Richard Widdess, who provided the original idea that led to the publication of this book. Our thanks go to our editor, Constance Ditzel, at Routledge; to all our chapter contributors for their patience in dealing with our repeated requests for extra information, and their tolerance of our often intrusive editing; to all the musicians who are featured in these chapters for their outstanding music-making and their tolerance of our often intrusive questions; and to our anonymous reviewers for their helpful feedback.

Rachel Harris
Rowan Pease
August 2014

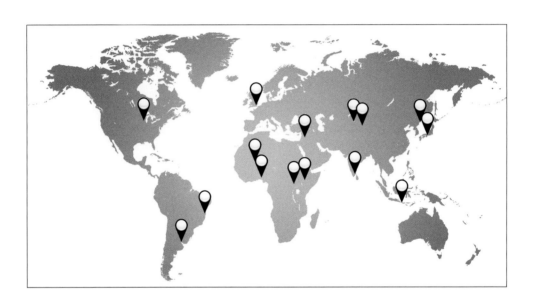

PART I

Music and Place

Protected Place

Introduction

Rachel Harris and Rowan Pease

The chapters in our opening section explore music's role in forming a sense of place and sense of identity, of belonging to a particular geographical location. They encompass notions of the soundscape, and explore how people use music to connect with their natural environment, to mark out physical or social space, to conjure up imagined ideas of place, carry local memories, and even store history. Together, these chapters reveal that music-making and listening are central to the ways in which people make sense of the place in which they find themselves, and the ways in which they think about the places that are crucial to their sense of identity.

We consider a range of sounds that go beyond the traditional European definitions of "music" through Abigail Wood's chapter on the Jerusalem soundscape. The term "soundscape" encompasses the whole sonic environment from natural to human and mechanical sounds, from "noise" to "music," from consciously to unconsciously produced sounds. Approaches to soundscapes emphasize the ways in which we listen to places. Sounds reveal physical spaces to us: sound is shaped by the environment in which it resounds, and contributes to our intuitive awareness of the physical environment. Sounds also tell us about time. Natural time is punctuated by daily changes in sounds: bird song at dusk and crickets after dark. Urban sounds change according to the rhythms of the seasons or the day, through annual street festivals, or the daily flows of commuters. These patterns of sound are linked to the economic or social functions of different neighborhoods and buildings within the city. They allow us to map the ways that sound "sticks" to places, and more broadly to conceptualize ecosystems of sound.

Music Marking Space

Thinking about the soundscape helps us to consider place and community in new ways. How are places characterized in sound? How are local geographies imagined by their inhabitants, and how is this reflected in sound? Wood's chapter on the Old City of Jerusalem explores how attention to its sounds can help us to understand its complex web of space and identity. Attentive listening is crucial in order to negotiate the narrow streets and intercommunal politics of Jerusalem's Old City. In urban environments such as this, where many different communities live cheek by jowl, the study of sound provides insights into coexistence and conflict. The Muslim call to prayer, for example, issued from the minaret five times a day, often aided by a loudspeaker, summons the faithful to prayer but may be heard as a noise nuisance by non-Muslims.

Music (sometimes defined as "humanly organized sound") has its place in these soundscapes: the clarinets at a bar mitzvah celebration and the singing pilgrims described in Wood's chapter. Other chapters in this section feature musics that are part of the modern urban soundscape, such as the Korean *t'ungso* flutes and drums played in city parks in northeast China as described by Pease, or the Malian *jeli* bards (and even our chapter author Lucy Duran) who might loudly "call the horses" by singing "Soliyo" on a Paris street or in an immigration hall, instantly invoking the social mores of the Mande world. To Western readers, the modern concert hall may be a more familiar context for music: the hall creates a space entirely devoted to music, and cut off from all the competing sounds of the outside world. This is where the Kazakh instrumental piece "Aqqu" (White Swan) in Saida Daukeyeva's chapter is now most commonly heard, although, paradoxically, *qyl-qobyz* music evokes the natural environment, bringing it into this enclosed urban space.

Our sense of place is embedded in networks of social relations and understandings; it involves hierarchies, difference, and boundaries, as mapped out so clearly in Old Jerusalem. In West African Mande society, "Soliyo" has an essentially ritual function. It may be sung at any time that a *jeli* encounters someone he considers a patron; it implies a sense of submission, but also expresses the power of the *jeli*. In China, the sound of the *t'ungso* instantly marks out the player as Korean, while to the local population it carries notions of the peasantry. In Brazil, the performance of Capoeira Angola takes place inside the physical space of the *roda*: a circle formed by members of the group who sing and play instruments while two people in the center of the circle attempt to trick and bring one another down. As Zoë Marriage explains, the *roda* creates a kind of temporary, moveable, ritualized space; a space set aside from the struggles of everyday life for marginalized communities in Brazil who were the originators of this genre. The sung responses by the chorus underline the sense of community created within the space of the *roda*. The music generates an emotional atmosphere that acts on the bodies of the players; it motivates their physical exercise (a form of "entrainment" not unlike that practiced by the Sufi women described in Chapter 7, in the spirituality section).

Music Evoking Place

Within this very present physical space, however, the Capoeira music traces an emotional journey to other places distant in geography and time: from Africa, homeland of the slaves, to their present environment in Brazil, finally leading to a joyful catharsis. Songs, sounds, and musical phrases evoke the personal and collective memories and feelings associated with particular places with an intensity and directness unequalled by any other social activity. Even history more distant than that of the slaves' journeys can be carried through the musical event. The Mande song "Soliyo" appears in performances of historical epics, such as in the story of Sunjata Keita, founder of the Mali Empire. Lucy Duran links this song to the archaeological site of Sorotomo, a thirteenth- to fifteenth-century capital of the Malian empire, and home of the ancestors of the *jeli* bards. Horses were the symbol of its military power. Duran argues that "Soliyo" preserves a musical memory of the might of this now forgotten kingdom. It conveys a sense of Mali's powerful past and serves in the present as an expression of collective identity. In Daukeyeva's chapter, too, instrumental pieces (*küi*) evoke collective memories: of a Kazakh nomadic past and their rootedness in the magnificent Central Asian mountains and pasturelands. This body of stories in sound serves as an important aspect of contemporary Kazakh identity.

It is precisely these qualities that forge the links between music, place, and identity that make music deeply political. During the revolutionary period of twentieth-century Chinese history, for instance, the *t'ungso* flute's raspy sound quality had no place in the official imaginings of what a modern, socialist nation should sound like. Its sound was too intimately linked to the earth, to China's peasantry, and it was completely sidelined in the state project to modernize and improve Chinese folk music. By the twenty-first century, however, China's new urban classes had developed a strong nostalgia for rural environments, which they imagined as places of spirituality, naturalness, and innocence against the consumerist lifestyle that reforms had brought to China. The now "authentic" sounds of the *t'ungso* provided them with these links to the land, and the instrument was drawn into the state system of Intangible Cultural Heritage and reconfigured as a symbol of nation, and a national cultural asset.

Music and the Environment

If music-making and listening practices form a part of the ways in which people order the world, they also contribute to the ways we think about and evoke the natural environment. The emerging sub-discipline of "eco-musicology" considers the relationships between music, culture, and nature as they relate to ecology and the environment. Eco-musicologists argue that we need to understand human musical expression as part of a sonic ecosystem. Music is not just a way of mediating between people and their environment; it is an enactment of the environment in which humans are a part. The Capoeira Angola group FICA thinks of itself as a part of the environment rather than as a distanced owner. Links with the land are central to its ethos, so alongside its work as a center for Capoeira, it maintains an organic farm and a strong commitment to sustainable agriculture. As travelling herders and pastoralists, the Kazakhs of Central Asia also lived in intimate contact with the natural environment and the changing seasons, and their musical performance is rooted in aesthetics and beliefs arising from this lifestyle. Their instrumental music (*küi*) both imitates and animates the environment: in the traditional animist belief system, mountains, lakes, caves, and wild animals all have spirits that can be addressed, placated, and persuaded through music. *Küi* pieces also relate, through musical sound, stories about people's relationships with nature.

In our contemporary globalized world, our social networks and our lived experiences are rarely confined to the physical locations that we inhabit; we exist simultaneously in a local, a regional, and a global context. Traditional notions of place as a bounded entity fixed in space and time have been largely replaced by a view in which the local and the global, the past and the present are inextricably bound together. Places are penetrated and shaped by distant cultural phenomena. Thus an encounter between a Malian *jeli* and a patron on a Paris street is shaped by half-submerged memories of the ancient West African city of Sorotomo. Likewise, our sense of identity increasingly traces trajectories across space rather than constructing boundaries. The resulting sense of dislocation impels people to find ways of relocating themselves, perhaps through roots-seeking or nostalgic remembering of past places, for instance, in the contemporary reworkings of *küi* pieces, or rediscovery of the *t'ungso* flute in China. Thus here, and in the chapters later on movement, "place" is not so much a physical location as a process of imagining, embedding, and relocating ourselves. Our authors reveal how music often plays a vital role in these processes.

Location: Israel/Palestine

"Soundscapes of the Old City": Listening to Jerusalem's Old City

Recorded by Abigail Wood, 2009 and 2010, Jerusalem; edited by Maria del
  Mar Hollis Oyaga

Chapter one

"Soundscapes of the Old City"

Listening to Jerusalem's Old City

Abigail Wood

Summary

Jerusalem's Old City is a complicated space. Thick stone walls built by the sultan Suleiman the Magnificent in 1538 enclose about a square kilometer of urban space, encompassing residential areas and market streets; some of the most important religious sites in the Holy Land for Jews, Christians, and Muslims; schools; museums, monasteries, hostels and pilgrim houses, bakeries, markets, sweet-shops, cafés; basic amenities and a heavy Israeli police and security infrastructure. Today's maps of the Old City usually follow the British Mandate's division of the walled area into four quarters—Muslim, Christian, Jewish, and Armenian, in descending order of size—yet these designations far oversimplify the complex social geographies of the walled space, whose 40,000 or so inhabitants also include minority communities such as Domari gypsies, an African-Palestinian community, Copts, Karaite Jews, and transitory communities including Christian monks and nuns of many denominations and Jewish religious students, among many others. This residential population is further complicated by the fluid movement of people into and out of the walled space, in which local populations are sometimes dwarfed by throngs of tourists and pilgrims from many corners of the world.

This chapter presents an aural postcard of the sounds of this city, and explores how they might help us to understand this complex web of space and identity.

KEY WORDS
- Christianity
- conflict
- experience
- identity
- Islam
- Judaism
- space

Why this Piece?

When I first visited Jerusalem's Old City, my overriding impression was of the bright colors, sounds, and smells of the street markets. I noticed sounds both familiar and unfamiliar: the many languages spoken by local people, tourists, and pilgrims, the calls of merchants; a tourist blowing a **shofar** (ram's horn) in a shop; the clacking of dice and game pieces as two elderly men played backgammon; the intermittent ringing of church bells and the call to prayer from local mosques; the clatter of kids running with carts through narrow alleyways, calling out to warn those on the streets to move aside. I also enjoyed the sound made by my feet as my sandals slid on the smooth stones of the uneven streets—the "clack" sound of the sole hitting the stone and the jingle of the buckle.

On later visits I paid more attention to the ways in which the sounds people made shaped the spaces around them. I sat inside one of the gates of the walled city, and saw, in succession, groups of Armenian priests, Western tourists, Palestinian shopkeepers, and strictly Orthodox Jews moving through the same space, each bringing different sound worlds into play, which, in turn, changed the character of the space and influenced the interactions of others. I noted that despite the lines on the map demarcating conventional divisions of urban space, sounds travelled over walls and through doorways. Often I could hear people and activities that I couldn't see and could hear indoor sounds seeping into outdoor spaces.

Jerusalem is well known in the Western imagination as a visually iconic city— you would probably recognize photographs of the golden Dome of the Rock rising over impressive stone walls. But as I began to research the soundscape of the Old City, I asked a different question: what would happen if I listened to Jerusalem rather than focusing on visual mapping of the city? How might sounds help us to understand this complex web of space and identity?

Attentive listening is crucial in order to negotiate the narrow streets and complex intercommunal politics of the Jerusalem's Old City: it is perhaps no coincidence that I don't remember ever seeing a passerby in the city listening to an

FIGURE 1.1 **Busy market in the Old City, Jerusalem**
Photograph by Abigail Wood

FIGURE 1.2
Sweeping the street in the early morning, Old City, Jerusalem
Photograph by Abigail Wood

iPod to block out unwanted street sounds. The soundscape narrates changing histories of power as well as contemporary realities at the symbolic center of the Israeli-Palestinian conflict: church bells of different **timbres** ring out across rooftops, joined five times a day by **muezzins** calling religious Muslims to prayer; meanwhile, the insistent bleeping of soldiers' radios accompanied by the tinny voices they relay punctuates street life, alongside the shouts of cart runners moving merchandise through the streets, and the quiet chat of shopkeepers in Hebrew and Arabic, articulating infrastructures of power, commerce, and knowledge in today's city.

Other sounds change more quickly: languages spoken on the street serve as a barometer of different waves of tourists and pilgrims and cue different patterns of interaction. The sound of a helicopter circling above immediately indicates an increase of tension. The textures of street life tell more finely grained stories: a Jewish tour guide points out structures from the Biblical era; Russian pilgrims chant in harmony, blotting out the distracting sounds of the market; a soldier asks a Palestinian man in his twenties for ID; a group of teenagers wash a car, blaring pop music onto the street. Such sounds mark new and changing geographies and sites of agency.

Sound and Social Context

This track is an aural "postcard," a patchwork of several distinct sounds and street scenes, which I recorded in public spaces of the Old City of Jerusalem between autumn 2009 and summer 2010. Read the following questions, then listen to the track and try to answer the questions (it may help to close your eyes):

- What can you hear? Try to pick out every sound.
- Which sounds are familiar, and which are unfamiliar or confusing?
- What do the voices and sounds tell you about the places in which these sounds were recorded?

After you have tried to answer these questions for yourself, play the track again and follow along with the listening guide.

Musical Features

TIMED LISTENING GUIDE

0:00	The recording begins with the sounds of everyday life. Entering the Old City through the Damascus gate, we come to a lively Palestinian market street (See Figure 1.1). A vendor calls out the price of his wares in Arabic: 'bi-'ashara'— for 10 (shekels)
0:15	In a different part of the market, shopkeepers are quietly preparing for the day ahead, opening the metal shutters of their stores. Two adjacent stores are playing recordings of the Qur'an, the voices of the two readers weaving together while a street cleaner sweeps the stone streets of a side alley (see Figures 1.2 and 1.3)

0:32	In a nearby courtyard, a group of schoolboys play outside between lessons. Their voices resonate between the stone walls that surround them
0:49	Back in the market, the first rainstorm of the year has arrived. The raindrops make a loud clattering sound on the corrugated iron roofs that jut out over the stores. Passersby start to talk loudly over the sounds of the rain
1:06	Moving along in the market, we pass the doorway of a busy souvenir shop. A number of languages are spoken
1:20	We are now approaching the Western Wall, a holy site for Jews. It's a Monday morning and two **bar mitzvah** ceremonies, celebrations of the coming of age of 13-year old Jewish boys, are taking place. First, we hear *djembe* drummers and a clarinetist playing in a resonant space below the pathway (Figure 1.4). A few seconds later, another group moves into the sound space, singing a Hebrew **psalm** text and drumming, their leader using a portable microphone
1:53	At the Jaffa Gate, an entrance to the Old City frequently used by tourists, a young Jewish Israeli student is busking, playing the *oud*, a Middle Eastern lute, in the resonant space. A small crowd gathers to listen to him
2:20	A group of Russian Orthodox pilgrims sing as they walk through a busy part of the market, following the path of the Via Dolorosa, along which Christians mark Jesus's final path through the city to his crucifixion. As they move through the market, they walk past a music shop; the sounds of their voices compete with an Arabic pop CD then separate out
3:18	On the Via Dolorosa, a bell rings above a Franciscan monastery. The street here is empty but the regular **rhythm** of the bell in the sonorous space is punctuated by the squeaking of its mechanism
3:33	On a nearby rooftop, church bells ring with a different timbre, as the muezzin calls religious Muslims to prayer (Figure 1.7)
3:55	Back in the market, later in the day a street vendor cuts sugar cane to make a sweet drink for those breaking their fast during the Muslim festival of Ramadan. In the evening, hundreds of Muslim worshippers from Jerusalem, the Galilee and further afield will walk down this street on their way to the al-Aqsa mosque and several people are setting up food stalls
4:10	Above the plaza of the Western Wall, the sound of hundreds of birds in a large tree cheeping as dusk falls
4:26	Walking back to our starting point outside the Old City walls, crickets can be heard loudly chirping. The sounds of traffic are also immediately noticeable

What did the recording reveal about Jerusalem's Old City? While recorded on different days during a year of fieldwork, the sounds you heard represented something of how a typical day might sound in this space. I'm sure that you noticed one major difference from most Western cities: inside the stone walls of the Old City, the noise of cars is rarely present. Most of the streets are reverberant stone alleys and market places that can only be traversed on foot. Perhaps the fact that you could hear many voices on the streets—traders, pilgrims, tourists—reminded you that Jerusalem has a warm, Middle Eastern climate, in which much public life takes outside.

Sounds reveal physical spaces to us: sound is shaped by the environment in which it resounds, and contributes to our intuitive awareness of the physical environment.

BIOGRAPHY

What is your favorite sound in the Old City?

During my field research in Jerusalem, I asked many people, both local residents and visitors, about their favorite sounds in the Old City. Their answers tell us not only about the soundscape of the city, but also about how different people think about the urban environment around them. Some mention religious sounds, marking Jerusalem's importance for Jews, Christians and Muslims; for others, mundane neighborhood sounds are more significant. One interviewee focuses on cosmopolitan coexistence between people from different countries; another juxtaposes everyday sounds with memories of violent conflict. Together, these responses suggest that there is no one, shared narrative of this complex space, but rather many different ways of making sense of a complex and ever changing soundscape:

> For me, actually the best sound that I can think of in Jerusalem, and I would be singing in my head when I hear it, when I walk in a neighborhood or courtyard or the back alley, where usually you don't see many people . . . Normally the best noise that you get there is church bells ringing. I love that. (Kevork, Armenian shopkeeper)

> My favorite sound is the minaret, al-Aqsa [mosque] minaret, because it is very close to my home, and it's emotional sometimes to hear it [. . .] During that period, I feel like I live with God for a moment, and I love to hear it especially outside my home, like I walk to the garden, where the voice is more clear, and more nice. (Amineh, Muslim resident)

> Excuse me, but I like to tell you, the best sound for me is small birds. When I'm coming from home to here, I like the sound when I'm coming, and you know, they are jumping, collecting their food. I *like* it! (Maria, Christian voluntary worker)

> The sounds of people, because what matters is people, the different languages and all the people passing—Brazilians you know, Portuguese—and all the languages you can think of. And that's amazing, in how many square meters? —in this tiny city, you hear all these different languages, and that's fascinating. (Charlotte, British tourist)

> On Friday nights at the Western wall, there are 100 different groups praying at the same time. And if it was one group, that would be very powerful. This is something else. There's a verse in Isaiah that talks about hearing the rush of angels, like rushing waters. That's exactly what it's like. It's like sound falling into sound, and melody falling into melody, and it's just this cacophony of sound . . . swelling. It's almost like being washed over with it. You don't really know what you're hearing, you don't really know what you're listening to. (Aaron, Jewish shopkeeper)

> Once, I was walking in the Old City. I closed my eyes, and I started to hear the people, what's going on around: an old man and an old woman, a young man, and a baby crying, a baby shouting, and some fight here or there, you know,

between two guys. So for me, this is the Old City and it *should* be like this. This is the sound that I like, the sound of people. The sound that I don't like is when there is something broken, like the sound of shooting. Because I remember at the Second Intifada time [Palestinian uprising, 2000–2005], people were walking on the street, and something happened, somebody threw stones at the soldiers, and they started shooting in the Old City, in the air, so the people started running, everyone the same way. They start running, the shooting calms down, they start to slow down, and they continue what they were doing, shopping, like nothing happened. (Izzat, Palestinian photographer)

We hear the sound of a squeaky bell, or of raindrops falling on a tin roof, and begin to put together a mental picture of our surroundings. Places are recognizable by their sounds: a number of the people I spoke to during my fieldwork told me about places that they liked to walk in at certain times to enjoy particular sounds (see Biography Box, above). Sounds also tell us about time. Natural time is punctuated by diurnal changes in sounds: birds at dusk and crickets after dark. On top of this are overlaid the timetables of work—the opening and closing of stores— and of religious activities: Jewish bar mitzvah celebrations on Monday and Thursday mornings; church bells and muezzins several times daily calling Christians and Muslims to pray; the special sounds of yearly religious observances such as Ramadan.

Yet while certain sound constellations might be typical of particular places and times, the soundstream itself is ever changing: we cannot replay it and listen again.

FIGURE 1.3 **Opening a store, Old City, Jerusalem**
Photograph by Abigail Wood

FIGURE 1.4 **Bar mitzvah**
Photograph by Abigail Wood

The story told by sounds *as we experience them* is incomplete and often ambiguous; listening does not only tell us about the space—it tells us about ourselves and our expectations. Take for example this extract from my fieldnotes, from a Friday in October. This was a time of acute tension in the Old City. The Israeli police had closed the city to Muslim men under the age of 50, and in response the al-Aqsa mosque cranked up the volume of the Friday sermon far beyond that of a normal week. Newspapers had been predicting a renewed outbreak of hostility between Israelis and Palestinians. There was a partial strike, and many predicted violence on the streets. As worshippers streamed towards the mosque, I sat on the nearby roof of the Austrian Hospice to record and write:

> At 11ish I go up onto the roof—I wonder what will happen. I sit there for a while and soon the call to prayer starts. A short time later, the sermon begins—I can hear it loudly. I listen—my Arabic isn't perfect but I can hear that it is discussing the contested sovereignty of Muslim holy sites in Jerusalem. Just before 12 the speech stops—I have been riveted all this time—and after a short pause, the church bells begin, equally loudly. As they continue, the voice starts again and the speech rises and rises in volume. The bells ring, a police helicopter circles overhead and I think, *this is it*. This is the conflict. I see smoke rise behind the Al-Aqsa mosque. I can't tell where it's coming from. It reminds me of how I felt while living in northern Israel during the second Lebanon war (2006)—I am geographically in the middle of a conflict situation but from here it's hard to know what's going on.

FIGURE 1.5 Christian pilgrims in the Old City, Jerusalem
Photograph by Abigail Wood

While I could have included here the recording I made on the roof that day, it's impossible to recapture the indeterminacy of the moment: the impact of the sounds, my interpretation, of course, influenced by my consumption of newspaper editorials. The lack of information is also striking—in contrast to news reports and academic discussions where events are melded into a complete, rounded narrative, here there is no complete picture. Caught in the midst of events, one simply cannot know what is going on.

Sounds also tell us about the people in the city. The Old City of Jerusalem is a particularly interactive physical space, one to which you have to pay attention in order to move around through busy streets and uneven surfaces, and in which the presence of others is intensely felt. In the recording, you heard vendors calling to customers, tourists asking the price of a souvenir and locals commenting on the weather, in at least four languages, revealing wider geographies of travel and migration. Sounds are also actively manipulated by street users to create a desired environment. While changing the visual street environment is out of the reach of most, the ability to repaint the street in sound is available to just about everyone. Particularly early in the morning, the sound of the Qur'an seeps through the street, at once creating a calm, slowed-down environment, and also marking personal space—the same sound that joins street users together into a shared acoustic environment also discourages extended conversation, maintaining personal space while each shopkeeper prepares for the day ahead.

The examples we have looked at so far focus on one sound event at a time. However, the soundscape also reflects the interaction or collision of many things happening simultaneously. How can one understand this complex, multi-layered environment? Thinking about this multitudinousness requires us not only to decide what the different elements are in the given mix, but also to consider the nature of the interaction between them.

Fosdick, Harry Emerson (1927) *A Pilgrimage to Palestine*. New York: Macmillan. 98–99; 243–244.

The first impression which Jerusalem makes upon the visitor depends largely on the visitor's previous familiarity with Oriental towns. If he comes fresh from Western scenes and customs and here for the first time looks upon the East, he will find many strange sights, sounds, and smells to which to adjust himself. Some will shock him; his appreciation of Jerusalem will stumble at the start over details distressing to his senses and his mind. . . . In the end even the traveler who at first is shocked discovers the real Jerusalem. Its narrow, winding, climbing streets; its thronged bazaars packed along the traffic ways or crowded under colonnades built by crusaders to house pilgrims; its endless riot of color in costumes that represent many faiths and races; its fascinating salmagundi [miscellany] of strange faces, strange animals, strange clothes, and strange accents—all these fill the eye until the Strand or Fifth Avenue seems by contrast very dull, drab, standardized, and monotonous.

Disturbances are frequent. On Good Friday night, while we were in the city, an Armenian Christian who brought a Jewess in his party to the church was set upon by Moslems and Christians alike and thoroughly beaten. Here is the very crux and center of all the rampant prejudices and bitter rivalries that rend Jerusalem asunder. . . . Such is the atmosphere of the Church of the Holy Sepulchre today and public worship is an unhappy advertisement of it. In gorgeous, ecclesiastical vestments the five sets of churchmen parade around the sanctuary, chanting, genuflecting, ringing bells. The groups proceed, each in its appointed course and order, about the rambling, meticulously apportioned church to swing

PRIMARY SOURCE

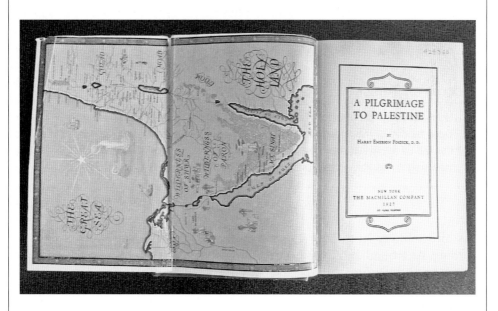

FIGURE 1.6 *A Pilgrimage to Palestine,* **by Harry Emerson Fosdick**
Photograph by Rowan Pease

censers before the holy places. The spot where Constantine's mother found the "true Cross," Golgotha itself, the stone of anointing for the burial, the place where Mary stood when she saw where they laid him, the Master's tomb, and Joseph of Arimathea's own sepulcher as well—such holy places within the sanctuary are venerated with swinging censers twice a day by every one of the five churches, and no one of them dares omit a single occasion lest it lose forever the prize privilege of sharing in the fivefold monopoly.

The church itself is bedlam [chaos] to the eye and ear. The garish, gawdy decorations, the competing din of five simultaneous services, the hideous **dissonance** from gongs, the very lamps which hang in multitudes from the roof, their differences advertising their fivefold sectarianism—all this represents a type of religion that Jesus disliked most and represents nothing that he pleaded for and for which he died.

Commentary

Beginning many centuries ago, and increasingly from the nineneenth century until the present day, European and American Christians have travelled to Jerusalem as pilgrims. A prominent American Baptist minister, Harry Emerson Fosdick (1878–1969)'s book describes his four-month trip to Egypt, Palestine, and Syria. Like many Western travelers to the Middle East, his impressions of the places he visits are strongly shaped by his sensory impressions of unfamiliar places. In the account given here, Fosdick recognizes how his impressions of Jerusalem changed as he became more used to his new sensory environment.

In recent decades scholars have paid increasing attention to the ways in which Westerners describe and depict the 'Orient.' In his influential book *Orientalism* (1978), Palestinian-American scholar Edward Said—himself born in Jerusalem—argued that romanticized images of the Middle East and Asia have stood in the way of the recognition of the depth of local cultures, and have served as justification for colonial rule.

Discussion Topics

- How does sound contribute to Fosdick's sensory description of Jerusalem?
- Does he depict the sounds he hears in a positive or negative light? Why? What does this tell us about his own religious assumptions?
- How might Fosdick's description of Jerusalem differ from that of a local resident?

As an example, let's think about the "sound clashes" that we heard in the recording. At around 1:42, you heard a musical collision of groups celebrating bar mitzvah parties. During the past five years or so, a new tradition has sprung up among Jewish Israeli family groups celebrating bar mitzvahs at the Western Wall: to accompany the boy from outside the Old City through the Dung gate to the Western Wall plaza with drums and singing, thus creating an opportunity for all the family to sing and dance together before more formal prayers at the Wall.

FIGURE 1.7 **Rooftops of the Old City, Jerusalem**
Photograph by Abigail Wood

On any given Monday or Thursday, lots of groups make use of the spaces between the gate and the plaza; each group is unified by its own creation of a moving acoustic space, but this space is permeated by the sounds of the celebrations of others. In the recording, we heard what happened when a group holding a celebration in a hollow near the gate were passed by a new group coming in. Here, there is no apparent conflict between the many simultaneous events, which move in and out of one another's sonic space. One might relate this to the **heterophonic** aesthetic of traditional Jewish prayer, where each congregant recites the prayers at his own pace, creating community from a rich **texture** of thick sound rather than from a unified recitation.

A second example highlights a more explicit conflict of sonic space. We heard a group of Russian pilgrims singing a slow **chant** in rich harmony as they walked the Via Dolorosa, a path that turned their journey through the Old City's streets into a religious act. As they pass through the market, their singing helps to keep them together as a group, avoiding the distractions of street life. As they pass a music store, the sound of an Arabic pop CD momentarily blocks out their singing; however, they quickly move onwards. In terms of sound, here we have a kind of cold conflict: there is no particular hostility between the two sound sources—but they do represent very different ways of using the street space, and it is not possible to listen properly to both at once.

Finally, sound is also political. Jerusalem's Old City lies at the symbolic heart of the Israeli-Palestinian conflict, and its religious sites are shared by people of different cultural and national backgrounds. In a contested space like this, politics are also manifest in the soundscape. Narratives, politics, and power relations are constantly entangled, and conflict can be manifested on every scale from the prosaic to the global. Inside the Church of the Holy Sepulcher, the Franciscans—a Catholic religious order—wage war against the loud Orthodox Christian Palm Sunday crowds filling the building, using loud organ music and the sound of their palm branches to open up a space for their procession. And near the Damascus gate, on a day of high conflict between Israeli security forces and Palestinians at the al-Aqsa mosque, in the Izheman coffee shop the sound of events taking place a few hundred meters away, broadcast live on al-Jazeera, mingles with the sound of coffee grinding—because it's business as usual this side of town—and the conversation of shop workers, which drifts between the topical and the mundane.

Studying Sound

You might have been surprised to find a chapter about sound in a book about music. Why should we pay attention to sounds? "Sound studies" is a relatively new area of interest for ethnomusicologists. While scholars have been studying the musics of the world for centuries, and while the acoustic qualities of sound have interested both physicists and musicians since ancient times, the idea of studying the sounds around us—not just those sounds labeled "music"—is relatively recent.

Perhaps, however, you noticed in the recording that it's difficult to distinguish entirely between sound and music. Some nonmusical sounds have regular rhythmic patterns: the hacking of sugar cane, the ringing and squeaking of a bell. Sounds can be memorable parts of everyday experience, and can evoke emotional responses. Many of the people that I met in the Old City had a complex imitative vocabulary to describe, for example, the calls of vendors in the market and even how these have changed since their youth. People often also described how they felt when they heard these sounds ("it's like I'm singing inside when I hear it; I like it!; it makes me feel happy"), an aesthetic response that we might also expect when we listen to music.

Other sounds in the recording were explicitly musical: the singing of Christian pilgrims and Jewish bar mitzvah groups; a CD recording of pop music; Turkish music played on the *oud*, a six-stringed Middle Eastern lute. Here, these sounds were embedded in the spaces and practices of everyday life, reminding us that music is always performed in a context: the ability to isolate sounds and play them through noise-cancelling headphones, and the reification of music as an object separate from its spatial and social context are rather recent concepts. Further, the definition of music depends on the listener. Perhaps the two voices reading the Qur'an sounded to you like music—and they played the same role in the street scene as recorded music might—but religious Muslims do not consider Qur'anic recitation to be music (see Rachel Harris's chapter in this book).

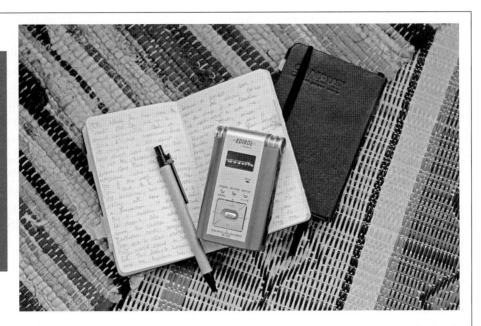

FIGURE 1.8 **Edirol and fieldnotes**
Photograph by Abigail Wood

What are the tools of an ethnomusicologist? On my first field trip, when I was still a teenager in the mid-1990s, I carried a huge four-track tape recorder with a large microphone around the Solomon Islands, hoping to record some local music, and returned with a shoebox full of cassette tapes. During the past couple of decades recording technologies have improved immeasurably, and most ethnomusicologists now use small, hand-held digital recording devices, which fit easily into a pocket and yet are capable of recording hours of CD-quality sound, whether musical events, sounds, or interviews. The location of the sound recording device is always important: when recording outdoor soundscapes, I usually place the sound recorder in several different places in order to capture different perspectives. How does a religious procession sound from the point of view of those taking part? How does it sound from the perspective of those standing outside as the procession passes by? Still and video cameras help us to capture the wider context of the sounds that we listen to, although to me it is an equally important challenge to listen without visual cues: what can we learn from sounds alone?

Of course, fieldwork is not all about recording sounds and images: no ethnomusicologist can be found without a field notebook, whether an old-fashioned notebook and pen or a laptop computer or tablet. Fieldnotes are the raw material of ethnographic writing. They are a place to record all the details that help researchers to remember our interactions with people in the field; or to reconstruct what exactly happened at a particular event. Further, writing ethnography is a process of reflection and interpretation. Fieldnotes give the space for us to note down the thoughts and ideas that we had when we were actually experiencing a musical event so that we can come back to these ideas and think through them later, perhaps when writing a chapter like this one.

The first prominent scholar to propose the systematic study of the sounds around us was the Canadian scholar and educator Murray Schafer. He used the word term "soundscape" to describe the acoustic environment, a term that has since gained wide currency. Schafer's research into environmental and human sounds was prompted by the blurring of the boundaries between sounds and music by composers of ***musique concrète***, including John Cage, in whose "silent" work 4'33" listeners only hear ambient sounds. His work also reflects an anxiety about changes in the soundscape caused by modernity: the rise of loud, industrial sounds and the simultaneous loss of the sounds of nature, of traditional crafts, and the invasion of the acoustic stillness of nature by mechanized sounds.

Since the 1980s, the field of sound studies has grown quickly among both anthropologists and ethnomusicologists. Steven Feld's research among the Kaluli people of the Bosavi highlands in Papua New Guinea makes an important bridge between these academic disciplines, exploring how Kaluli songs and speech sounds interweave with the natural acoustic environment of the rainforest, mimicking bird

FIGURE 1.9 **A street in Jerusalem's Old City, 1914**

Photograph courtesy of Elia Photo Service, Jerusalem

calls and interacting with the sounds of waterfalls. Others have turned to urban sound environments. Rowland Atkinson proposes that urban sound, like the natural soundscape, forms a "sonic ecology," within which recurring sounds in certain places—from commuter cars to house parties and street festivals—help us to understand the spatial patterns of the city. Sound artists have sought ways to represent the aural qualities of urban spaces in sound maps, soundwalks, or films. Other scholars have studied particular aspects of the urban soundscape: church bells and the Islamic call to prayer, recorded music, and iPod use in public space; traffic sounds; the acoustic properties of buildings.

In my own work, I suggest that sound offers a productive way to think about how shared spaces are both shaped and interpreted. Much of the academic literature on Jerusalem takes a top-down, map-based sociopolitical approach that emphasises physical, religious, and ethnic divisions between communities and tends to focus on narratives of conflict. However, despite the harsh and ever present realities of conflict, the ways in which people actually use the spaces of Jerusalem's Old City frustrate straightforward mapping. The moments of sound production and listening that I outline here disrupt some of the conventional ways in which Jerusalem is described: they do not conform to the contours of a map, they are often not narratable, and they disregard the "boundaries" between text and practice; art and politics; performance and everyday life, both reinforcing and undermining ingrained narratives of conflict and structures of power.

Recommended Reading

Atkinson, Rowland (2007) "Ecology of Sound: The sonic order of urban space." *Urban Studies* 44/10: 1905–1917.
> The paper discusses the power of music, sound and noise to denote place and demarcate space, and attempts to theorize the spatial and temporal patterning of the city.

Bull, Michael (2007) *Sound Moves: iPod Culture and Urban Experience*. London and New York: Routledge.
> This book uses the example of the iPod to investigate the way in which we use sound and technology to construct key areas of our daily lives.

DeNora, Tia (2000) *Music in Everyday Life*. Cambridge: Cambridge University Press.
> This book uses a series of ethnographic studies and in-depth interviews to show how people use music to construct individual and group identities.

Lee, Tong Soon (1999) "Technology and the Production of Islamic Space: The call to prayer in Singapore." *Ethnomusicology* 43(1): 86–100.
> Explores the relationship between technology and the spatial organization of social life focusing on the use of the loudspeaker and radio to mediate the Islamic call to prayer in Singapore.

Samuels, David, Louise Meintjes, Ana Maria Ochoa, and Thomas Porcello (2010) "Soundscapes: Toward a sounded anthropology." *Annual Review of Anthropology* 39: 329–345.
> Major overview of anthropological studies relating to soundscapes.

Schafer, R. Murray (1977) *The Soundscape: Our Sonic Environment and the Tuning of the World*. Rochester, VT: Destiny Books.

> A pioneering early exploration of the acoustic environment, with explanations of how to classify sounds, exercises and "soundwalks" to help us become more discriminating and sensitive to the sounds around us.

Wood, Abigail (2013) "Sound, Music and Migration in Jerusalem's Old City." In Jane Garnett and Alana Harris, eds. *Rescripting Religion in the City: Migration and Religious Identity in the Modern Metropolis*. Aldershot: Ashgate.

> Further discussion of the themes introduced in this chapter.

Wood, Abigail (2013) "Urban Soundcapes: Hearing and seeing Jerusalem." In Tim Shephard and Anne Leonard, eds. *Routledge Companion to Music and Visual Culture*. London: Routledge.

> Further discussion of the themes introduced in this chapter.

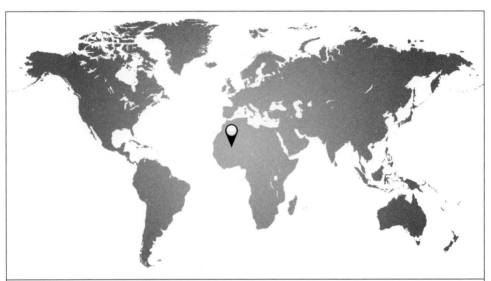

Location: Mali, West Africa

"Soliyo" (Calling the Horses): Song and Memory in Mande Music

Piece sung by Hawa Kasse Mady Diabaté; recorded by Lucy Duran, December 2012, Mali

Chapter two

"Soliyo" (Calling the Horses)

Song and Memory in Mande Music

Lucy Duran

Summary

A Malian woman in her mid-thirties, wearing a traditional gown of embroidered damask, crosses a road early one morning in a busy neighborhood of Paris. She has spotted a fellow Malian, recognizable by his dress and way of walking, and she approaches him. During a brief exchange of greetings in Bamana—Mali's main language—she learns the man's surname. As if on cue, she stretches out one arm with a theatrical gesture, and in a piercing, declamatory style that can be heard over the roar of traffic, she sings an age-old song from the Mande tradition, whose title may be translated as "Calling the horses":

> Horses, oh! Jimbe! The horses of Silamakanba Koita! A patron of a *jeli* is better off than someone who has no *jeli*. I bless the person who has shown me love. If you are a true noble, you will love those who love you. Horses, oh horses!! War goes well for you. You seized him, you killed him. War is not good for cowards!

The song has only lasted about 40 seconds, a blast of fiery and piercing melody, during which the man has been rooted to the spot. There is not a horse in sight, only lots of cars whizzing through the streets, and people going about their daily tasks in the French capital. Who are Jimbe and Silamakanba Koita, why are their names sung for this person, and which war goes well for whom? The recipient of the song, looking rather dazed, reaches into his pockets and hands the singer a wad of bank notes before hurrying off to work, to earn back some of the money he has just given away.

KEY WORDS
- gender
- identity
- improvisation
- Islam
- oral history

Why this Piece?

I cannot remember when I first heard the "Calling the horses" song. It may well have been one of the very first pieces of music I was exposed to when I began to study Mande music back in the late 1970s. Since then it has been a constant part of the musical environment around me during my many periods of fieldwork; first in the Gambia and Senegal and later, from the mid-1980s onwards, in Mali.

The Mande are a Muslim people, and men and women occupy different but overlapping social spheres. **Jelis**, the Mande term for a person born into a hereditary lineage of musicians and wordsmiths, are assigned with the task of most professional music, and the division of musical labor according to gender is strict. Instruments are played by male **griots**; female *griots* (known as **jelimuso**, *jeli*-woman) are the preferred singers, (although male *jelis* do sing as well). My initial purpose was to study the **kora**, a 21-string harp, very much a male instrument, and, as a foreigner, I was permitted to cross this particular gender barrier. In most other ways, however, I was expected to be part of the women's world, helping out with domestic chores, and participating in song and dance.

One of the best things about that experience was going along with the women to the joyous music parties that mark every birth, circumcision, and wedding. These are lively, noisy, colorful occasions, known as **sumu**, organized by women for women, usually held in the courtyard of the house or outside in the street under a canopy. The only men present were the instrumentalists, all men. From the 1990s

FIGURE 2.1 Hawa Kasse Mady Diabaté (right, holding microphone) sings the "Soliyo" to the accompaniment of *djembes* and *dununs* at a wedding party

Photograph by Lucy Duran, Bamako, 2013

FIGURE 2.2 Babani Kone, Mali's most popular *jelimuso*, at a wedding party, calling the horses for the bride's relatives, who prepare to give her money

Photograph by Lucy Duran, Bamako, 2008

onwards, in Bamako, Mali's capital, the music would be heavily amplified, especially at wedding parties, which were the most lavish of all lifecycle events. I would sit at one end of the canopy with the musicians. On the other three sides were seated the female guests and relatives, some dressed in brightly colored matching gowns, who would leap to their feet to dance whenever a song was dedicated to them. As they shuffled by the singer, they would give her money. When the singer spotted someone special, such as the bride's "godmother," she would belt out the "Soliyo," which raised the temperature of the event by several notches.

The women I was staying with taught me a basic version of "Soliyo," and encouraged me to sing out as confidently as I could, adding improvised text where possible. "A *jelimuso* can't be shy," they would say. "Do you think the horses will hear you if you sing quietly?" Of course, I took this as a reference to the opening line of the song ("horses, oh!"), which I had been told was how the *jelis* would praise their patrons. I doubted that any amount of my singing would have attracted a real horse's attention.

My gate-crashing of wedding parties as honorary *jelimuso* meant that at some point I had to justify my presence to the guests. All eyes would turn to me as if to say, "well? You're a *jelimuso*? Prove it!" I would be handed the microphone, and mustering all my courage (I am not a singer), one arm outstretched, I would launch into as powerful and elaborate a rendition of the opener, "horses, oh!" in my most strident voice. This invariably provoked a gasp of astonishment, with some people even coming up to give me money.

No other song had the same impact. On many occasions, it helped me through difficult moments, such as going through roadblocks on country roads. Once when crossing the border into Guinea overland—a notorious spot for having to hand out bribes—just by "calling the horses," I sailed through the various police checks. In fact, I came out with my pockets stuffed with money—given to me by immigration officers who were astonished to hear me sing the song. These were gifts to me for reminding them of their social obligations.

Background to the "Soliyo"

Mande music, like Mande culture in general, has not developed in a vacuum. It has been in contact with many different styles across North and West Africa for centuries, to such an extent that it is sometimes hard to unravel what is indigenous and what comes from elsewhere. It is tempting to think that "Calling the horses," with its **melisma** and free rhythm, is in some way influenced by the Muslim call to prayer. But the descending and declamatory melodies are shared with the Mande repertoire in general, especially in the improvised sections (known as *teremeli* in Maninka and Bamana, and *sataro* in Mandinka). These sections, which are undoubtedly part of a centuries-old style, are the true test of a *jeli*'s skill and knowledge. The more likely explanation for any similarity between the "soliyo" and the *adhan* or call to prayer is that the region is located on the trade routes between subSaharan Africa and the Middle East, and has absorbed elements from both.

"Soliyo" does have musical features that set it apart from other Mande *jeli* songs. These are: its **a cappella** performance; its short length (between 30 seconds and two minutes); and its opening and closing phrases, which are exclusive to the song. It must begin with the exclaimed word "*Soliyo!*" (or "*Soruwo!*"), which usually starts on the 5th and goes down to the **tonic**; and it must close with some version of the following text: "*y'a muta, y'a faga, kele*" ("you seize him, you kill him—that's war"), which falls from the 3rd degree of the **scale** to the 5th below tonic, finally ending on the tonic. In between these two "musical bookends," the singer will insert any number of formulaic phrases. In addition, individualized textual material related to the regional background, knowledge, and skill of the singer, and the person to whom he/she is singing, is inserted. The scale may include both a major and **minor** 3rd, and both flat and natural 7ths, and each phrase tends to go downwards, or go up and down rapidly within a range of a 4th. (This is also a characteristic of other Mande *griot* melodies.)

"Calling the horses" is the only piece in the Mande repertoire that is performed a cappella. When inserted into another song, however (as described above), the scale and rhythm may be adapted accordingly, but it fits best with a major key accompaniment such as *Jawura*.

The tonal center (tonic) for the "Soliyo" in our listening guide is F, and the melody is in a major **heptatonic scale**, with both a flat and natural 7th. The melodic range is a 10th; it goes up to a flat 7th (E flat) above the tonic, and down to the 5th (C) below the tonic. This is fairly typical of performances of "Soliyo." Most of the phrases are in syllabic and descending contour, following the rhythm of the spoken word, in an **improvisation**al style known as *teremeli*. This texture is varied by a few words such as "horse" being drawn out with melisma, sustained notes, heavy **vibrato** and some **microtonal variation** (presumably a legacy of the literal "call to horses"), to dramatic effect.

Musical Features

TIMED LISTENING GUIDE

0:00   *Soliyo*
     —Calling the horses
     Begins with a rapid **glissando** up to C in the treble clef on the syllable *So-* and descends in a melismatic phrase to the tonic F

0:07   *iyehehe*
     —(a meaningless exclamation, probably a call to horses)
     Drawn out over **pitches** 3, 4 and 5, with sustained vibrato on the last note 3 (note A)

00:12   *Jalitigi ni jalitan mankan/Mògòtigi ni mògòtan mankan/Mògò lakali mand'i konyògòn ye*
     —A man/noble with *jelis* is not comparable to the one without *jelis*/A popular noble is not
       comparable to a man without followers/A man is not always best praised by his peers
     A recitation of three phrases with an almost identical melodic profile: using one note per syllable on pitches 3, 2 and 1 of the scale, and a dropped almost spoken final syllable, characteristic of much of the Mande *griot* repertoire

0:23   *N'bè soli welela*
     —I call the horses
     The singer adds intensity by going up to the 6th (high D) and then descends down to the 3rd (A) with some ornamentation on the last syllable

0:26   *jatigi baro/i ka di jatigi min ye/ni ye jatigi jugu baro*
     —Entertain a patron who likes you/if you entertain a bad patron
     Three phrases that start on the high 6th (D) and descend to the 3rd (A) with some tonal inflection and vibrato on the last syllable of each phrase

0:32   *N'a ma f'i ye son ye, a b'a f'i ye fana ye*
     —They will either accuse you of being a thief or a gossiper
     Two phrases, the first descends from the 5th to the 3rd, and the second goes from the 2nd to the 4th and then down to the tonic

0:37   *Jatigi jugu la baro man di n'ye abada*
     —I do not like entertaining bad patrons at all
     The phrase starts on the 3rd and goes up to the 5th before descending to the tonic. The last six syllables are all on the tonic (F). There is a longer pause between this and the next phrase

0:41   *N'bè jigi barika da*   —I thank my patrons

	A syllabic phrase that starts on the high 6th (D) and descends to the 3rd (although the last syllable is almost spoken)
0:44	*ah n'bè kanu barika da – yi* —I give thanks to love This single phrase, which goes across an whole octave, goes up to the flat 7th (E♭) and down to the E♭ an octave below, also has some longer held notes performed with a rich vibrato on the first and last syllables of the phrase
0:51	*A ye hòròn nyumannu barika n'ye* —Please give thanks to all good nobles The phrase descends from the 5th to the tonic
0: 55	*Ala mògòlu da/Ala ma mògò bè lakanya/kè mògò fè min b'i fè/fara mògò de la/mògò min t'i fè* —God created men /but God not make them equal/love someone who loves you back/and avoid those who do not love you Four syllabic phrases descending from the 6th to the 3rd
1:06	*Ne bè n'ka jigi barika da jatigi nyumannu ye lon o lon/Kanu ka wusa ni fa ye/jigi ka wusa ni fa ye* —I give thanks to all patrons every day for all their good deeds. Love and good deeds from a patron is better than having a father Three phrases in syllabic recitation with descending lines across the notes that fall between the 5th and the tonic
1:14	*I dali so nina hee-yi* —Get used to this horse This phrase signals that the song is coming to an end, as the singer is calling the horses for a last time. There is a pause between the two parts of the phrase; the second part of the phrase ascends from the tonic up to the 4th, and then glides down to the 2nd with heavy vibrato before dropping in almost spoken **mode**
1:21	*ahh kèlè yi fè/i y'a muta o i y'a faga/ kèlèeee* —The battle is yours/when you capture someone, you kill them, that's war! This is the standard formulaic ending to the piece, with melismatic melody descending an octave down to the 5th below tonic, via the flat 7th, and ending on the sustained tonic with the word "war/"

The Social Context

The woman described in our opening anecdote who sang the song in Paris was a *jelimuso* or *griot*. The man she sang to was a *horon*, or "freeborn," a descendant of Mali's precolonial rulers and warriors. It is the *jelimuso*'s business to know the genealogy of every Malian surname; it is the *horon*'s business to reward this act with some kind of a gift, nowadays usually money.

The *jelimuso* automatically considered this man a patron merely by virtue of his surname, even though she had never met him before and might never see him again. Neither he nor she understood the exact meaning of the song's rather obscure lyrics, except that they refer to the heroes and wars of the great Mali Empire of many centuries ago. But clearly, some exchange happened that is considered meaningful by both protagonists.

Scenes of this kind, with a *jelimuso* "calling the horses" for a patron, are played out wherever there are Mande people. The song is archaic and unique, but also ubiquitous. No one except a *jeli* may sing it. It is fundamental to the expression of *jeli* culture, and yet little has been written about it. At worst, the song is formulaic and predictable; at best, it is an exhilarating vocal tour de force, technically demanding, powerful, improvisational and highly individual—a "calling card" of the *jelis*.

"Soliyo's" musical features, along with its unique textual features—the emphasis on horses, their power, and the mention of the name Silamakanba Koita—suggest that it has an essentially ritual function, and acts as a statement of the relationship between the *jeli* and other members of Mande society. It is widely performed by *jelis* across a vast geographical area, from the Gambia in the west to Burkina Faso and Côte d'Ivoire in the east. This broad diffusion of the song and the consistency of its features, language and social function, suggests that it is very old indeed. One of the problems in identifying and understanding the piece is the variation in language and dialect across the geographical area where Mande culture exists, which means that it may be referred to by different titles. It would appear, judging from musical features, that the piece comes from the west of Mali. As we shall see, however, some elements in the song point to a different regional origin, further east.

Girls in *jeli* families are trained to sing the basic lines of "Soliyo" before they can even speak, and certainly before they can understand the meanings of the words. There is something surreal about hearing these archaic lines, glorifying war and conquest, coming out of such tiny mouths; particularly since the Mande are well known for being a peaceful people. From the age of about 10, *jeli* girls begin to sing with their mothers in public, often at wedding parties, and will perform the "Soliyo" in a reasonably complex version. This song is how girls begin to learn the skill of improvisation, which is so intrinsic to the *griot*'s art.

"Soliyo" crops up in performances of Mande epics, such as in the story of Sunjata Keita, who founded of the Mali Empire in c. 1235. Singers will tend to place it at

PRIMARY SOURCE

Interview with the *jelimuso* Kandia Kouyaté

Kandia Kouyaté (b. 1958 in Kita, western Mali) was considered one of Mali's most knowledgeable and greatest voices of the 1980s and 90s. I conducted a lengthy interview with her in 1998 which was published in a magazine called *fRoots* in 1999.

LD. What is the importance of the "soliyo" why do you sing it all the time?

KK. Soliyo? You know, in the old days you couldn't do anything without horses. All the big things that happened, were with horses. The religious wars of Almamy Samori Toure happened with horses. The religious wars of Cheikh Oumar Tall were fought with horses! So when the *griots* saw horses, they would sing:

(sings) "Soru-wo! Yeh, Su kele mansadingo nyara yariyariyari" (Horses oh, the princes' war horses were beautiful).

[speaks] *yariyariyari* means the horses have left like this, *yariyariyari*. The horses were well dressed—yes! The king's horses were well dressed. So when they rode off, they went like this: yari - yari - yari. That's why when I sing "soliyo," I put this into my song.

Soliyo, soliyo—all the *griots* start with soliyo. Because one can never "sing a king" if he has no horses. He always has horses. In the old days there were no cars! One travelled from country to country with the horses . . .

LD. Is this "soliyo" a fixed song or can you sing anything?

KK. You can sing anything but it must be things that the great warriors have done, involving horses. For example, "soliyo" is the Magan [Makan]. The Magan was someone who had many horses, Makanba Koita, that was before the time of Sunjata. He was a great warrior. You can never sing "soliyo" without singing Soru Siramaganba [Silamakanba] Koita . . .

LD. There are many things in your songs that are not everyday language. When I asked your sister-in-law what you sang, she said she didn't know, it was *jelikan*.

KK. (laughs) Yes. But what I mean is that there are many words [in my songs], expressions one doesn't hear elsewhere—words that I learnt from the elders. They're not just any words, they're words that are carefully controlled. Not everyone can understand.

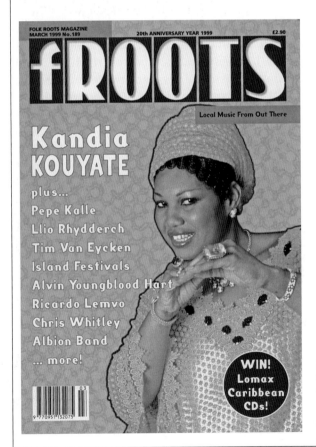

FIGURE 2.3
Cover of *fRoots*, March 1999, featuring Kandia Kouyaté

Courtesy of Ian Anderson

strategic moments in the story, for example, when narrating the events of a battle. Often it sounds more like a praise song for horses than for the warriors who rode them. Versions of the "Soliyo" are also embedded in thousands of recordings of vocal music by Mande *jelis*—a song within a song, serving to heighten the emotional intensity of the performance. Sometimes just the opening or closing lines of "Soliyo" are sufficient to add what is like a dose of strong pepper.

Obscure Words, Powerful Sounds

The senior Malian *jeli*, Wa Kamissoko says that "Calling the horses" is the song with which the *jelimuso* ritually begins her singing, but he comments, "most *jeliw* don't even know its meaning any more, nor can they pronounce all of it."

"*Jelikan*" (literally, the language of *jelis*) is the name for the special vocabulary and phrasing that the *jelis* use in both speech and song during particular ritual moments. Some of the vocabulary is extremely obscure because it has been retained from a much earlier period of history, possibly even going back eight centuries to the founding of the Mali empire: like hearing words and grammar from the time of Chaucer, but passed down through the ages via word of mouth. Inevitably, words have been transformed and given new meanings. There is also the belief that the *jeli*'s spoken or sung word contains an esoteric force, known as **nyama**.

The author Patrick McNaughton notes that blacksmiths, who are also powerful hereditary artisans, share this power as well as many aesthetic concepts with the *jelis*. He writes:

> Bards, called *jeliw* [the Bamana plural of *jeli*], are the genealogists and epic poets of Mande society. They are at once historians, musicians, and political motivators . . . while the great bards pride themselves on knowing history most authoritatively, they are rarely interested in its accurate public presentation. They manipulate the details of history to motivate their audiences. One of their most important tasks is to inspire the Mande citizenry, to fill people with the desire to live up to their potential so that society remains solid and vital . . . For the Mande, words are full of special energy, which can be dangerous if misused. Bards are believed to possess great reserves of this same power, and they are trained to manipulate it. Thus their songs become more than inspirational. They are instrumental. The power in them can inhabit an audience and literally drive it to all manner of acts.

McNaughton's insight into the way that songs have "power" and can "inhabit" the audience, helps us to understand why a song like "Calling the horses" can produce such a strong impact on the listener. One important concept shared by blacksmiths and *jelis* is the importance of clarity and obscurity: blacksmiths apply these ideas to the lines of their masks. Veteran *jelis* likewise emphasize the importance of clear delivery of text and melody; each word and phrase must be heard distinctly. Most information in Mande culture has circulated orally rather than in written form, and song has played a vital role in this for centuries. The flow of the words and phrases should determine the melodies in the improvised, **recitative** sections, while the choruses are more rhythmic in *jeli* song. By the same token, the actual words used may be obscure, allowing performers and listeners to provide various interpretations, according to the situation. This conforms to the concept of obscurity.

"Something happens when you improvise the great songs of the past" comments Hawa Kasse Mady Diabaté, one of the finest singers of the younger generation of *jelimuso*, whose version of "Soliyo" is analyzed in this chapter. Each time she performs a song from the Mande repertoire, she does it differently, as she told me in Bamako in 2013:

> I myself sometimes don't even know what I've just sung. It comes from deep inside me. Maybe they're words I've snatched out of my memory from having heard my parents and grandparents perform. Others will ask of me, "what is that name you sang then?" and to be able to answer, I may have to listen back to a recording of myself, and even then I may not know. These are names from a long time ago.

The Mande have a strong belief in something they call *yeredon*—to know yourself, which means, to know who your ancestors were and what they did, and the *jelis* have always played an important role in imparting such information. Hence the line, "A patron of a *jeli* is better off than someone who has no *jeli*." "If you know who you are, and what your origins are, you'll never do bad things," Bako Dagnon, a veteran *jelimuso*, told me when we met at her home in Bamako in 1997:

> The *jeli* sings to his patron, "you are so and so, your father did this, your grandfather did that, you don't have the right to do something bad." If you see someone doing something bad, the *jeli* says to them, this is unworthy of your culture, of your country . . . Women observe much more than men. Men go straight for the action, women check it out first, they have lots of little ways of doing things. The *jelimuso* is a good commentator.

Why "Call Horses"?

There is no doubt that the tradition of singing this song goes back to precolonial times, when horses were highly prized because of their prowess in the battlefield. But when and why did this tradition come about? Who are the horses and why call them? To answer, evidence must be pieced together from a number of sources— oral literature, live performance, recordings, interviews, observation, the culture of horses in the Mande world and even, as it turns out, archeology.

Horses have been in the West African savannah at least since the ninth century, probably introduced by Berber traders. They are still widely used for transport in rural Mali. For some populations of the middle Niger valley, such as the Fulbe neighbors of the Mande, skill in the saddle is an important aspect of cultural identity to this day.

In the precolonial era, that is, up until the late nineteenth century, Mande warlords practiced equitation, and fought wars on horseback. According to oral tradition, they trained their horses to prance to the music of *jelis* when returning victorious from battle. It is, of course, well known that horses have an ear for music, as in the Spanish and Viennese riding schools, where horses dance to waltzes and pasodobles.

There are many songs that tell of horses dancing to the sound of two of the *jeli* instruments, the **balafon** (Mande xylophone) and *kora* (a 21-string harp). The popular *balafon* piece "Keme Bourama," dedicated to the nineteenth-century warlord and Muslim cleric Almami Samory Toure (1830–1900) and his half-brother Keme Bourama, is sometimes also called "So Bala" (the horses' *balafon* tune), because its lively interlocking melody made the horses spring in time to the rhythm. One of its refrains reflects how much Keme Bourama valued his horse—comparing it to his wife. It says: "Keme Bourama has three brides: Yoro [his horse], Mariama Sire [his wife], 'enemy-slayer' [his sword]."

Another well-known Mande song, "Kuruntu Kelefa," supposedly the first piece ever composed specifically for the *kora*, has the refrain, "Ah, see the horses dancing/Look, the war is over, the horses are dancing."

The horse is depicted in "Soliyo" as a creature of awe, a "fearsome thing" (*so man nyin de*). Some of the lines describe horses as "traitors," because they are more

FIGURE 2.4 **A young Fulbe man shows off his riding skills**
Photograph by Lucy Duran, Bamako, 2013

powerful than their riders: "the horse can betray, even the horse's reins can betray" (*so ye jamfati ye, so nugulen ye jamfati ye*). The *jelis* explain these lines as follows: "Even if a rider tries to hold tight to the horse's reins, the horse may not obey. Or the horse may die, leaving its rider on the ground, vulnerable."

Some lines in the Mande epics attribute horses with almost human qualities:

> This is how we praise the horses, we say
> Master of the wild bush,
> Host-killing hunter.
> Stranger in the afternoon and village chief by morning.
> Mouth full of chain and back full of saddle,
> Your forefeet dig a grave and your hind feet close it.
> Your tail fans misfortune away from your neck.
> Your spine tramples misfortune,
> The pupil of your eye blinks at misfortune,
> Your nose snorts at misfortune,
> Your ears twitch at misfortune.

Whenever I asked about the meaning of "Calling the horses," singers and listeners alike would describe it in metaphorical terms; there have been no battles on horseback for well over a century, not since the precolonial era. The reference to horses was not considered important per se, except as a signifier of the power of the person to whom the song was dedicated, because kings also rode horses. "The opening call *soliyo* establishes a sense of grandeur," was how some *jelis* put it.

However, I began to wonder if this elongated musical cry could originally have been quite literally a call: a call that a horse would be trained to recognize and respond to. This would explain why the song is so short, and a cappella. Perhaps the real protagonist of the song is not the patron after all, but the horse itself. This would explain a recitation by Bamba Suso of the epic story of Sunjata, recorded in the Gambia in 1970, where Sunjata asks his *jeli* to call the horses, and a white stallion appears:

> Sunjata said to Bala Faaseega Kuyate [his *jeli*]
> "Haven't you called the horses for me?"
> Bala asked, "What sort of a thing is a horse?"
> Sunjata said to him, "A *griot* is an impatient fellow,
> Just call the horses."
> "Come horses! Oh horses! Mighty Sira Makhang" . . .
> When he called the horses,
> a white stallion appeared,
> and Sunjata said, "This is a fine looking horse."
>
> (Suso and Kanuteh, 1999: 17–18)

FIGURE 2.5 Horses wearing the traditional ornamental tack on parade at the Segou Festival

Photograph by Lucy Duran, 2006

Sorotomo, City of Horses

This opens up an exploration of how song can throw light on history and vice versa. It may also provide a missing clue as to the specific origins of "Soliyo."

As already stated, Mande *jelis* belong to hereditary lineages of specialist families who have been entrusted with the art of music for centuries. These families have special surnames, one of which is Koita. The Koita *jeli* lineage traces its ancestry to Soro, an ancient city, which now remains only as an archeological site in central Mali, and to its most prestigious ruler, Silamakanba Koita. The site of this city is known as Sorotomo ("the ruins of Soro") and has long been uninhabited. It is a huge field of mounds in a rolling plain not far from the Niger river to the west of Segou, near a market village called Konodimini (a name which means "stomach pain").

In my interview with *jelimuso* Ami Koita (see Biography box, pp. 40–1), she says that her ancestors moved from Soro into the Manden region (present-day western Mali and eastern Guinea). Why would they migrate and leave the powerful kingdom of Soro? The study of "Soliyo" is a rare instance where a song can contribute to the findings of conventional archeology in Africa.

BIOGRAPHY

Some Malians believe that the only truly authoritative versions of "Soliyo" are those sung by *jelis* of the Koita lineage, because they are considered descendants of Silamakanba Koita. Ami Koita was one of the most popular and innovative *jelimuso* in the 1990s. Born in 1952 in Djoliba, a village some 40 kms west of Bamako, she is an example of how female *jelis* are grounded in the tradition but find ways of innovating as well. Ami grew up in a celebrated family of *jelis*: her mother, a noted singer, was from Kirina, one of the major centers of *jeli* learning. Kirina was founded by two lineages—the Koitas (*jelis*) and the Keitas (nobles), according to Ami. Her maternal uncle, Wa Kamissoko (1925–76), was probably the greatest orator of his time, famous for his knowledge of ancient Mande history and for his recitations of the story of Sunjata Keita, which were published in 1975.

In 1969, aged 17, Ami won a competition to join the state-sponsored Ensemble Instrumental National of Mali, where she stayed for two years. In 1971 she composed and recorded "Wadjan," a song in honor of her uncle Wa Kamissoko. Only a few years later, this became one of the most successful tunes of the Mande repertoire, when Salif Keita recorded a version with the title "Mandjou," in praise of Guinea's first president, Ahmed Sekou Touré.

With her background in the deep traditional styles and songs of *jeliya*, Ami Koita was also a modernizer, changing the sound of the traditional *jeli* ensemble by adding

FIGURE 2.6
Ami Koita holding one of her music awards

Photograph by Lucy Duran 1993, Bamako

an electric guitar, drum machine, synthesizer, and global rhythms. Her most successful album was *Tata Sira*, in praise of a woman patron, in 1990. Because she sometimes used Latin rhythms in her music she was called "*jeli pachanga*," and also was known as "*jeli* finesse," because of her dress style. During this period she was in great demand on local television and at concerts in West Africa, and also received generous financial support from several patrons including "Concorde" Gaye, a Senegalese businessman, so-called because he always flew by Concorde.

I interviewed Ami Koita in Bamako back in 1991, asking her about the Koitas and her connection to the "Soliyo":

LD. Can you explain about calling the horses? Because the song mentions the name Koita, and that is your surname.

AK. This song is uniquely for the Koitas: it's dedicated to Soro Siramakanba Koita, the first warlord. The *jelis* used to sing for him and call the horses because he loved horses—he used to speak to them. So whenever someone does something good, the *jelis* will "call the horses"' for that person, but always remembering Sira Makanba Koita. Jimme was his brother: That's why we sing Soliyo Jimme. This was long before Sunjata's time, it happened at Sorotomo near Segou. At Konodimini there's a museum which tells the story of Siramakanba Koita. These are my ancestors. They were originally from Segou during the Wagadu Empire, but then they moved west to Manden, at the time of Sunjata. There are Koitas who were noble and others became *jelis*, they are my ancestors.

The meeting point between archeology and ethnomusicology is often referred to as music archeology, and focuses primarily on reconstructions of a non-extant musical past through material culture—sound artifacts such as musical instruments, and depictions of music performance. Looking at a West African past through song texts and melody is more problematic because of the dynamic nature of oral tradition. In this case, work on the archeological site of Sorotomo has begun to reveal the story of a prosperous city whose power was based on its cavalry. This may well unlock the meaning of the obscure references and musical features in the piece "Soliyo," which, in turn, provides further evidence to support the findings of archeology in West Africa.

Sorotomo only began to be excavated in 2006, by a team led by the UK-based archeologist Kevin MacDonald and Malian historian Seydou Camara. Their excavations and research into local oral traditions suggest that Silamakanba Koita—whose name features in many versions of "Soliyo"—was its most prominent ruler. He was a warlord who owned an enormous cavalry; some say he had as many as 100,000 horses.

Oral traditions collected by the team from elders in villages around the site, provide a colorful account of the culture of horses in Sorotomo:

When he [Silamakanba Koita] rose up to go and conquer another place, he would have trees cut down and placed across the road. His cavalry would then pass over them. So numerous were the horses that they would continue until their hooves had cut the tree trunks in two. At that moment he would say "Stop, that's enough horses!"

It is possible that the horses may have been called to the road by women singing some version of what is now known as "Soliyo," a song equally in praise of the ruler and his horses.

Both Ami Koita and Kandia Kouyaté place the time of Silamakanba Koita from before the Mali Empire, in other words, before the thirteenth century. But MacDonald's excavations at Sorotomo suggest that it was founded in the early thirteenth century, and "abandoned in the 15th century at the time of imperial Songhay's initial military surge into the region . . . [suffering] a brutal and sudden abandonment, with possessions—from pots and grinding stones, to spindle-whorls and cowries—left in place."

Perhaps this "brutal and sudden abandonment" gives us another key to the mysteries of "Soliyo." Could it be that the fall of Sorotomo was predicted, as a result of which the *jelis* called the horses to get ready for battle? The belief in the power of diviners and omens is a running theme in the Mande world to this day. The words *kawuru* (or *kauru*) *santigi*, occur in many different performances across geographical space and time. Although difficult to translate, *jelis* believe they refer to an omen of some kind, connected with the "bearer of far-away news." They occur in another version of "Soliyo," also by Hawa Kasse Mady Diabaté, which is on the companion website. (Hawa Kasse Mady Diabaté was brought up in Kela, a village in southwest Mali that is famous for its oral traditions. Her father, Kasse Mady Diabaté is considered one of the finest voices of the Mande world, and his family is well known for powerful performances of "Soliyo.")

Could it be that the *jelis* used this song as a special melody to call the horses when the city was threatened, and its inhabitants then scattered and slaughtered? Could the *jelis* of Sorotomo have then moved westwards, sometime in the late fifteenth century, keeping alive the memory of Sorotomo with its giant cavalry—a musical reminder of its extraordinary might and power?

This very short piece of music, "Soliyo," holds many stories across a long period of time and a wide geographical space in West Africa. Its unique qualities lead me to suggest that it began life during the early period of the Mali empire some 700 years ago as, quite literally, a musical call to horses, performed exclusively by the *jelis*.

"Calling the horses" conveys a sense of Mali's powerful past through both its obscure words and its special melodies; the a cappella performance gives it a raw power and evokes a feeling of bygone times. It is sung to remind people of their place in and their obligations to society; its value is as an expression of individual and collective identity. "Soliyo" has thus played a crucial role in the continuity of Mande history and cultural values across the centuries.

Discussion Topics and Activities

- Listen to the second version of "Soliyo"—link and lyrics provided on the website—and compare it with the version discussed in the timed listening guide. Notice how different the lyrics can be, even if the melodic contours and some of the textual imagery remain roughly the same.

- Read the article on music archeology by Arnd Adje Both and discuss the differences and the relationship between the methodologies of this sub-discipline with core methods in ethnomusicology.

Recommended Reading

Charry, Eric (2000) *Mande Music: Traditional and Modern Music of the Maninka and Mandinka of West Africa*. Chicago: University of Chicago Press.
   The most comprehensive source available on this rich music culture, drawing on research in Mali, Guinea, Senegal, and the Gambia. It covers Mande music from its thirteenth-century origins to the recording studios of Paris and New York. The author focuses on the four major spheres of Mande music: hunter's music, music of the *jelis* or *griots*, *djembe* and other drumming, and guitar-based modern music.

Both, Arnd Adje (2009) "Music Archaeology: Some methodological and theoretical considerations." *Yearbook for Traditional Music* 41: 1–11.
   Key article about this emerging discipline by its leading theorist.

Conrad, David (1990) *A State of Intrigue: The Epic of Bamana Segu According to Tayiru Banbera*. Oxford: Oxford University Press.
   Another Mande epic: a traditional history of the eighteenth- and nineteenth-century Bamana kingdom of Segu. The story describes daily life in Bamana Segu, as well as its military strategy, taxation, law enforcement, and, as quoted here, horses.

Duran, Lucy (2007) "Ngaraya: Women and musical mastery in Mali." *Bulletin of SOAS* 70(3): 569–602.
   An analysis of the concept of musical mastery and the esoteric power of the *jelimuso's* singing.

MacDonald, K.C., Camara, S., Canós Donnay S., Gestrich, N., and Keita, D. (2009–11) "Sorotomo: A forgotten Malian capital?" *Archeology International* 13–14: 52–64.
   This presents new collaborative research based on the archaeology and oral histories of Sorotomo, quoted here.

McNaughton, Patrick R. (1988). *The Mande Blacksmiths: Knowledge, Power, and Art in West Africa*. Bloomington: Indiana University Press.
   Like *jelimusow*, blacksmiths are more than simple artisans, able to wield great power through their control of *nyama*. This acclaimed ethnography examines their lives and aesthetics, as well as the rhythms of their work.

Suso, Bamba and Kanute, Banna (1999) *Sunjata*. Edited by Graham Furniss and Lucy Duran. London: Penguin Classics.
   Translations of live performances of the Mande historical epic by two leading Gambian *jalis*, one of whom is quoted in this chapter. Banna Kanute's exciting version is about violent action, supernatural forces, and the struggle for mastery, while Bamba Suso features more dialogue and human relationships.

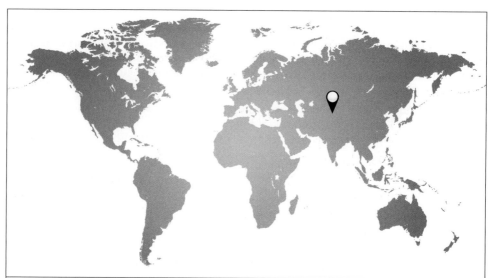

Location: Almaty, Kazakhstan

"Aqqu" (White Swan): Sound Mimesis and Spirit Evocation in Kazakh *Qobyz* Performance

Played by Raushan Orazbaeva on the *qyl-qobyz*; recorded by Kairat Zhünisov, January 2014, Almaty, Kazakhstan

Chapter three
"Aqqu" (White Swan)

Sound Mimesis and Spirit Evocation in Kazakh *Qobyz* Performance

Saida Daukeyeva

Summary

The **qobyz** is a two-stringed horsehair fiddle, ascribed ancient origins and considered sacred among the Kazakhs, whose versatile mimetic sound was once used in shamanic rituals and epic narration to evoke nature and animal spirits worshipped by the nomads. Adopted into narrative art performance in the nineteenth century, the instrument underwent a dramatic history of suppression, decline and revival as a national cultural symbol in Soviet and post-Soviet Kazakhstan, and has more recently reached worldwide audiences, eliciting new responses to its sonic mediation of the spirit realm. This chapter traces the historical evolution and recent journeys of the *qobyz* in the changing political and cultural contexts of Kazakh society, exploring the social roles and sacred connotations of sound mimesis in *qobyz* performance. The narrative centres on "Aqqu" (White Swan), an early instrumental piece based on a legend, performed by acclaimed *qobyz* player, Raushan Orazbaeva. Orazbaeva's compelling depiction of the "Aqqu" legend in sound recreates shamanic ritualized evocation of spirits in an art concert setting. Her interpretation of the piece is emblematic of the contemporary rediscovery of the *qobyz* tradition, rooted in nomadic spirituality, in Kazakhstan and beyond. The chapter examines the structure and aesthetics of Orazbaeva's mimetic performance in order to elucidate the nature of modern *qobyz* musicianship and situate it in relation to both local and global music culture and discourse.

KEY WORDS
• cultural policy
• identity
• Islam
• national revival
• ritual
• sound mimesis

Why this Piece?

1998, Almaty

The young talented Kazakh musician, Raushan Orazbaeva, who plays the horsehair fiddle, *qobyz*, the instrument of former shamans and epic bards, takes part in a concert of folk music at the Kazakh National Conservatory in Almaty. She performs a narrative instrumental piece (**küi**) from the early *qobyz* repertory, called "Aqqu"

(White Swan). This is a legend *küi* (*aŋyz küi*) linked to a form of shamanic ritual practice that is now largely discontinued in Kazakhstan. It relates the story of a boy whose abandonment of a hunt for swans, sacred among the Kazakhs, ensures his victory over the enemies of his homeland and brings better fortune to his family. The legend behind the *küi* is not told before the music performance, but the listeners, mostly conservatory students, tutors and music connoisseurs, are all aware of the narrative. They can distinguish in the music the words spoken by the boy, the galloping of his horse, his sister's joyful cries, his grandmother's wailing, and the sounds of the boy's fight with the enemies. The most vivid image captured in the *küi*, however, is that of the swan, the legend's central character, believed by the Kazakhs to embody an ancestor-spirit. The diverse array of imitative sounds that Raushan derives from her instrument recreates the voice and movements of the swan, emplacing the listeners in the legend's soundscape and enlivening the ancestor-spirit. One listener, herself a *qobyz* player, tells me that after the concert Raushan's interpretation of the *küi* made such a powerful impression on her that she visualized the performer herself transform into a swan and rise above the stage, a vision that led her to believe that Raushan's ancestor-spirit, and the spiritual guardian of her instrument, was the swan.

2008, London

The master *qobyz* player, Raushan Orazbaeva, one of only a few Kazakh musicians who have made this shamanic instrument known beyond Kazakhstan, gives a solo recital, called "*Qobyz*: Spiritual Journeys through Music," at the Royal Academy of Music in London. I organized this concert to take advantage of Raushan's brief visit to the city. The recital was publicized at short notice, yet on the night of the concert the venue is packed full. The audience is diverse, ranging from Kazakh diplomats, students and expatriates to people of various other ethnic and cultural backgrounds, and from experts in music and Central Asia to those who are little acquainted with either. Some have come out of general interest in Kazakhstan and Kazakh music, others have been drawn by the shamanic aura surrounding the instrument and its link with ancient healing and soothsaying practices. Yet, as the concert progresses, and I introduce the artist and the pieces performed, I sense the *qobyz* music drawing in and spellbinding these disparate audience members, and the atmosphere becomes elated. The evening reaches its climax with the closing piece, "Aqqu." The listeners, who are provided with a written summary of the *küi*'s legend, may not be able to follow each episode of the narrative in sound, but Raushan's extraordinary imitation of the swan affects them all, leaving no one unmoved. After the concert my inbox is flooded with enthusiastic responses to the concert: "a mesmerizing recital," "a memorable experience," "really moving," "fabulous," "Raushan's achievement is of inestimable value," "I hope her visit to the UK will introduce many more people to the very special instrument she plays with such consummate skill." An English rock and folk musician, writing about the "non-human music" of "Aqqu," notes: "In an age of the hyper self-conscious

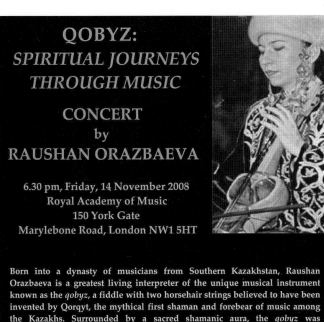

FIGURE 3.1 Poster for Raushan Orazbaeva's London Concert
By Saida Daukeyeva

X-Factor talent shows and computerized all-in software perhaps all music for, and by, and influenced by, animals is the way forwards!"

    As I reminisce over Raushan's performance and my conversations with her and other *qobyz* players over the years, I wonder how to capture the essence of this ancient, yet contemporary, music that appeals to both local and global audiences. To what extent is this neo-traditional music rooted in older practices on the instrument or influenced by the subsequent historical evolution *qobyz* performance has undergone? Indeed, what is *qobyz* "tradition" in the twenty-first century, as sought after by musicians and their listeners? Does the mimetic and expressive power of Raushan's performance arise from mediation with spirits or finely honed artistry? And how does it create a sense of place and identity for its diverse listening audience?

Musical Features

Before listening to "Aqqu," read the legend of the White Swan on page 53. Once you are familiar with the story you will hear how it is depicted in music. In traditional performances, the story always precedes the instrumental playing.

TIMED LISTENING GUIDE		
00:00	Bowing of the instrument's open strings tuned to a fifth (D–A). Pitches are designated according to the modern nomenclature for *qobyz* tuning and scale	
00:04	*Motif 1*: sounding of the strings at D–A an octave above (D^1–A^1), bowed with separate strokes for each note	The swans in flight
ca. 00:13	Production of harmonics by slightly lowering the left-hand fingers along the neck and moving the bow closer to the bridge, reinforcing E^2 and $C\#^2$	
00:31	Striking of E^2 on the A string with the hand from above, reinforcing $C\#^2$ The performer's left hand visually imitates the flapping of a swan's wing, varying in trajectory, amplitude, and rapidity	
00:39	Vibrato on E^2, emphasizing $C\#^2$, played with a full bow The performer imitates the swans gliding down with wings outstretched	Swans circle around . . .
00:55	Stepwise movement between E^1 and $F\#^1$ in an alternating heavy-and-light rhythm	. . . and land on the lake
01:04	Repetition of vibrato	Swans take off and fly away
ca. 01:15	The performer slows down, raises and releases the bow, while continuing to strike the strings with the left-hand middle finger, to convey the retreating flutter of the swans' wing movement	
01:21	*Motif 2*: a **melody** in the D major scale with an opening octave leap to A^1 (the 5th step), followed by a movement between $F\#^1$ and A^1 (the 3rd and 5th steps) on the A string, articulating the boy's words	The boy shouts: "Hey! Swans! The place where you are going is the Balkan mountain. We, too, have seen that mountain." ("*Ei! Aqqu-au! Barar jerin Balqan tau. O da bizdiŋ körgen tau*")
01:30	*Motif 3*: leaps of a 4th with **grace notes** between E^1 and A^1 (the 2nd and 5th step) on the A string with an open D string, bowed with separate accentuated strokes for each note	Köksholaq's galloping, as the boy rides after the swans
01:38	Closing motif: leaps and a stepwise whirling movement between D^1 and A^1 (the 1st and 5th steps), affirming the tonic	

01:56	*Motif 4*: a variation of motif 2, followed by a sharply articulated phrase between E^1 and G^1 (the 2nd and 4th steps), enunciating the sister's words	The sister's exclamation: "Oh, hurray, hurray! Brother is coming back, and he's shot a swan! Brother is bringing a swan!" ("*Alaqai-au, alaqai! Agham aqqu atyp keledi, agham aqqu äkeledi!*")
02:14	Closing motif	
02:32	*Motif 5*: a lament-like melody in the low register, embracing D to G (the 1st to 4th steps) on the D string	The grandmother's wailing
03:10	*Motif 3*	Köksholaq's galloping
03:19	Closing motif	
03:37	*Motif 6*: a melody comprising a leap from A^1 (the 5th step) to D^1 (the upper tonic), and a stepwise movement back to the 5th by way of a flattened 7th on the A string, played smoothly with long strokes of the bow	The enemies are sounding the *kernei* trumpet
04:01	*Motif 7*: temporary modulation up a fifth to the A major scale, exploring steps 1 to 5 of the new mode with an emphasis on C♯^{1} (the 3rd step), followed by a short plucking of the open A string	The boy's challenge to combat: "One-to-one, one-to-one" ("*Jekpe-jek, jekpe-jek*"), followed by a shot
04:15	Repetition of *motif 7*, followed by three plucked snaps on the open strings, A, D, A	The enemies' response: "Come on then, come on then" ("*Kelseŋ—kel, kelseŋ—kel*"), followed by an exchange of shots
04:30	*Motif 3*	Köksholaq's galloping
ca. 04:37	Transition to *motif 1*, emphasizing harmonic E^2	The swans in flight
04:54	The performer imitates the shrill honking of a swan's cry by pressing the index finger hard against the side of the A string at E^2 and lightly touching it with the little finger from above at A^1 to produce harmonics (e.g. A^2)	The cry of a swan
5:07	The performer lightly touches each string from above alternately with the index and little finger, emphasizing the move of harmonics F♯^{2}–D^2 on the D string and C♯^{2}–A^2 on the A string	Several swans' cries, as they take off and fly away
05:14	The performer simulates the discordant tumult of the birds' cries by damping the A string with the palm at the base of the left-hand index finger to produce a squeaky sound, and randomly twanging the D string over the open resonator out of time with the bow movement	The swans' cries, fading into the distance
05:30	She presses with the index finger curled round the strings, and lightly touches the D string with the middle finger to produce an impure E^2–F♯^{2} with grace notes. The slowing down and moving of the bow up the strings towards the resonator imitates the dying away of the swans' cries	
06:08	Short plucking of the A string	A rifle shot

Instrumental Onomatopoeia and the *Qobyz* Sound

"Aqqu" exemplifies the genre of programmatic music, *küi*, in which a story told by the performer is depicted solely by means of instrumental sound. Among a diverse *küi* repertory, legend *küi*s like "Aqqu" are thought to represent an early layer of Kazakh instrumental music. Drawing on legendary subjects that evoke images of animals and birds, these *küi*s reflect an ancient worldview among the Muslim Kazakhs that fuses Islam with indigenous shamanic and animist beliefs, such as the worship of animal ancestor-spirits. Thus, the legend of "Aqqu" is rooted in the cult of the swan, and is symbolic of the special place this totemic bird holds in Kazakh culture. According to a mythical interpretation of the Kazakh people's origins, a white swan or goose (*aq qaz*, cognate with *qazaq*) turned into a princess and bore a boy child who became a forebear of the Kazakhs.

Besides their reflection of ancient beliefs and mythology, legend *küi*s are characterized by a close interrelation between verbal and musical elements, whereby instrumental playing serves to depict successive episodes in the narrative. A vestige of the earlier practice in which storytelling was interwoven with corresponding passages of music performance, the musical structure of such *küi*s is therefore episodic. The primary musical device of instrumental legends is **onomatopoeia**, or imitation of the images and characters featured in the narrative and its individual episodes. Looking at the role of onomatopoeia in the cultures of Turkic-speaking hunter-pastoralists of Central Asia, ethnomusicologist Theodore Levin coined the term "**sound mimesis**" to designate what he defined as "the use of sound to represent and interact with the natural environment and the living creatures that inhabit it, and the exploration of representational and narrative dimensions of sound-making." The musical means of mimesis are diverse, ranging from representation of an image or a scene, to stylized rendition of sounds that are described in the narrative, to articulation of specific words and phrases spoken by the characters.

"Aqqu" displays a variety of these mimetic means. Each of the characters and actions in the story is depicted in sound in a compelling and graphic way. So listeners aware of the legend have no difficulty following the plot, while those who are unfamiliar with it may envisage its content from the music. Thus, Köksholaq's galloping (motif 3) is expressed by means of leaps of a fourth in the melody, bowed with separate accentuated strokes in a regular **duple metre**. The musical portrayal of the boy and his sister, and the depiction of the boy's fight with the enemies (motifs 2, 4, and 7), involve precise rhythmic articulation of words spoken by the characters. The grandmother's wailing (motif 5) is imitated by a sorrowful, freely articulated melody in the low register resembling folk laments. The appearance of enemies playing the *kernei*, a long natural trumpet used during military campaigns, is signaled by a short descending motif in a bass drone emulating the sound of this instrument. Rifle shots are aptly conveyed by short plucking of the strings. Last but not least, the *küi* offers a picturesque imitation of movements and sounds made by swans, the main figures of the legend (motif 1): their flapping of wings and gliding down with wings outstretched, as they circle and alight on the lake

TECHNOLOGY

Qobyz

The name *qobyz* derives from cognate words in Turkic languages that refer to hollow objects. Indeed, the *qobyz* is hollowed out from a single piece of wood in a ladle-like shape, with an open resonator, and a lower extension covered with camel skin. It is strung with two horsehair strings, tuned a fourth or a fifth apart, and played with an arched horsehair bow. Hence, its fuller name, *qyl-qobyz*, *qyl* meaning horsehair.

Historically, the *qobyz* and similar fiddles current across Central and Inner Asia, such as the Kyrgyz *qyl-qiyaq* and Mongolian *morin khuur*, are thought to have been the precursors of bowed stringed instruments in general. In oral tradition, the invention of the *qobyz* is ascribed to Qorqyt, a legendary hero among Turkic peoples and the protagonist of the Oghuz epic *Dede Korkut Kitabi* (The Book of Grandfather Korkut) whom Kazakhs regard as their first shaman, epic bard and musician. As the story goes, Qorqyt was foretold his imminent death, and, in search of immortality, he travelled to all four corners of the world, eventually returning to his homeland, the banks of the Syr Darya river, at the centre of the earth. There he devised the *qobyz*, covering it with the skin of his sacrificed she-camel, Jelmaya, and played the instrument on the waters of the Syr Darya day and night. His playing enchanted nature, animals, and birds, and, as long as he played, death could never approach him.

Depicted in the legend as a medium between the human and spiritual worlds, protecting from death and establishing equilibrium in the universe, the *qobyz* came to signify a sacred instrument (*kieli aspap*) among the Kazakhs, and was adopted in the ritual practice of shamans and epic performance of bards. The shape of the instrument, perceived as an *alter ego* of the shaman and a vehicle for transporting him to other worlds during the ritual, was likened to a living creature and associated with totemic animals and birds—the camel, horse and swan—embodying ancestor-spirits. The exterior decoration of the shamanic *qobyz*—a mirror set within the open resonator and metal pendants and bells attached to its head—was believed to attract helping spirits. The sound of the *qobyz* was also assigned a sacred meaning. Distinguished by the ample use of reinforced harmonics, **melodic** ornaments and extra sound effects, it was thought to resemble the swan's voice, considered the most beautiful in nature. Within the ritual and epic performance it served a mediative and transformative role, contributing to the air of magic and mystery surrounding these practices.

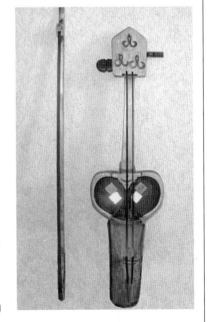

FIGURE 3.2 *Qyl-qobyz*

Photograph by Saida Daukeyeva

(00:04–01:03), and the flutter of their soaring pinions, as they take off and fly away (01:04–01:20). Its imitative **coda** (from about 04:37) realistically renders the honking of one swan followed by the cries of a flock of swans, as they disappear into the distance.

The depiction of the legend's diverse cast of characters is facilitated by the richness and versatility of the *qobyz* sound. Its key feature is the abundance of harmonics—reinforced overtones of a fundamental **tone** sounded on a string—generated by the friction of horsehair bow against horsehair strings, especially near the bridge, and light fingering of the strings at certain nodal points. This technique is known as *flageoletto*, a term adopted from the European stringed instrumental tradition. Owing to the acoustic properties of the horsehair strings and bow, and the *flageoletto* technique, the *qobyz* lends itself to the production of a wide range of harmonics, both natural harmonics derived from open strings and artificial harmonics on stopped strings. Virtually every tone on the *qobyz* can be harmonically amplified to produce striking sound effects. This, along with the frequent use of articulation and **ornamentation** techniques, such as vibrato, trills and grace notes, creates a complex and heterogeneous sound. Described in traditional sound aesthetics as *qoŋyr* (dense, velvety), it is deep and warm in the lower and middle registers and bright in the upper register, with flute-like, silvery harmonics.

Social Context

Sound Mimesis as Spiritual Mediation in Ritual and Epic Practice

The exploration of mimetic qualities of the *qobyz* in the contemporary repertory of legend *küis* goes back to earlier practices on the instrument, that is, to shamanic rituals and performance of epic tales among the Kazakhs. In both these traditions, the horsehair fiddle was ascribed special powers and significance as a means of mediation with the world of spirits. Kazakh shamans, **baqsys**, played the *qobyz* and sang invocation tunes (*saryn*) to its accompaniment to establish contact with and appease the ancestor-spirits, with the purpose of ensuring a successful hunt, healing a patient, or foretelling the future. The use of instrumental onomatopoeia during a shamanic ritual, as well as the shaman's vocal imitations of the sounds of nature and the human world, signaled the shaman's possession by his helping spirit, which was often personified as an animal or a bird. At that point the shaman would receive information from the spirit world through the medium of his instrument. Bards, *jyrau*s, who served as advisers to rulers, clan leaders, and military heroes, used the *qobyz* to accompany their recitation of epic tales (*jyr, dastan*), as well as didactic and philosophic poetry (*terme, tolghau*). In their performance, the instrument, with its distinctive versatile sound, depicted images and episodes in the narrative, and helped summon ancestor-spirits to guide individuals or a community, and to foretell and affect the outcome of important events.

PRIMARY SOURCE

"Aqqu" (White Swan)

FIGURE 3.3 "Aqqu" (White Swan)
Courtesy of X-Print Design Studio, Almaty

Long ago, at the time of enemy raids, a nomadic clan has to migrate from its homeland, leaving behind a poor orphaned boy with his grandmother and younger sister. To help save his family from starvation, the boy goes hunting for animals and birds. One day, as he hunts by the lake, he hears a flapping of wings above his head and sees a flock of white swans circling around and landing on the lake. He wants to catch one of them but misses his aim. Startled, the birds rise up from the lake and fly away. The boy shouts towards the swans, "Hey! Swans! The place where you are going is the Balkan mountain. We, too, have seen that mountain." He jumps on Köksholaq, his Blue Bobtailed horse, and rides after the swans. Failing to catch up with them, he returns home. Seeing him from afar, his sister runs towards him shouting, "Oh, hurray, hurray! Brother is coming back, and he's shot a swan! Brother is bringing a swan!" But his grandmother, seeing him empty handed, starts wailing, "What are we going to do now? We shall die from hunger." Witnessing their sorrow, the boy says, "I'd rather die than hear this wailing," and, taking his father's rifle, he mounts his horse, Köksholaq, and rides off. On his way he meets his people's enemies who surround him playing the *kernei* (trumpet). The boy shouts out the challenge to military combat, "One-to-one, one-to-one," and fires a shot. The enemies respond, "Come on then, come on then." They exchange a few shots, and the boy defeats the enemies in spite of the overwhelming odds against him. He takes all their possessions and rides home with his trophies. His grandmother and sister rejoice at his victory, and they live happily ever after.

Scholars in Kazakhstan have suggested that the distinctive timbral complexity of the *qobyz*, enhanced on the shamanic instrument by the jingling of metal pendants and bells, served as a sonic representation of the multi-layered structure of the universe in Kazakh cosmology. The symbolic implication of this rich resonant sound, amplified with harmonics, would be to set in motion the layers of the universe, thereby facilitating the shaman's journey to the upper and lower worlds during the healing ritual and the bard's calling on spirits during epic performance.

Consistent with the special status assigned to the *qobyz* as an instrument of mediation with spirits, in Kazakh society its use was forbidden outside the domain of ritual and epic practice. A similar restriction was placed on the appropriation of shamans' personal tunes, held to be their individual means of invoking spirits. The taboo stemmed from a fear of dangers involved in crossing the border from sacred to profane, since, when used in an improper context or by the uninitiated, the *qobyz* could reverse its inherent magic powers, causing harm to both performer and listeners.

Art Performance on the *Qobyz* and its Social and Musical Evolution

Formerly reserved for ritual observance and epic recital, the *qobyz* was adopted into the sphere of art performance through the development of the *küi* genre in the nineteenth century. This followed the decline of epic narration to *qobyz* accompaniment in the late eighteenth century and changes within shamanic practice brought about by transformations in Kazakh nomadic society resulting from Russia's colonization of the steppe, and the influence of Islamic proselytizing, which discouraged local spiritual beliefs and practices.

The musician credited with the development of the *küi* genre was Yqylas Dükenuly (1884–1916), a master *qobyz* player of a *baqsy* lineage, originally from southern Kazakhstan. His own *küi*s and renditions of folk instrumental pieces, such as "Aqqu," as far as we can judge from their contemporary versions, were musically autonomous and cohesive programmatic compositions, which in their structure and aesthetics departed from older ritualised music-making on the instrument. Nevertheless, they drew on the same musical and expressive resources of the *qobyz*, notably the characteristic techniques of sound production on the instrument, which lent themselves to the use of harmonics, and onomatopoeia. The latter, in particular, became a frequent artistic device of Yqylas's *küi*s.

A more drastic social and musical change was, however, to affect *qobyz* performance in the twentieth century, with the establishment of Soviet Kazakhstan. Soviet cultural policy aimed at modernizing the culture of the indigenous peoples of the Soviet Union by eradicating local practices viewed as backward and patriarchal, and promoting Western models of music performance and pedagogy, including musical **notation,** European-style music institutions and orchestras. The traditional horsehair fiddle, an instrument of shamans and epic bards, was condemned as a "vestige of the dark feudal past," and its related performance practices were suppressed and marginalized. At the same time, a new, modified version of the *qobyz* was introduced into mainstream, state-supported music practice. This was the *prima-qobyz*, modelled on the violin, with a closed wooden sound table, four metal strings and a violin bow. Intended for playing solo and in newly established folk orchestras, it was adjusted to the pure pitch of orchestral instruments and lacked the harmonic richness and timbral diversity of the traditional *qyl-qobyz*.

FIGURE 3.4
Prima-qobyz
Photograph by Saida Daukeyeva

The 1960s saw a political "thaw" in the Soviet Union, and a relaxation of some of the more extreme cultural policies. Now began a process of restoring traditional Kazakh culture, music, and musical instruments, including a revival of the original *qobyz* and its *küi* repertory. Two traditionally trained master *qobyz* players, Däulet Myqtybaev (1905–1976) and Jappas Qalambaev (1909–1969), were invited to teach the *qobyz* at the Kazakh National Conservatory in Almaty. They taught students using conventional oral methods, and thereby helped to preserve a body of traditional *küi*s for the *qobyz*. However, the assimilation of the *qobyz* into the Europe-influenced system of education in Kazakhstan led to changes in training and performance. The *küi*s recorded by Däulet Myqtybaev and Jappas Qalambaev were disseminated in notated scores, and *qobyz* players began to be taught using teaching methods and technical vocabulary adopted from Western art music. The migration of *qobyz* playing onto the concert stage also entailed a break with the past in the style of performance. Instead of sitting on the ground, holding the instrument in front of them, performers now sat on a chair, gripping the instrument between their knees. Storytelling, which used to be a vital part of *küi*s, was abandoned in concert performance, turning *küi*s into purely musical pieces. Although the oral tradition related to *küi*s and the knowledge associated with *qobyz* musicianship continued to be passed down to younger generations of performers, interpretation of the small surviving repertory of *küi*s for the *qobyz* became a matter of debate among Kazakh musicians. Central to this debate is the question of "tradition" in *qobyz* performance.

"Aqqu": Art or Mediation?

Raushan Orazbaeva's artistic interpretation of "Aqqu" reflects the contested nature of the *qobyz* tradition today. Some critics argue that Raushan has moved away from the tradition by adopting new techniques and stylistic features. Indeed, her virtuoso manner of playing, which bears witness to her technical mastery of the instrument, exhibits some influence from performance on European stringed instruments, particularly the cello, in the way of holding the instrument, fingering and articulation. The quality of her sound contrasts with the open and strained sound production typical of earlier *qobyz* performance, as described by ethnographic accounts and captured on some early recordings of *küi*s. Her judicious contouring of phrases and clear structuring of musical form are not typical of earlier *qobyz* music-making, where musical expression was integrated into the ritual context or alternated with storytelling. She aspires to render traditional *küi*s musically persuasive and structurally cohesive in a way that reflects her awareness of European classical music, and her wider musical knowledge and listening experience.

The distinctive traits of her performance style become apparent if a comparison is made between Raushan's version of "Aqqu" and that of Däulet Myqtybaev, which she initially learnt. Myqtybaev's version is longer (08:32 against Raushan's 06:09 minutes); it contains a greater number of reiterations of the same motifs and an additional transitional motif played after the performer retunes his *qobyz* midway through the *küi* (05:25) so that the strings are a fourth apart. His *küi* thus begins and ends in different tunings, and is structured in an open-ended, episodic fashion. By contrast, Raushan maintains the tuning in fifths, as retuning the instrument would not be appropriate in a concert performance. Her interpretation of the *küi* is more succinct and integrated, and has a well-shaped tripartite form, with the framing introduction and coda imitating swans, and the main section consisting of a series of contrasting motifs, reminiscent of structural procedures inherent in European classical music (see below).

Introduction	Exposition		Development		Recapitulation	Coda
	Main theme group	Contrasting theme	Transition	Modulation	Return to the main tonality	
Motif 1	Motifs 2, 3, 4	Motif 5	Motif 5	Motif 6	Motif 2	Motif 1

Representing as it does an example of modern *qobyz* musicianship developed in the mainstream professional scene, Raushan's evocative performance nevertheless recaptures the traditional essence of *qobyz* music as spiritual mediation. Its imitative dimension, besides being crafted with a view to its aesthetic appeal for contemporary audiences, is intended to enhance the mediating and transformative power of the music, to "enliven" the animal spirit. Akin to the former *baqsy*, Raushan derives her mimetic skills from a close observation of nature and the experience of engaging with it. She relates how she came to use previously unknown playing techniques and achieved specific sound effects after noticing peculiarities of the birds' flight and cries. When she played "Aqqu" beside a pond full of birds in Almaty, the birds became anxious and responded to her imitation of the swan with similar calls, mistaking the sound of the *qobyz* for the swan's voice.

Thus, Raushan's "Aqqu" is a confluence of artistry and mediumship. It transcends the boundaries of the tradition, reflecting the performer's wider musical awareness and experience, while at the same time being rooted in the age-old shamanic tradition of *qobyz* music.

Qobyz: Spiritual Journeys through Music

Raushan Orazbaeva's performance demonstrates the multifaceted role of *qobyz* music in contemporary global culture, and the many ways in which it evokes a sense of place and identity. For audiences in Kazakhstan, this music and the instrument itself are closely associated with the locality of Qyzylorda on the banks of the Syr Darya in the south of Kazakhstan, from which the *qobyz* is said to originate. It transports its listeners to the realm of legends and tells of a Kazakh antiquity, of an archaic nomadic past, and of ancient spiritual beliefs centered on the worship of nature. The presumed ancientness of the *qobyz* has made it a potent national cultural symbol. In contemporary independent Kazakhstan its image has been invoked in narratives of the ancient historical origins of the Kazakh people and their culture. Besides creating a sense of local and national identity, the *qobyz* is also perceived in current nationalist discourse as a link to the wider Turkic world, and a symbol of the Kazakhs' ancient racial roots. Scholars in Kazakhstan point to the affinity of the *qobyz* sound to other forms of drone-overtone music-making— from playing on jew's harps and end-blown flutes to throat-singing—which are all believed to have a long history among the Turkic-speaking nomads of Eurasia.

The enthusiastic reception of the *qobyz* outside Kazakhstan has proved that it also appeals to global audiences. Raushan says that when she started to perform abroad it was surprising and liberating for her to discover that this instrument, so closely bound up with Kazakh culture and sacred beliefs, could also be appreciated by listeners worldwide. She tells of the many instances when her performance was met with a warm reception by people in, say, Holland or Belgium, who had never heard *qobyz* music before and were unfamiliar with the content and meaning of the *küi*s performed. In her view, the reason for this lies precisely in the mediating power of the *qobyz*, its ability to provide a "key" or a "bridge" linking people, nature and the supernatural. Raushan reflects that the *qobyz* can serve as a medium for people across the world, because its sound awakens in the listeners memories of their own roots (*tamyr*). For her, the purpose of *qobyz* performance is the exchange of spiritual energies that leads to purification and catharsis. She concedes that in Islam it is forbidden to call on spirits, and admits the danger of disturbing them and opening up a way into the other world. "Yet," she says, "since this instrument endowed with magic powers was given to humanity, there must have been a reason. It bestows valuable things on the human soul, and the soul is immaterial and connected with the cosmos."

BIOGRAPHY

Raushan Orazbaeva: Neo-traditional Master

An acclaimed contemporary master of the *qyl-qobyz*, Raushan Orazbaeva comes from a dynasty of musicians originally from Qyzylorda, a region in southern Kazakhstan stretching along the Syr Darya river, the legendary birthplace of the *qobyz*. Her great-grandfather played the *qyl-qobyz*, and her great-grandmother was a *baqsy* shamanic healer.

She belongs to the younger generation of Kazakh female artists who have challenged traditional notions of *qobyz* musicianship as a male preserve. Having inherited the family inclination for music, she received formal training on the *qyl-qobyz* from Äbdimanap Jumabekov, first at the Jubanov Republican Music School and later at the Kurmangazy Kazakh National Conservatory in Almaty. She recalls that notated scores were consigned a subsidiary role in the transmission of *küi*s, and the teacher encouraged students to engage individually with the music. Through this training and continuing performance, Raushan therefore developed a creative approach to interpreting traditional *küi*s.

Now she is herself an experienced teacher, having tutored at the Conservatory in Almaty and more recently at the Kazakh National University of Arts in Astana, she believes that conservatory training can only equip a *qobyz* player with technical expertise in the craft. A genuine mastery of the art, which implies a performer's ability to go deeply into the musical material and communicate by that means, can only be attained through independent practice and personal experience by someone who is constantly seeking new ways of expression and who is destined for this art.

In the spirit of traditional musicianship on the *qobyz*, Raushan is both performer and composer. She has devised her own idiosyncratic renditions of existing *küi*s, enlarged the current *qobyz* repertory by arranging *küi*s for the two-stringed lute, *dombyra*, and composed her own *küi*s. She understands contemporary performance as a rediscovery and creative interpretation of old instrumental tunes (*saryn*).

FIGURE 3.5
Raushan Orazbaeva
Photograph courtesy of Raushan Orazbaeva

My dream is to retrieve the ancient sound of the *qobyz*. The more time goes by, society advances and civilization develops, the more one has to keep to one's own roots and seek out one's own sources. The repertory for the *qobyz* is small, and our generation should leave something of its own, but in such a way as to restore. This is possible through entering into an ancient *saryn*, through mediation with spirits. As you play, all of a sudden you realize, 'This is how it should be,' as if the spirits tell you. We say that we compose but in fact we restore: just as an ancient castle can be restored from ruins, so it is possible to take fragments of a *saryn* and make a *küi*.

Raushan is equally well known at home and abroad, having contributed to the revival of the instrument in Kazakhstan and at the same time to its growing popularity beyond the country. As a sign of her recognition, she has won awards at a number of republic and regional competitions, including the Grand-Prix in the Yqylas Dükenuly competition for *qobyz* players in 2008, when she was granted the opportunity to perform on a *qobyz* that belonged to Yqylas himself. She has also performed widely across Central Asia, the Middle East, Southeast Asia, Europe, and America, and is known through her recordings, in particular her solo disk *Akku* released in Italy in 2004. Whether at home or abroad, she keeps to the traditional repertory and contemporary pieces in the earlier style, and eschews adapting traditional tunes to the aesthetics of "world music." Her choice—to perform music in the former style—is deliberate. She sees it as her vocation to preserve the integrity of *qobyz* music, to assimilate the traditional style into her own creativity, and to bear it to new generations and wider audiences.

While her musicianship has absorbed broader influences, Raushan's understanding of *qobyz* music touches on its original sacred role, purpose, and significance. She views

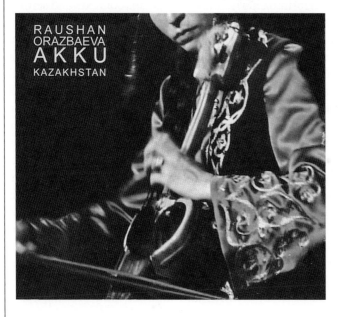

FIGURE 3.6 *Akku* **CD cover**
Courtesy of Felmay Records

the *qobyz* as "a magic power," "a bridge by which one comes into contact with spirits, with the other world." "Its very sound," she observes, "brings the listener, and even more the performer, into a state of trance. I myself, as bearer of this instrument, am also a bridge to the other world, a vessel through which information is transmitted by spirits."

The most striking feature of her personality is her self-identification as a *baqsy*, and her deep attachment to her instrument. She recollects how her favorite *qobyz*, that has been her companion for many years, split apart in her hands before her performance at a competition. Her teacher thought the instrument had taken on itself the evil eye intended for its performer. She then fell ill, and for a long time could not find any master who would repair it. At last, she made a pilgrimage to the shrine of the Sufi saint Sunaq Ata, her clan's forebear, in Jaŋaqorghan in the region of Qyzylorda. After that journey she met an unknown young master who revived her instrument.

Raushan says that "the *qobyz* world is a universe," and that her calling is to explore it as much as the spirits will allow her. She describes her performance experiences as meditations, journeys into different worlds, whereby she surrenders herself entirely to the music, entering another time and space dimension where she can mediate with the spirits. "I have played and played, but not yet reached the summit. The *qobyz* sound is like an ocean bed. Can it ever be fathomed?" Still in pursuit of this ideal sound she believes that revelations are only possible in the course of performance, in the "here and now" of a performance event, during the immediate contact between performer and audience.

Raushan's experience of performing *qobyz* music in various contexts and settings all over the world—a concert at a church in France, a therapeutic séance at an abbey in Germany, and spiritual festivals in Fes (Morocco) and Jodhpur and Nagaur (India)—demonstrates that the *qobyz* has moved away from its former attachment to a specific ritual and cultural context. It has revealed an affinity with other spiritual, ecstatic, and transformative practices from around the world, such as neo-shamanism and **Sufism**, and in this way it aligns with the emergence of new religiosities and spiritual communities. Listeners worldwide have responded to the sacred power of its sound in ways that confirm that it is no longer solely a regional or national phenomenon. For them, too, this instrument creates notions of place and belonging in an emotional and spiritual sense. Raushan is glad that *qobyz* music can now travel to other parts of the planet, generating an exchange of energies in the way that was not possible before. "I used to communicate with spirits on Kazakh soil. But now I perform all over the world. I am called upon to play where there is a spiritual need for it. I believe that this is arranged by spirits."

A local instrument that has achieved global recognition and has a universal appeal, the *qobyz* facilitates journeys in time and space, transporting from the past to the present, mediating between this world and another, and evoking local, national, cross-regional and global senses of identity.

Discussion topics

• Watch the video of Raushan's performance on the accompanying website and follow the legend as it is depicted in sound in the timed listening guide. Discuss the musical means of onomatopoeia employed by the performer, paying attention, in particular, to the techniques for producing harmonics and other sound effects used in the imitation of swans.

• Listen to the audio recording of "Aqqu" performed by Däulet Myqtybaev on the website and compare the two interpretations. What differences do you find in terms of their sequencing of the motifs and overall form?

Further Listening

Kazakh Music: Songs and Tunes from across the Steppe (SOASIS CD15 and CD16, P&C SOAS, 2008).
Double disk introducing regional traditions of Kazakh music, including *qobyz* performance from southern Kazakhstan by Aqnar Shäripbaeva.

Kazakhstan: Music from Almatï (VDE Gallo, Lausanne, 1996).
Collection of Kazakh *küü*s, mainly performed on the plucked lute *dombyra*, with useful sleeve notes.

Raushan Orazbaeva. *Akku*. Kazakhstan. Kyl-kobyz (Felmay, 2004).
Raushan Orazbaeva's solo disk, including a 15-minute video with concert footage:

Kazakhstan. The Kobyz. The Ancient Viol of the Shamans. (INEDIT Maison des Cultures du Monde, 2004).
Disk featuring performances by the *qobyz* players Smagul Umbetbaev and Saian Aqmolda.

Rough Guide to the Music of Central Asia. Uzbekistan to Kazakhstan: Sounds of the Silk Road (World Music Network, 2005).
An introduction to music in Central Asia, including Raushan Orazbaeva's performance of "Aqqu."

Songs from the Steppes: Kazakh Music Today (Topic World Series, 2005).
Album of Kazakh music featuring a performance of Yqylas's *küü* "Zhez kiik" (The Copper-Colored Antelope).

Recommended Reading

Daukeyeva, Saida (2007) "Kazakhstan. Le kobyz. L'ancienne viole des chamanes. Smagul Umbetbaev, Saian Aqmolda," "Raushan Orazbaeva. Akku." *Asian Music* 38(1): 155–161.
Review of two CDs of *qobyz* music.

Daukeyeva, Saida (2015) "The Kazakh *Qobyz*: Between Tradition and Modernity." In Theodore Levin, Saida Daukeyeva, and Elmira Köchümkulova, eds. *Music of Central Asia*. Bloomington and Indianapolis: Indiana University Press.
Textbook chapter overviewing the history of the *qobyz* against the backdrop of political and social change and evolving ideologies and concepts of identity among the Kazakhs.

Kunanbaeva, Alma (2002) "Kazakh Music." In Virginia Danielson, Scott Marcus, and Dwight Reynolds, eds. *The Garland Encyclopedia of World Music*, Vol. 6: *The Middle East*. New York and London: Routledge.
>   An encyclopedia introduction to Kazakh music.

Levin, Theodore with Valentina Suzukei (2006) *Where Rivers and Mountains Sing: Sound, Music, and Nomadism in Tuva and Beyond*. Bloomington and Indianapolis: Indiana University Press.
>   Book exploring the relationship between music and sound-making and the natural and social environments of nomadism in Inner Asia, accompanied with a DVD/CD.

Mukhambetova, Asiya (1995) "The Traditional Musical Culture of the Kazakhs in the Social Context of the 20th Century." *World of Music* 37(3): 66–83.
>   Journal article examining the impact of Soviet cultural policy on Kazakh traditional musical culture.

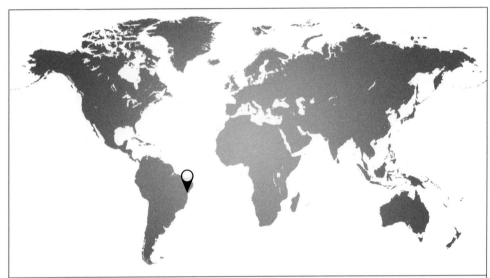

Location: Bahia, Brazil

"Grande Mestre" (Great Master): Longing and Celebration in Capoeira Angola

Performed by Mestre Valmir (Valmir Santos Damasceno), accompanied by Mestres Jurandir and Cobra Mansa on *berimbau*s, with two *pandeiro*s, *agogô*, *reco reco*, *atabaque*, and chorus; recorded by International Capoeira Angola Foundation (ICAF/FICA), 2011, Bahia

Chapter four

"Grande Mestre" (Great Master)

Longing and Celebration in Capoeira Angola

Zoë Marriage

Summary

"Grande Mestre" is the opening track on the first CD released by the International Capoeira Angola Foundation (FICA), and as such it is crucial in defining the group's identity and sound. **Capoeira Angola** is an art form that combines physical play, fighting, and dance with music. Capoeira groups present a history that traces their roots to communities of escaped slaves in northeastern Brazil. Elements of capoeira may have derived from combat games or initiation ceremonies practiced on the African continent. Capoeira is played by two people who attempt to trick and bring each other down. Around them, other members of the group sit in a circle (*roda*) and sing and play instruments. "Grand Mestre" opens with a melancholy solo song about being enslaved and forcibly transported to Brazil. It then passes through a praise section, at which moment the chorus joins in, before moving to the more up-beat **call-and-response** songs that accompany the physical game of capoeira. In this chapter, I situate the group, FICA Bahia, in terms of its music, history, and geography, and discuss the spectrum of emotions associated with Capoeira Angola, which range from longing to celebration. This spectrum of emotions is indicative of the way capoeira adepts reject or transcend material constraints, and use music as a source of continuity and identity.

> **KEY WORDS**
> - African religion
> - identity
> - memory
> - migration
> - spirituality

Why this Piece?

In 2012 I went to Brazil for five months to train with FICA Bahia as part of a piece of research I was conducting on capoeira. I went to training between three and five times a week for two hours at a time, and attended the weekly game, the *roda*, on a Saturday mornings. The *roda* lasted for around three hours, and players took turns to play instruments, engage in the physical game, and sit in the circle (also called the *roda*) supporting the players with singing. The *roda* has a ritual and spiritual element to it, although is not necessarily associated with religious practice:

FIGURE 4.1 A training class at the International Capoeira Angola Foundation, Bahia
Photograph by Hugh Marriage

there are conventions relating to respecting the physical space (for example: entering and leaving the game from the "mouth," where the musicians sit, not walking across the circle), and respecting the nature of the game (controlling aggression, and acknowledging hierarchy within the group). There are no rules in capoeira, so adherence to convention is what maintains coherence.

My training included physical and musical instruction, and took place in a large hall near the centre of Salvador, the capital of Bahia. I was part of a group of around 10 or 15 students, many of whom came from outside Brazil: FICA has satellite schools around the world and many students go to Bahia to train for a few weeks or months. All training was conducted in Portuguese. Different classes focused on different parts of the game: moves, interaction, and general fitness. The physical element was intense, not least because of the heat in Bahia, and this intensity generated a form of exhilaration that is crucial to capoeira. Musical training included instruction on the core rhythms and variations, and practice with songs and improvisation. The first *ladainha* I learnt was "Grande Mestre," under the instruction of Mestre Valmir, who sings on the CD.

Musical Features

TIMED LISTENING GUIDE

0:01	*Gunga* enters	The largest *berimbau*, the *gunga*, played by the mestre (master), sets the speed and intensity of the game
		Gunga enters straight into Angola *toque* (rhythm), playing two *chiada* (buzz note, made by holding the coin lightly on the string) quavers followed by crochet G and A (rising tones)
		Tempo around 112 BPM
0:06	*médio* enters	The middle *berimbau* enters with a series of open notes, and then plays the inverse pattern of tones to the *gunga*
		The *médio*'s *toque* (rhythm) is two *chiada* quavers followed by C♯ and B (falling tones)
0:09	viola enters	The smallest *berimbau*, the viola, enters with an open note, then moves straight into variations on the core *toque*, which is two *chiada* quavers followed by D and C (falling tones)
0:15	*pandeiros* enter	*Pandeiro*s are tambourines. There are two *pandeiro* players and they sit either side of the three *berimbau*s. They mark three crochet beats (accenting the second of these with a slap tone) and fill or part-fill the gap with jingles
0:19	*agogô* enters	The *agogô* is a double-headed metal bell (the same instrument is used in samba). Sometimes an instrument made out of coconuts or wood can be used instead. The important element is that it has two tones and produces short percussive notes; the pattern being low-high-low crochets
0:21	*reco reco* enters	The *reco reco* is a scraped instrument similar to the Cuban *guiro*. It is made out of a thick bamboo cane with grooves carved into it and a small stick is drawn over the grooves
0:25	*atabaque* enters	The *atabaque* is a large foot drum, similar to those played in southern Africa. A single conga is sometimes used. Its rhythm and tones overlay the crotchet notes played by the *pandeiro*s
		The entrance of each instrument in turn exhibits the part they play in building up the sound. The rhythms largely overlap but the texture and volume change as each instrument is introduced
0:30	'lê'	'lê' is the call to capoeira—the start of the song and the invitation to play. The style and length of the call defines the mestre and the group. This one, at six seconds, is quite long
0:39	*Ladainha*	*Ladainha* starts. The *ladainha* is the long song that opens a *roda* and is used to draw in the attention of the players with a story. Generally, the song line starts on the fourth beat. In this *ladainha*, the lines in the first half of each stanza start alternately on the second and fourth beat; in the second half the lines start on the fourth beat
		This *ladainha* relates the story of a slave who is reflecting with nostalgia on an unnamed place that he has been forced to leave. It opens "*ai que saudades*" meaning "oh, what longing!" and the slow sonorous music supports the melancholic words
		Tempo around 122 BPM at this stage

2:20	*louvação*	The *louvação* (also called *chula*) invites the chorus to respond and prepares for the physical game. It tends to be quite formulaic as it needs to be simple enough for people to hear over the ***batería*** and respond. As a rule of thumb, the *louvação* starts with a spiritual element ("long live God"' being the most widely used), moves to praise of the mestre, and ends with a celebration of capoeira
3:13	*corrido* 1	*Corrido*s are shorter songs that accompany physical play. In the *corrido*s, the lead singer improvises verses and the other players respond with the chorus
		The first *corrido* is, "*O pandeiro o viola*" and presents the instruments involved in capoeira
		Tempo about 126 BPM
6:09	*corrido* 2	The second *corrido* is "*Bahia de todos os Santos, Bahia de todos Orixás.*" This references Bahia, the cradle of capoeira, but also indicates the syncretic nature of capoeira. Bahia is the "bay of all saints," but also the "bay of all Orixás," the west African deities venerated in the Afro-Brazilian religion of **Candomblé**
		Tempo around 134 BPM
8:18	fades	This is not a typical ending. In practice, *corrido*s are called off by the mestre, either with a series of continuous open notes on the *berimbau* or with a short vocal call of "iê"

Capoeira Angola is a Brazilian art form that traces its roots to the slave quarters and communities of runaway slaves of Bahia, a coastal province in northeastern Brazil. More distantly, elements of capoeira can be traced to combat games or initiation ceremonies practised on the African continent, particularly the central-southern region including Angola. It combines physical play, characterized by kicks, escapes, head butts, and sweeps, with music. The physical game of capoeira is played by two people who attempt to trick and bring each other down. The intent is not to kick the other person to the ground but to catch them off balance or feint a kick that demonstrates superior cunning or malícia. Around them, other members of the group sit in a circle (*roda*) and sing and play instruments. The musical ensemble is composed of eight instruments that form the *batería*: three *berimbau*s, two *pandeiro*s, one *agogô*, one *reco reco*, and an *atabaque*. The songs are in Portuguese, the language spoken in Brazil, which was adopted following European colonization.

Capoeira music relies on participation, and most of the instruments in the *batería* are easy to manipulate. The *berimbau* requires technique and instruction, and is also associated with power, so there are technical and political obstacles to the beginner playing the *berimbau* in a *roda*. The singing relies largely on the **pentatonic scale** and the intervalic range remains usually within an octave. Stresses in the lyric fall within the rhythmic pattern provided by the *batería*. These factors make participation and improvisation accessible. The *ladainha* (litany) introduces play and often has a prayer-like or reflective quality. It is sung as a solo with instrumental accompaniment, but thereafter all songs are call-and-response.

TECHNOLOGY

The Capoeira Angola *batería*

The *berimbau* is an instrument that originated in the central and southern areas of Africa and was introduced to Brazil by people who were enslaved. It is a bow, approximately 1.5 meters in length, held curved by a wire. The *cabaça*, a gourd that acts as the sound box, is moved towards and away from the player's stomach to vary the resonances from its aperture. The player holds a small stick (*baqueta*) and a *caxixi* (rattle) in one hand and strikes the wire with the stick while using the other hand to move a large coin (*dobrão*) or stone on the wire to change the notes and sound texture. The three *berimbau*s have different sized *cabaças*, and are known as the *gunga* (with the largest *cabaça*), *médio* (medium), and viola (smallest). The *gunga* commands the speed and intensity of play with its *toque* (rhythm), and is usually played by the master (mestre).

The *pandeiro* (tambourine) was brought by the Portuguese colonizers to Brazil and is central to many Brazilian folk traditions. Frame drums are also found in West Africa, from where the two-headed bell, the *agogô*, originates. The scraped instrument, the *reco reco*, is understood to have been played by indigenous Brazilians. It is made out of a thick bamboo cane that has grooves carved in it, and a small stick is run over the grooves to make a scraping sound. The *atabaque* is a foot drum, this deriving from the Congo-Angola region of Africa.

FIGURE 4.2 **FICA** *batería*
Photograph by Hugh Marriage

Rhythm

There is practically no tradition of learning from written music in capoeira groups; students learn aurally, usually from their mestre or teacher. Nonetheless, the music can be conceptualized with reference to two concurrent rhythmic cells that produce accents and intensity.

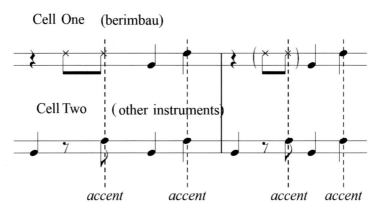

MUSIC EXAMPLE 4.1   **Rhythmic cells**

Transcription by Zoë Marriage

Identifying these cells allows the most basic form of the rhythm to be analyzed and understood by non-practitioners, but does not enable them to reproduce the music as variations in rhythm, tempo, and intonation are integral to the genre. Further, the *berimbau* has notes of indeterminate tuning and generates various percussive and resonant rather than melodic sounds, rendering the stave inadequate to capture all elements.

The first cell in the music of Capoeira Angola is defined by the *berimbau* and is, in its most elemental form, a one beat rest followed by two quaver notes and two crotchets. The quaver notes are *chiada* tones (buzz notes, played by holding the *dobrão* loosely against the string while striking the string with the *baqueta*), and the two crotchets either ascend or descend the two melodic notes of the *berimbau*. This rhythm is often rendered vocally as, "chi-chi dong ding," with "dong"' representing the open note and "ding" the higher note achieved by pressing the *dobrão* on the string. The second cell forms the basis of all other instruments and consists of a longer base note and a shorter louder or higher note, followed by another base note and a higher note of equal length. This can be sung as "pum - pap pum pap."

The rhythmic patterns played on the various instruments are overlaid rather than being interlocking and the shape of the sound is given by the combination of instruments that play on each beat. The *berimbau toque* leads the music. Navigating the cell with respect to the songs, the *berimbau*'s two *chiada* quaver notes fall on the second beat of the cell or bar. The second of these quavers is often picked up on the *pandeiro*, *agogô* and *atabaque*, giving the music a little kick. All instruments mark the third and fourth beat, accenting the fourth with a slap tone (*pandeiro*s and *atabaque*) or with the higher note (*agogô*, coinciding with the high note on the *gunga*, lead *berimbau*). The first beat is less intense, as it is not played by the *berimbau*s. The effect is to produce a subtle accentuation on the second and a half and fourth beat; these are the beats picked out in other Afro-American traditions, including by the bass in Cuban son.

Structure

The structure of "Grande Mestre," which includes the introduction of the instruments and the sequencing of songs, and the themes that are covered reflect the way that music is played during a capoeira game. The track is also instructive. This is a CD that is used by FICA and other capoeira groups to practice musical techniques as well as being played to generate atmosphere and pace during physical training.

The track opens with a long and sonorous "iê": this is a commonly used call in capoeira and, aside from prefacing songs, it is used to gather people together and to catch attention during a class or game, as well as to signal the end of a song. As the intonation, length, and volume of the "iê" are open to interpretation, it also identifies the singer, as people develop their own rendition of the call. In more practical terms, the "iê" allows the singer to engage the vocal chords before embarking on the song.

There are three forms of song in Capoeira Angola: *ladainha*, *louvação* (or chula) and *corrido*. The sequence remains the same: one *ladainha* followed by a few lines of *louvação*, followed by any number of *corrido*s, which can last an hour or more. If there is a break between capoeira games, and someone decides to sing a solo, the sequence returns to the *ladainha* and starts again. Improvisation on lyrics and melody is core to all three forms of song, and no combinations of songs are scripted.

The *ladainha* is a relatively long and slow song. It is generally sung by the mestre who is leading the *roda*, or by a player who is about to play in a game. It can be sung as a learnt piece, an improvisation, or an adaptation; adaptation with respect to place (where the song is being sung), and gender (of the singer) are common practice. The *ladainha* provides the opportunity to tell a story or set the mood for play. Many *ladainha*s deal with the fact that capoeiristas (capoeira players) exist outside mainstream society. Songs address a history of political and legal marginalization in Brazil: capoeiristas are confused, frustrated or threatened by the world. Capoeira Angola offers them an alternative reality with a different set of priorities— it is liberating and exhilarating to play and it celebrates natural and supernatural beauty—and the *ladainha* is the gateway to the game.

The *ladainha* "Grande Mestre" is sung on the FICA CD by Mestre Valmir. The song recalls the "Great Master" (who is not identified), foregrounding the authority vested in the title and the significance of lineage. The *ladainha* falls roughly into five verses, with a slight pause between each. It is melancholic in content, with a slave longing for his home and describing the horrors of the Middle Passage, the crossing from Africa to South America, and the violent conditions of slave life. The pauses allow the singer to breathe and the listeners to reflect on the story.

The *ladainha* is followed by the *louvação*, a praise song, and the soloist calls the other players to join in the singing. The *louvação* has an explicit praise element often, as on this track, starting with "Long live God." Whatever the soloist sings, the chorus responds with the same words, adding "*camará*" (meaning "comrade") to the end of the phrase, reinforcing the sense of community amongst the players. The lead singer introduces the line with a short "iê" and sings over a bar and a half. The chorus respond, picking up with a longer "iê" on the second beat of the second bar and singing through to complete a four-bar phrase. The *louvação* often makes reference to the game, particularly towards the end, and phrases are used such as "Let's go! Let's play capoeira." After a few exhortations of this sort, the physical game starts. On the track, Mestre Valmir sings, "Capoeira has principles, now is the time [to play]."

Capoeira groups place a premium on live music during *roda*s (recordings are used for training), so the CD is an artistic representation of the musical structure rather than a literal tool. Nonetheless, the interaction between the music and the physical play is bound by tradition and the introduction of the *corrido*s on the recording informs listeners that the physical play would start at that moment. The *corrido*s are often four or eight bars long and cover a range of themes, including capoeira, market or laboring jobs, and the natural world. The lead singer then improvises verses that are usually of the same length as the verses. *Corrido*s tend to be more up-beat than *ladainha*s and motivate those engaged in the physical game. Sometimes a *corrido* is chosen to give instructions to the players on the type of game they should play (faster, closer, more intense, lower), or to warn one player about the other.

The *corrido*s sung in the "Grande Mestre" track, like the *ladainha* and the *louvação*, present and situate FICA as a group. The first takes as its theme the instruments in the *batería*, with the chorus singing, "*o pandeiro, o viola,*" referring to the tambourine and the smallest of the three *berimbau*s, and the improvisations work around the theme of capoeira music. The second *corrido* is "the Bay of all saints and all Orixás." This situates the group geographically in Bahia (Bahia is the Portuguese for "bay" and is the name of the province in which the group is based), and reinforces the spiritual element to the track, as I will discuss below.

Social Context

The Social History of Capoeira Angola

The history of capoeira during the nineteenth century in Bahia is little known, but by the early twentieth century, capoeira was a word used to describe a range of activities from relaxation from physical labor in plantations and docks to street fighting with knives and guns. It was played by people of African descent and was banned by the Brazilian state, as African-derived cultures were considered debasing for the modern European-style configuration. Capoeira was also associated in law with vagrancy and brawling. Capoeiristas were incarcerated or punished harshly, and the suppression of capoeira rendered it ineffective as a fight and practically meaningless as an art form in the early twentieth century.

In the 1930s Mestre Pastinha, a capoeira player from Bahia, codified Capoeira Angola by regularizing the ensemble and instrumentation of the *batería*, introducing uniforms (yellow t-shirts and black trousers), teaching in an academy and placing parameters on the physical and musical improvisation. This was largely in response to the creation of Capoeira Regional by another master, Mestre Bimba. Mestre Bimba had prioritized combat elements of the game and had introduced the art to white students. Mestre Pastinha's approach was the opposite, developing the theatrical and ritual elements and resisting the modernization and assimilation that was being promoted by the Brazilian state in the first half of the twentieth century.

The artistic developments made by these two men restored respect for the game and capoeira was decriminalized. Pastinha and Bimba reclaimed capoeira from a custom that was declining in popularity and cultural significance, and galvanized interest in playing, particularly in Bahia. The re-engagement with capoeira (particularly Capoeira Regional) spread across Brazil in subsequent decades, and the pace of its growth led to divergences in the style of the physical play and its accompanying music. Capoeira Angola experienced a revival in the 1980s, led by the Pelourinho Capoeira Angola Group (known by its Portuguese acronym GCAP). In the 1990s Capoeira Angola gained popularity outside Brazil, and it is now played all over the world.

Capoeira Angola can be read, throughout its history, as a form of resistance. The early practice of capoeira in the face of the Brazilian law that banned expressions of Afro-Brazilian culture was resistance. Pastinha's work was largely concerned with preserving capoeira from appropriation by a white-dominated Brazilian culture. Association with other black-led movements, including Rastafarianism and the civil rights movement informed a black consciousness that was crucial to the growth of Capoeira Angola in the 1980s. Capoeira Angola did not sit easily with the military dictatorship, but its popularity increased when Brazil returned to civilian rule in 1985.

Resistance is detectable in the continual recreation of alternative histories and futures: in the twenty-first century FICA's mission combines the promotion of Capoeira Angola's heritage alongside permaculture. Mestre Cobra Mansa lives and works an organic farm—named Kilombo, after the term used to refer to maroon slave settlements—in Bahia. Capoeira students visit to train with him, work on the farm and learn about permaculture, the use of sustainable agricultural and architectural systems.

The Capoeira Angola *batería* was assembled by Mestre Pastinha. Previously, various instruments—or none—were used to accompany capoeira games. The formalization of the *batería* and the rhythms assigned to each instrument instituted defining characteristics, and the continuation of the same ensemble distinguishes Capoeira Angola from other styles. The continuation of the style and sound is reinforced through the melodic and lyric components of songs. The songs on the "Grande Mestre" track do not explore new topics or melodies but reiterate the significance of classic themes and conventions. The first *corrido* is in the public domain, but is made specific to the group in the improvisation: Valmir, playing the *médio*, name-checks his FICA colleagues on the other two *berimbau*s by singing, "Jurandir is on the *gunga*, Cobrinha [Cobra Mansa's nickname] on the viola." The second *corrido* is composed by Mestre Boca Rica, who is based in Salvador, and the references to the city reinforce the historical lineage with the notion of geographical continuity.

BIOGRAPHY

FICA was founded in 1994 by three mestres: Cobra Mansa, Valmir and Jurandir and has satellite groups across the world. Their musical collaboration on the CD, using the ensemble and rhythmic patterns established by Mestre Pastinha, situates the group within the lineage and conventions of Capoeira Angola.

The centrality of Mestre Pastinha's legacy and the **oral transmission** of Capoeira Angola combine to attach particular significance to lineage (see Figure 4.3). The founding mestres of FICA trained at GCAP, which is headed by Mestre Moraes. Moraes is the only mestre teaching in Salvador, the capital of Bahia, who trained with Mestre João Grande. João Grande was a student of Mestre Pastinha.

Lineage is referenced and demonstrated in various ways including by the conventions of the *roda*, the style of the game, and use of the uniform introduced by Pastinha, but the primary marker of lineage is the music. The ensemble, songs and *berimbau toque*s define a group and its relationship with others.

Mestre Valmir, with whom I trained, and who leads the singing on this track, was one of the founding members of FICA Bahia in 1994. He has been playing capoeira for 30 years, and gained the title of mestre in 2003. Like his FICA colleagues, he trained with Mestre Moraes in GCAP and was part of a generation of capoeiristas who oversaw the revitalization of Capoeira Angola in the late 1980s. Mestre Valmir's teaching incorporates many references to Candomblé and particularly to Ogum, his Orixá. All the mestres in FICA are men, but women are not excluded from the hierarchy: at the next level of seniority, there is one woman, Contra-Mestra Gege.

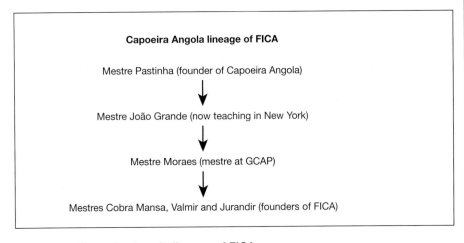

FIGURE 4.3 **Capoeira Angola lineage of FICA**

The *berimbau*, as the lead instrument in the *bateria*, defines the music by its *toque*, and plays the classic Angola *toque* on this track. *Toque*s are generally taught by the mestre to students to ensure the faithful transmission of the art. Improvisation is also taught: students learn variations on each of the *berimbau toque*s and their inversions for the *médio*, which plays the inverse of the *gunga*'s pattern. These variations are deployed at the discretion of the player, in concert with the variations used by the players of the other two *berimbau*s.

Significance of the "Grande Mestre" Track

The songs on the "Grande Mestre" track trace the emotional spectrum of capoeira, which ranges from longing to celebration. This reflects capoeira's slave origins and its expression of joy, which is not dependent on material conditions or personal experience but on the strength to play despite conditions of hardship. The longing is closely associated to the theme of migration as reference to Africa recalls forced displacement and loss. Africa is also established as the spiritual home, the realm of the Orixás, the West African deities referenced in songs. Africa is also the home of the ancestors and the way of life they represent—one that is marked by freedom and power rather than slavery and marginalization. This ancestral home is not temporally defined: it is both where one comes from and where one is going to, as well as being a continuous present, encountered through spiritual experiences. As such, it is synonymous with the other side of death: the realm before life and after physical demise, and this links the theme of migration to that of spirituality.

Migration

The use of the name "Angola" preserves reference to Africa and migration from the continent. The *ladainha* exposes the horrors of crossing the Middle Passage, the journey between Africa and the Americas, as experienced by a person who has been enslaved. The opening line, "*ai que saudade*," means, "oh what longing." This is not a slave song, it was written by Mestre Angolinha, who trained in GCAP, but its first-person narrative situates the singer within the story. As the song progresses, the singer reveals his longing not only for his mestre, but also for the place from which he has been taken, and the power of which he was deprived. In doing so, the song builds up a layered description of loss; "if the mestre were here," he sings, "this would not happen."

The *corrido*s develop the theme of migration, but through celebration rather than longing: the first celebrates capoeira music and the second the geographical location in Bahia, where Pastinha lived and where FICA has its headquarters. The corrido, "*o pandeiro, o viola*," celebrates the assemblage of the *bateria* that embodies the transmission of cultures from across the African continent and from Europe. The *berimbau* is totemic as a symbol of the African roots of capoeira, and the *pandeiro* was brought to Brazil by the Portuguese colonizers.

The second corrido picks up the migration theme. The significance of Bahia as the destination for people trafficked from Africa is intensified by the fact that it is the contemporary site of pilgrimage for capoeira players. FICA has an international reach with affiliated groups in the USA, Mexico, Costa Rica, Sweden, France, Denmark, Germany, Italy, Japan, Russia, and Mozambique, and study groups elsewhere, including in the UK. The improvised verses suggest, "If you don't know Bahia, come and see what it's like, it's a beautiful place, I'll live here until I die." Bahia is the seat of the group's identity and many capoeira students from elsewhere travel to Bahia to train.

Spirituality

Capoeira Angola has strong spiritual elements to it, although it is not aligned to a particular religious practice. Spirituality is the antidote to the chance or misfortune that rules the physical lives of people who are marginalized. Referring to the slave trade, the *ladainha* narrates that "Africans were arriving by chance, or had died on the crossing." Emanating from and alluding to experiences of slavery or extreme marginalization, spirituality is frequently expressed in terms of the need for protection.

The *louvação* signals a change in emotional pitch from longing expressed in the *ladainha* to celebration. Praise of God, the mestre and capoeira provide three spheres of potential protection and happiness; there is a hierarchy, but all three are venerated. Capoeira is a celebration of life and the triumph of joy over adversary, which constitutes a kind of spiritual activity in itself. The participatory nature of the *louvação* generates shared understandings and values and, by singing and playing together, the group is united in its experience, and in the happiness that this community brings.

The *louvação* and *corrido*s mix religious references. The "God" named in the *louvação* is not specified, but Nkossi, a deity from southern Africa, is called on for protection before entering the *roda*. The theme of spirituality is revisited in the second *corrido*, which opens with a Catholic appellation: the Bay of all Saints. The second line, however, introduces the syncretic nature of spirituality in north-eastern Brazil, changing the name to the "Bay of all Orixás," replacing the Catholic name with reference to Candomblé, the West African religion that was brought to Brazil by people who had been enslaved. The song then moves to Mãe Menininha do Gantóis (ineffectively translated as "Mother Little Girl of Gantóis") a spiritual leader from Salvador and follower of the Orixá Oxum, deity of love. The combination of spiritual references and its association with the geographical feature of the vast natural harbour serve to sanctify Bahia.

The prayer elements in capoeira songs prepare the players for the game; the physical space is understood by many in spiritual or quasi-spiritual terms: players are required to attend to various conventions. Having a spiritual connection underscores the discipline of the *roda* not as a threat but a common practice that people engage in together: how to enter the game with respect to the mestre and the art, and how to play.

PRIMARY SOURCE

Capoeira Angola is immediately visually distinct from other forms of capoeira on account of its use of yellow t-shirts. This was a uniform initiated by Mestre Pastinha, and the yellow is taken from the strip of the Ypiranga football team, which he supported. Capoeira Angola groups that trace their lineage to Pastinha tend to adopt this color and it is also used on the sleeve of the FICA CD.

The CD sleeve depicts cowry shells (used in Candomblé rituals) alongside depictions of capoeira and *berimbau* players. The CD itself shows a zebra (superimposed on a map of Africa) kicking a capoeirista (superimposed on Brazil). This references the N'golo "zebra dance," the Angolan initiation dance that has been identified as a possible root of capoeira. There are a number of t-shirt designs; this one shows two swords, the insignia of Ogum, the warrior Orixá.

FIGURE 4.4 **FICA CD**

Photograph by Zoë Marriage

FIGURE 4.5 **FICA CD sleeve**

Photograph by Zoë Marriage

FIGURE 4.6 **FICA t-shirt**

Photograph by Zoë Marriage

Capoeira is a game and has aesthetic dance elements to it; it is also a fight, a martial art, and it can put players in danger. Capoeira music is the medium by which stories and principles are conveyed. They are open to interpretation and maintain no distinction between the game of capoeira and life. A call for protection, however it is voiced, marks this consonance, and makes sense of the most fundamental goal in life: staying in the game.

Discussion topics and activities

- The chapter says that "Resistance is detectable in the continual recreation of alternative histories and futures." How does FICA aim to do this, and what kind of histories and futures does it imagine?

- What is the *roda*? What kind of space does it create, and what kinds of transformation occur within it?

- "Grande Mestre" might be described as an emotional journey through time and space. Can you explain why? What places do the lyrics reference, and why?

- Divide into two groups, recite and beat out the basic rhythmic cells, paying attention to the accents.

Further Listening

Das Voltas que o Mundo Deu às Voltas que o Mundo Dá (FICA Fundação Internacional de Capoeira Angola, 2011).
> This is the CD from which "Grande Mestre" is taken. It was recorded in 2011 and includes tracks by the three FICA mestres: Cobra Mansa, Valmir and Jurandir. Available from FICA affiliated groups.

Capoeira Angola from Salvador Brazil (Grupo de Capoeira Angola Pelourinho (GCAP), 1996).
> The defining CD of the Grupo de Capoeira Angola Pelourinho (GCAP) group in which the mestres who formed FICA were trained. This is more widely available than the FICA CD and represents elements of the same tradition.

Recommended Reading

Capoeira, Nestor (2002) *Capoeira: Roots of the Dance-Fight-Game.* Berkeley, CA: North Atlantic Books.
> Nestor Capoeira came to the Europe in the 1970s and was the first to teach capoeria in the UK. This is a creative book about the history and meaning of capoeira, told from the perspective of a practitioner.

Galm, Eric (2010) *The Berimbau: Soul of Brazilian Music.* Jackson: University Press of Mississippi.
> A book dedicated to the *berimbau*. This follows the history of the *berimbau* from an instrument despised by the Brazilian state on account of its African origins, to an iconic symbol of Brazilian cultural identity.

Lowell Lewis, J. (1992) *Ring of Liberation: Deceptive Discourse in Brazilian Capoeira.* Chicago: University of Chicago Press.

> This book explores the play in capoeira through the optics of the music, lyric, and physical game. It analyses the discourses of the game, and the meaning and role of trickery in capoeira.

Röhrig Assunção, Matthias (2007) "History and Memory in Capoeira: Lyrics from Bahia." In N.P. Naro, R. Sansi-Roca and D.H. Treece, eds. *Cultures of the Lusophone Black Atlantic.* New York: Palgrave.

> A chapter exploring the meaning of lyrics within capoeira songs, drawing on and analyzing particular examples to construct a theory of their function within the game more broadly.

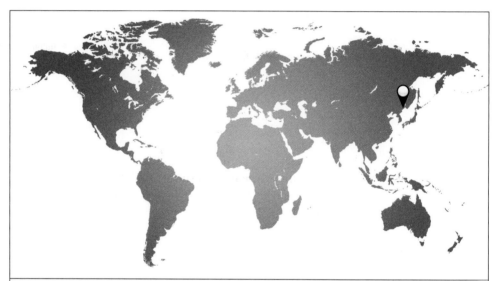

Location: Yanji City, China

"Asŭrang" (Dance Music): Buzz, Modernity, and Tradition in China

Played by Kim Ch'angnyong (*t'ungso*), accompanied by Kim Yisŏn (*puk*); recorded by Rowan Pease, August 1999, Yanji City, China

Chapter five

"Asŭrang" (Dance Music)

Buzz, Modernity, and Tradition in China

Rowan Pease

Summary

Sometimes it's good to sound rough. In "Asŭrang," we hear dance music played on a home-made vertical flute that seems purposely designed to make producing a note difficult. Ever since 1945, on the borders of China and North Korea where this flute music is found, folk music has been enlisted in the service of politics, "to serve the millions of working people," in the words of China's former leader Chairman Mao. Such music has been adapted for staged performance, whether in village square or town hall, "modernized" using Western techniques, and given political themes. However, Communist Party cultural officials did not find all instruments suitable for the modern age. The *t'ungso* flute generally slipped under the radar for political appropriation, because it sounded too "earthy," too close to the peasants. It continued to provide music to accompany drinking and dancing at parties, untouched by official ideology.

The last two decades have seen remarkable economic change in China, with a rapidly urbanizing population that is cosmopolitan, exposed to global popular culture, but also patriotic. The new consumer class explores traditional music as part of a tourist experience. In the twenty-first century, urban Chinese have rediscovered a taste for "authentic" sounds, and the state has embarked on a large-scale project for documenting and preserving Chinese "Intangible Cultural Heritage" (**ICH**), including music. The *t'ungso* has been drawn into this project, and is being transformed in ways that reflect new ideals relevant to the post-revolutionary period, but which are as radical as any of the changes wrought under Maoism.

KEY WORDS
- ethnic identity
- politics
- preservation
- timbre

Why this Piece?

When I first visited northeast China, home to China's Korean minority, back in the early 1990s, I could find no *t'ungso* players in any public places. My curiosity was piqued by a picture of these flute players in a local book, but they did not appear in cultural shows I saw, and the instrument was not taught in music schools. I was told that players gathered in the main city park in Yanji City, or at a pavilion near the river where old people met early in the morning to chat or play chess. It sounds rather romantic, but the pavilion is on one corner of a major intersection, across the road from the main city market. Since all drivers passing through that intersection beeped their horns constantly, it was, in fact, rather noisy. Perhaps that is why there were no *t'ungso* players whenever I visited. But the old fellows sitting there knew who I was looking for, and eventually in 1999 I got a phone number for Kim Ch'angnyong and arranged to visit his house. I was initially disappointed that Kim played what seemed to me simple folk-song standards, and that he was no virtuoso, but I later learned that this is in keeping with the *t'ungso*'s amateur standing. Nevertheless, when I produced a video camera, he changed into a traditional Korean jacket and mesh hat, symbolic of his ethnic heritage. He told me that he continued to play and teach this difficult instrument into his late 70s because it was an important part of being Korean.

Fifteen years later it is no longer hard to find *t'ungso* players. Indeed, the newspapers are full of them (see the article on p. 94). In 2011, I visited Mijiang, a village on the Chinese side of the River Tumen which forms the border between China and North Korea. Mijiang has been designated "The Land of the *T'ungso*" with a statue of the instrument in the heart of the village. Villagers here claim a history of over 80 years playing the *t'ungso*, since they first crossed over the river border from neighboring Hamgyŏng province in present-day North Korea. Now they were preparing for a new role as bearers of China's Intangible Cultural Heritage. With the help of a music teacher, they were formalizing their teaching and playing techniques, as well as adopting modern stage craft and professional performance gestures. Moreover, they were looking at ways to modernize the instrument to suit new venues, in particular by increasing its volume. They aimed to promote *t'ungso* nationally and internationally, and so increase cultural tourism to the area. Although I had been initially disappointed by the amateurish performance in the recording I had made in 1997, I was no more pleased by the slickness of the second recording. But for elderly players like Kim these changes in sound and style were perhaps less important than the official attention that vindicated the long years they had spent trying to preserve the instrument for their people in the face of indifference.

Musical Features

TIMED LISTENING GUIDE

0:00	Warm-up	
0:05	"Asŭrang"	The drum takes a few moments to settle in. Since this piece would be used to accompany dancing at parties, the pattern is fast, regular and lilting, with a rim stroke to accent the 5th and 11th quavers
0:15		The low A is always vibrated, by the player shaking his head sideways. The same is true of the lower E, at 0:20

0:24	Repeat	The first note of the tune, a held E, is each time articulated halfway through by flapping the fingers briefly over the neighbouring note
0:31		The C, here and each time the tune is repeated, is particularly "buzzy"
0:45	Repeat	
0:47		Some neighbors pop in to see what the party is, but are sent away
1:05	Repeat	
1:32		This is just one of several places in the piece where Kim does not have enough breath pressure to sustain the note
1:48	Repeat	
2:07–2:09	End of "Asŭrang"	A dramatic slowing, and the piece ends on the core note, E (so). Kim says "next piece"
2:13	"Rajilga"	The new mode is immediately obvious. This section starts on a G♯, which had no place in the previous tune, but is the main note of the new *kyemyŏnjo* mode (mi so la do re). There is often a falling pattern to the main note (mi), here G♯
2:18		The drummer has to slow down a bit to allow Kim more time. The rhythm is still settling
2:22		The second phrase moves up to circle around the "la" C♯
2:28		The third phrase moves up into a higher register, to circle the "do" (E). Not every note "speaks"
2:41	Repeat	
3:03	Repeat	At 3:21–3:24 you can see the drummer striking with her stick on alternate skins
3:26	Repeat	Kim replaces the third higher phrase at 3:36 with improvisation around the lower middle register, and then extended upwards. He continues to improvise on the "Rajilga" tune
3:56		The melody is breaking up into fragments. It is very energetic, if a little breathless, particularly here and again at 4.30
4:45	"Hullari"	Kim introduces another short tune, popular in North Korea as "light music," which he repeats at 4:59, 5:15, and 5:30. The mode has shifted to a brighter *pyŏngjo* mode, with do on E, and emphasis on the 3rd and 5th degrees
5:41	"*Orae orae anjuseyo*" (Come in and take a seat)	Kim introduces a well-known popular song, a local "Happy birthday," as it were. It uses a simple pentatonic mode used for much local pop music—like a major scale missing the 4th and 7th degrees—which easily fits to conventional Western (I, IV, V) harmonies
6:15		Repeat of tune above
6:17, 6:23		Usually it is the drummer's job to offer up some words of encouragement. Here however, she is urging him to take a rest—perhaps anxious for his health, or maybe tired of drumming and needing to get on with something else!
6:54		The drummer signals the end with three firm strokes. "Is that enough?" he ends

MUSIC EXAMPLE 5.1 *Asŭrang* melody

Transcription by Rowan Pease

MUSIC EXAMPLE 5.2 *Rajilga* melody

Transcription by Rowan Pease

The *t'ungso* is not a sophisticated instrument, and neither is its repertoire. Kim mainly played short well-known folk songs, often strung together to accompany dancing. When I recorded him, Kim warmed up with two folk songs: a "Farmers' Song" (*Nongbuga*) that celebrates a bumper harvest, and *Toraji* (Bellflower), a standard folk song praising the Korean national flower (both these can be heard on the website accompanying this book). These songs are well known throughout the Korean peninsula, although they are often adapted to reference local places or products: their themes of rural prosperity and contentment suited all political regimes.

Kim then launched into two dance pieces: "Asŭrang" and "Rajilga," which continued the themes of peasant celebration. These are pieces that make partygoers "dance like crazy," and are the focus of the chapter.

Kim Ch'angnyong's performance exhibits many of the features of Korean traditional music: a compound rhythm, vibrato, the noises of breathing, and a raspy

TECHNOLOGY

This *t'ungso* (lit.: hole flute, sometimes spelled *t'ongso*) was handmade by Kim, using a long, thick piece of bamboo, bound with thread (he said it was made from human hair for its strength) with a notch cut into the top as a mouthpiece, and metal joints. The whole is stained and varnished inside and out. It is 72 centimetres long, and the diameter of the bore is 30 millimetres at the top, 20 mm at the bottom. The gauge of the tube itself runs from 5 mm at the top to 8 mm at the bottom. There is one thumb hole and four finger holes, each 12 mm diameter and they are spaced 6 centimetres apart (there is one unused hole at the bottom of the flute). The *t'ungso*'s construction makes it incredibly hard to play. The thick bamboo is not particularly vibrant, the size and length of the bore require a great deal of breath, and the player needs long arms, a wide handspan, and must cover the finger holes with the second joint of the fingers, rather than the fingertips, which are too small! Some players turn the lower, right hand, to support the *t'ungso* from underneath, the third finger covering the upper hole, the thumb the lower hole. You can see one more hole above the finger holes that is covered by a very fine membrane (from the inside of a reed), and on top of that a moveable thin metal plate, attached by wires. The reed vibrates to give a raspy buzz, which can be modified by the metal plate.

As you listen to the recording, you can hear Kim breathing often, every two beats (in the middle of the beat), and you can notice the breaks in lower notes where the pressure of air causes the membrane to slacken and the sound to drop out. Given the clear and even resonance that we are accustomed to in much Western music, you might think this is incompetent instrument-making, but both the timbral complexity and the audible physical effort of the player are prized by Kim and his fellow musicians. Since 1945, many instruments in North Korea and China have been "reformed" to bring them closer to Western timbral ideals (which are considered more "scientific"). Many traditional instruments are now factory produced, but the *t'ungso* in this area remains a home-made artisan instrument.

The *t'ungso* once belonged in court orchestras and is clearly related to other East Asian end-blown notched flutes, such as the Chinese **xiao** (*xiao* and *so* are written with the same character), Japanese **shakuhachi**, and the smaller Korean *tanso*. But in its social context and repertoire, timbral qualities and playing style it is quite different from each. The mellow *xiao* is a refined instrument of the literati, the meditative *shakuhachi* has long been associated with Buddhist mendicants, while the brighter *tanso* is used chamber groups, and nowadays as a beginner instrument in Korean schools. The *t'ungso*'s vibrating membrane and other ornamental techniques are, however, shared with the other East Asian horizontal flutes such as the Korean *taegŭm* and Chinese *dizi*.

FIGURE 5.1 *T'ungso*

Photograph by Rowan Pease

FIGURE 5.2 *Puk* drum
Photograph by Rowan Pease

quality provided by a vibrating membrane which covers the air hole. The *t'ungso* is very hard to play due to the large diameter of the notched mouth piece, and the long distance between finger holes. Moreover, players sit cross-legged on the floor, which allows less freedom of movement, and surely constricts the diaphragm. All this tell us something about local musical aesthetic preferences. The voice of a Korean singer of traditional **p'ansori** tales, for instance, is similarly husky, and is also strained, audibly effortful. Kim repeatedly told me how tiring it is to play the *t'ungso*, and you can hear this particularly in the first section as he warms up. The width of the mouth hole means that the player cannot alter the shape of the lips and tongue much, and vibrato is produced by actually shaking the head, most usually from side to side, but sometimes up and down.

"Asŭrang" is a simple, 20-second melody (see Music example 5.1) that uses a pentatonic mode (so la do re mi), called *pyŏngjo*, which is characteristic of central Korea. A mode is not just a selection of pitches, but about the relationship between them and the way each is played. In the *pyŏngjo* mode, the emphasis is on so, do, and mi (here, E, A, and C♯, respectively) and these are the notes that are longest held in "Asŭrang." The tune starts on a high E and ends an octave lower. Most notes have grace notes of some kind, but you typically hear more vibrato on the A and the low E, while the C is particularly "buzzy." The second section of the dance music, "Rajilga" (see Music example 5.2) is in the more plaintive "lower *kyemyŏnjo*" mode, which emphasizes the mi, la, do (G♯, C♯ and E, here). Despite the limited number of notes, the shifting weight gives each tune quite a different character. Kim then moves onto two more pieces in the so-called "higher *pyŏngjo*" mode with the do on E and the mi (G♯) and so (B) emphasized. In fact, this mode, with its emphasis on the notes of a Western triad, is close to a major scale with the 4th and 7th degree removed, and fits easily with simple **diatonic** harmonies. It is not surprising then that the last section of the piece is a local well-known (and

FIGURE 5.3 **Dancing in the park**
Photograph by Rowan Pease

very cheesy) 60th birthday song. The 60th birthday is a major celebration among Koreans, and such parties were the natural context for *t'ungso* playing.

Drumming is an indispensable aspect of Korean music: the drummer's job is not only to provide the **rhythmic structure** of the piece, but to offer support to the singer or instrumentalist. The **puk** barrel drum used here is played with the bare left hand and with a stick in the right: the stick beating on the main skins of the drum for strong beats, and crisper patterns on the rim of the drum (see Figure 5.2). Korean music is underpinned by rhythmic patterns called **changdan** (lit. long-short). Many *changdan*, like those in the first two sections, use groupings of three notes into cycles of two, three, or four beats (6/8, 9/8, and 12/8), but the third section uses a more unusual fast 2/4. *Changdan* are associated with certain speeds and can involve complex patterns of accents. The ones in these pieces are simple, but still you can hear that each beat is played a certain way each time, for instance, struck on either side or with both heads, in the centre or on the rim. The first dance uses *kŭtkori*, a typical moderately fast dance rhythm with accents on 5th quaver of each six-note group (Music example 5.3). The second is a more unusual driving 2/4 rhythm known as *hwimori* (Music examples 5.4a and b).

MUSIC EXAMPLE 5.3 *Asŭrang* drum pattern

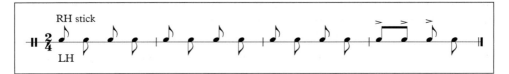

MUSIC EXAMPLE 5.4A AND B *Rajilga* drum patterns

Social Context

Folk Music in China and North Korea

When I recorded "Asŭrang" in 1999, the *t'ungso* was associated with the parks of this Korean region of northeast China, and with traditional village life. Kim met with about five friends regularly to play in a pavilion in the city park. There was a saxophone player in the group—Kim said it was a good substitute for the Korean double-reeded *p'iri*. Mostly they played for fun, but sometimes they were paid to provide music for people to dance to at 60th birthday parties, earning about 50 yuan each (about US$7 at the time, which was similar to nightclub musicians in the same town), and they performed in street or park parties for the Old Folks festival or other city festivities. They had no contact with the local cultural bureau, and the *t'ungso* did not feature in professional cultural life.

This contrasts starkly with many other folk traditions, which were used to serve political ends by the communist governments in both China and North Korea. Cultural workers throughout China still followed the policy outlined by Chairman Mao Zedong in 1942: "We should take over the rich legacy and the good traditions in literature and art that have been handed down from past ages in China . . . old forms, remoulded and infused with new content, also become something revolutionary in the service of the people."

Likewise, North Korean leader Kim Il Sung said in a 1970 speech, "Our party's consistent policy on socialist national culture is that the peculiar national form of our culture should be preserved and properly integrated with the socialist content."

Hence musicians had to adapt traditional genres to express the ideals of modern international communism—for instance, removing titles or lyrics that they considered sexual, "superstitious," "feudal," or pessimistic—while maintaining musical markers of their ethnic identity. Both North Korea and Chinese cultural policy influenced the music of the border region of Yanbian, but cultural workers in both countries ignored the *t'ungso*, for reasons I discuss later.

Under the Radar: *T'ungso* Music in China

After the founding of the People's Republic of China in 1949, China's constitution guaranteed the right of its 55 recognized ethnic minority peoples (which include the Tibetans and Mongolians) to preserve and develop their own indigenous cultures. The local government of Yanbian, an Autonomous Korean Prefecture set up in 1952, therefore set about developing local Korean culture.

Yanbian at the time had a Westernized music culture, a legacy of the Japanese occupation of northeast China (1931–1945) and its modernizing agenda. Many townships had brass bands, pedal organs, and accordions, and in Yanji City there was even a professional choir and orchestra. But in the late 1950s there was a push to promote and modernize traditional cultures throughout China, a policy announced by Chairman Mao in his 1956 "Talks with Music Workers." In accordance with this "nationalization" policy, Yanbian cultural cadres went out to collect traditional music and recruit local folk musicians to perform with the local state-run song and dance troupes and teach at the schools of arts. Where no local players were available, they borrowed professors from North Korea's Pyongyang School of Music to teach Korean instruments such as the **kayagŭm** zither.

The local government commissioned a *Korean Folk Art Investigation Report* (1959), which stated that *t'ungso* was the most prevalent instrument: "widely taught and played amongst Koreans living in the border region of China." The writers described the *t'ungso* as cheap to make, portable, flexible in use, capable of expressing both sorrow and joy, and particularly suitable for the kind of festive music that Yanbian people enjoyed at parties. Despite these many advantages, the state did not recruit any players to their professional troupes or to the art school. Indeed, there was no official development of the *t'ungso* over the next half century there. We don't know exactly why this was, but we can speculate that it was because of its earthy sound and its association with the peasants. For all the idealization of the workers and peasants, professional musicians and cultural decision makers often regarded peasant culture as "backward," and were attracted to more refined, urban Korean instruments like the *kayagŭm* zither. Kim recalled playing music such as *Toraji* and "Farmers' Song" at rural festivals, as well as at parties during this period. He agreed with the report that there were plenty of amateur musicians enjoying the *t'ungso* in rural and township areas then.

Then came the Cultural Revolution (1966–1976), when Chairman Mao completely upturned the previous policies, and called for a complete cultural renewal and the destruction of old arts and culture. During this chaotic and dangerous period, the *t'ungso* could only be played discreetly. China's central government worried that the Korean population in the border area might shift its loyalties to North Korea, and accused local leaders of reviving Korean traditional culture to stir up ethnic nationalism. High-profile musicians were disgraced, beaten, and shunned. Even in villages, traditional music could only be played with caution. One woman told me that she was rejected by the Communist Youth League because neighbors had reported her playing the *kayagŭm* in her own home. In such a situation, the lowly status of the *t'ungso* was an advantage. There are no reports of players being persecuted, or their instruments destroyed.

BIOGRAPHY

Kim Ch'angnyong was born in 1919 in a village near Yanji. As you can see in this picture, taken when Kim was nearly 80 years old, he was a strong man, with large hands browned by years of labor.

Kim's family had been among the earliest migrants from North Korea, coming to seek land in Manchuria, a vast, sparsely occupied region of China in the late nineteenth century. Many other Koreans followed: escaping the Japanese occupation of Korea from 1910, or forcibly migrated by the Japanese in order to populate their growing empire after they invaded Manchuria in 1931. When Japan surrendered in 1945, Kim's hometown returned to Chinese rule, and was soon under communist control. Peasant families such as Kim's were very poor, but they received land as part of the Chinese communist land reform program, and so they saw little reason to move back to Korea.

Although originally a peasant, Kim lived in Yanji City, working in a factory until his retirement in 1985. Kim first played the horizontal flute *chottae*, but took up the *t'ungso* when he was 40.

It took him 10 years to master the instrument, he said, which he learnt by copying one particular older player, Kim Changchun, by rote. In turn, he was told he must pass it on before his own death, and he already had a favored successor. Kim used to be accompanied by his wife, but after she died in the late 1990s, his brother's wife replaced her on the barrel drum *puk*. When I met her, she said I did not need to know her name. It was not uncommon in Yanji for people, particularly but not exclusively women, to be addressed not using personal names but as so-and-so's wife/father/mother. Kim lived to be 93 years old, dying in 2012. I tried to track Kim and his partner down in March 2013. The local police eventually led me to the new flat they had shared after their house was demolished. She had died two weeks before. It was only then I learned her name, Kim Yisŏn.

FIGURE 5.4
Kim Ch'angnyong
Photograph by Rowan Pease

Kim said that after the Cultural Revolution, during the late 1970s and 1980s, he played again more openly. In 1982, trying to undo some of the damage done by the Cultural Revolution, China embarked on a large-scale project to record music that had almost been destroyed in previous decades: the national *Anthology of Folk Instrumental Music*. Collectors recorded several *t'ungso* players for the project, but the lowly instrument still escaped official development. District cultural officials sometimes invited Kim to play at local state festival days or for documentaries about Korean–Chinese culture. But as China rapidly modernized and pop music spread, people gradually lost interest in traditional music, and by the time I met Kim in 1999 there were few under the age of 40 who had even heard of the *t'ungso*. Kim felt it was a duty to continue to play, saying "However tired I am, I must keep playing for our people. Without our culture what do we have?" His incorporation of the saxophone into his group shows that he was not dogmatic about tradition. A lot of Kim's paid work still came from private parties, or "wherever old people wanted to get together and dance": "Young people don't like to listen to it, but the over 40s come here and dance like crazy." The group used music to stir up an atmosphere of excitement (called *hŭng* in Korean), with generous quantities of rice wine for the men. "Asŭrang" and "Rajilga" could be played for hours on end. Even when there were no parties, Kim played regularly for the pleasure of making music with his friends.

Symbolic, but Silent: The *T'ungso* in North Korea

The North Korean countryside, where the *t'ungso* was once widespread, is closed to foreign researchers, so it is hard to determine its fate under the communist regime that has ruled since 1945. The little that *is* written about the *t'ungso* is highly politicized. In a 1989 book called *Ancient Instruments* (*Ko akki*), Korea's "eternal" president Kim Il Sung is quoted praising it, saying "Since ancient times, the *t'ungso* has been one of the national instruments that has been loved by our people." It is the only instrument singled out for such praise in this book. *Ancient Instruments* speaks of its fourth-century roots in the kingdom of Koguryo (which was in the region now occupied by North Korea), and of its spread to the south of the peninsula, reflecting North Korea's ideology of unification with the south. Its revolutionary credentials are sealed by the suggestion that it played a role in the anti-Japanese struggle. The North Korean leaders owe much of their legitimacy as rulers to their role in fighting the Japanese, who occupied the whole of Korea from 1910 to 1945, and as a result the country and its culture are infused with militarism. Of the *t'ungso*, we hear that its sound is "manly," "thick," and "plaintive," and that great players among "our ancestors" created music that "raised morale" and "gave voice to the people's courage, intelligence and combative spirit" that ultimately defeated the Japanese invaders. The book illustrates the *t'ungso*'s music with the "Farmers' Song" that Kim opened his session with.

Despite this lavish praise, I have so far found no North Korean recordings or performances of the *t'ungso*, no teaching materials, and no scores. This is puzzling. Some instruments have disappeared in North Korea because of their links to the court or aristocracy, but the *t'ungso* had no such associations. Neither is the difficulty in playing the *t'ungso* a reason to abandon it. Since the 1960s most instruments have been reformed in North Korea (for instance, using steel strings, more resonant hardwood bodies, and metal keys like Western instruments). Korea's Dear Leader Kim Jong Il (son of Kim Il Sung) wrote in his 1992 book *On Music*, that "deficient" Korean instruments with small volume and unclear sound "should be reformed to overcome their weak points, to modernize them so that they too can splendidly form the music of our age, which will suit the people's taste." Why was the folk *t'ungso* not developed in these ways? Perhaps some clue is in the description of the timbre as "manly" and "plaintive." North Korean modernized instruments usually sound very bright. The music is unrelentingly optimistic (befitting a socialist paradise), and traditional music is now mainly performed by women, so perhaps those inherent qualities make it "unsuited to the modern age." Home-made bamboo instruments may still be enjoyed among rural communities, but whatever its symbolic role, the *t'ungso* has not been adopted for the national stage.

Detected . . . and Protected

In northeast China, the late 1990s saw a gradual recognition of the *t'ungso* as worthy of official promotion. This was spurred by the resumption of diplomatic relations between South Korea and China in 1991 and the opening up of Yanbian as a tourist destination to South Koreans, who eagerly sought signs of a nostalgic rural past in this remote area. Mijiang village, near Tumen, the town where tourists look across the bridge to North Korea, was declared by the Yanbian Bureau of Culture to be "the land of *t'ungso*" in 1997. This was the start of a process of institutionalization that is transforming the instrument and its place in society. A group of friends making music became an officially recognized Mijiang *t'ungso* Association in 1999, and they now perform at trade fairs and tourism expos. In Yanji City, where Kim Ch'angnyong lived, a *t'ungso* enthusiasts' club was formed by the government in 2006, and an annual one-day *t'ungso* festival has been mounted every August since.

In the first decade of the twenty-first century, China has enthusiastically participated in UNESCO's Convention on Intangible Cultural Heritage. It is an initiative that encourages nation states to submit to UNESCO plans for the preservation of recognized cultural and artistic "assets." UNESCO judges each nomination and gives financial support to those it accepts. China nominated just one or two items each for inclusion in the 2001, 2003, and 2005 lists of "Masterpieces of the Oral and Intangible Heritage." By 2009 China's enthusiasm for heritage had increased to the extent that 25 Chinese items were accepted onto the renamed "Representative Lists of Intangible Cultural Heritage," including the "Farmers' Dance of the Ethnic Koreans living in China." Besides those cultural assets that were accepted onto the UNESCO list, many others were approved for the Chinese State Council's internal list of items worthy of recognition and protection.

FIGURE 5.5 *T'ungso* player statue, Korean Folk Culture Village
Photograph by Rowan Pease

Alongside this official process of preservation, there has been a more general shift in musical taste among Chinese audiences and media, away from the modernized folk musics of the revolutionary period towards more authentic folk traditions, which have been dubbed "original ecology" (*yuanshengtai*) cultures. The audiences for this style of music originated among young urban professionals, and spread among China's new middle class. They expressed nostalgia for rural living, which they felt to be more spiritual, natural, and innocent than the consumerist lifestyle that reforms had brought to China (some of these attitudes can be detected in the news report shown on p. 94). Many "original ecology" musics were found among ethnic minority populations, such as Mongolian overtone singing and Kam long song from southwestern China, and most featured exotic vocal techniques and non-Western timbres. "Original ecology" performances regularly featured on televised variety shows, although their polished presentations were often quite at odds with their claims to authenticity. In this climate, *t'ungso* music, which had remained unprofessionalized all through the revolutionary period of modern Chinese history, was ripe for rediscovery. But in order to present their music publically, the local bureau of culture guided players to add some "performance artistry": adopting modern stage gestures, costumes, and playing in unison.

In June 2008 Mijiang's *t'ungso* music was one of 11 Chinese–Korean assets formally recognized as an ICH asset by the Chinese Ministry of Culture; Mijiang was designated a "Chinese Folk Culture Art Township," and later a "Chinese–

PRIMARY SOURCE

FIGURE 5.6 China's "Cultural Heritage Day"

China Web news, 11 June 2011

A trio of Korean *t'ungso* players: Transmitters of cultural heritage

(Caption)Trio of Korean *t'ungso* players: Jin Shengjun (right), Jin Xiangguo (middle) and Li Zongfan (left) at the Chinese–Korean Intangible Cultural Heritage Exhibition Hall in Tumen, playing traditional Chinese–Korean *t'ungso* music. Behind them the passage has been designed in the form of a *t'ungso*. China Web news: 11 June 2011 (China's "Cultural Heritage Day")

Translation: The recently inaugurated Chinese–Korean Intangible Cultural Heritage Exhibition Hall has become a huge attraction even beyond China's borders. This is the first such ICH exhibition hall among China's 55 ethnic minorities.

At the *t'ungso* demonstration area, I met a white-haired, 70-year-old Korean man, Jin Xiangguo. He was clad in a white ethnic costume, holding a *t'ungso*; a piece of melodious *t'ungso* music lulls us into an intoxicated mood of dream-like fantasy.

The old fellow Jin Xiangguo said that the national level ICH item *t'ungso* is just one of 52 items in the eight major ICH halls. Most days there are transmitters on the spot demonstrating and performing the few ICH items among these that are best able to represent the characteristics of Korean culture. There are three people in the *t'ungso* group. Each person takes it in turns to do this demonstrating for 10 days. The performance fees are symbolic, the three divide between them 500 yuan (about US$80) per month, "I would still do it without payment, for our ethnic group."

Old Jin Xiangguo is a typical ethnic Korean, from a young age he liked to play *t'ungso*. He says that Koreans are a nationality good at singing and dancing, their daily life cannot escape music and dance. Every time there is a celebration like a wedding, or a 60th birthday party, he and his friends like to go and do their duty for their neighbors and friends by playing. Over the last few years, in order to raise the standard of *t'ungso* playing, they have personally paid to make the return trip from Tumen to Yanji City, to become "apprentices" at a Folk Performance Troupe. Even now, Jin Xiangguo is still continuously studying: every morning the "*T'ungso* trio" make an appointment to practice together and compare notes. Jin Shengjun and Li Zhongfan separately are provincial-level and city-level ICH transmitters, Jin Xiangguo has still not registered, and so he is not yet a transmitter. "Live till old, study till old," 70-odd-year-old Jin Xiangguo says: "Playing the *t'ungso* improves my mood, my health, and also pleases others, going to Dali shows that I have an important responsibility to act as a transmitter of ethnic culture. I am very proud to take this on."

(Source *Zhongguo wang* China.org.cn)

Korean nationality *t'ungso* art township." Investment followed from the township council: approximately US$8000 for a transmission and performance center, where tourists can visit and film crews can record their playing. It includes changing rooms, a concert hall, and exhibition room. According to UNESCO's guidelines, applicants for the ICH program must designate a line of inheritance for their asset. In the case of Mijiang *t'ungso*, three generations have been identified from the 1930s until now (Han Sinchŏn, Kim Kwansun, and Ri Kilsŏng). Ri, the last of these, is not a native of Mijiang but came to the area in 1983 as a music teacher. He was a graduate from the Yanbian University School of Arts, where he is now an associate professor, but taught himself the *t'ungso*. He is a proficient player of many wind instruments, including the Chinese bamboo flute **dizi** and the Western flute, and borrows teaching and playing techniques from those instruments, using them for the amateur players of *t'ungso* in Mijiang. He modified his own *t'ungso* using metal keys taken from a clarinet. As the sole official "transmitter" of Mijiang's tradition, he is responsible for teaching future generations of players. Neighboring cities and townships have also set up transmission halls, with Ri as teacher, and you can read a news article about a nearby ICH exhibition centre (see above).

There are over 50 members of the Mijiang association, ranging in age from primary school children on the smaller notched flute **tanso** to the original players in their 70s. The association even has female members, although these generally play drums rather than the *t'ungso*, due to the large handspan and strength it requires.

China's ICH program not only requires that cultural heritage is preserved and transmitted through education and research, but that it can be used for public leisure, for the development of tourism and for international cultural exchange. The Mijiang *t'ungso* group has performed in the cities of Beijing and Chongqing at international festivals of ICH, and hopes to tour abroad. China uses ICH to develop its "soft power" (cultural influence) internationally, portraying itself as a nation of cultural riches to counter fears about its economic and military power. Through ICH, China also displays its support for ethnic minority cultures, such as Tibetan music, and claims them as their own, although this can be contentious. Many South Koreans objected to the classification of Korean farmers' music as China's cultural heritage. *T'ungso* music, which is associated with North Korea, has not yet been listed internationally by China, and North Korea does not participate in the UNESCO program.

For Kim Ch'angnyŏng, playing his homemade *t'ungso* was a pleasure but also a duty towards his people, particularly as he saw it being replaced by karaoke and pop music at local parties. Like other *t'ungso* players, he was largely ignored by the state cultural apparatus. *T'ungso* music escaped transformation under the communist revolution, but in the last decade, it has undergone a radical shift in meaning, from amateur pastime to cultural commodity. This has led to a change in style: to a defined repertoire of fixed pieces with start and finish, a cleaner sound, unison playing, and use of performance gestures. On the website that accompanies this book, you can see the influence of this increasing stagecraft in a short extract from a video I recorded of the Mijiang group playing "Asŭrang" in 2011: a unison version, much statelier, smoother, and less ornamented.

The *t'ungso*'s future as a symbol of Korean cultural identity is for now assured, as Kim hoped in 1999. But for the spirit of revelry, *hŭng*, the *t'ungso* is no longer a vital musical ingredient.

Discussion topics

- In the China.org article, Jin Xiangguo uses two clichés about the Koreans' fabled musical ability. Why is it that China's ethnic minorities are often assigned these attributes? (Reading suggestion: Dru Gladney's seminal 1994 article critiques the exoticized images of the "singing and dancing" ethnic minorities in China, which contrast with, and therefore construct, the normalcy and modernity of the Han majority.)

- Jin Xiangguo talks about traveling to the city every day to study with a professionalized, state-supported folk troupe. The UNESCO international ICH program's stated aims of preserving authentic folk culture seem at odds with this training. How can ICH programs best deal with such contradictions?

Further Listening

There are many CDs introducing Korean folk music, but not the *t'ungso*. For an all-round sample, try *Four Thousand Years of Korean Folk Music* (B000002NTU, Legacy International, 2008).

http://www.youtube.com/watch?v=2LxajHDxbEQ&feature=youtube_gdata
> In this video of a masked "lion play" (Bukchŏng saja norŭm), performed by North Korean refugees living in South Korea, you can see and hear *t'ungso*.

http://www.youtube.com/watch?v=PBefwiVa5eQ&feature=related
> An example of North Korean modernized folk instruments. The reformed fiddle (*haegŭm*) with four rather than two strings and played using a horsehair bow, with a bass version behind.

Recommended Reading

Blumenfeld, Tami and Silverman, Helaine (eds) (2014) *Cultural Heritage Politics in China.* Honolulu: University of Hawai'i Press.
> A collection of articles that examine the impact of China's ICH policies on a range of cultural activities (although not the Korean ethnic group).

Gladney, Dru (1994) "Representing Nationality in China: Refiguring majority/minority identities." *Journal of Asian Studies* 53(1): 92–123.
> The seminal article on musical representations of minorities in China.

Howard, Keith (1988) *Korean Musical Instruments: A Practical Guide.* Seoul: Sekwang.
> This book gives a general survey and playing instructions for the six best-known Korean instruments, but not the *t'ungso*.

Korean Music (Seoul: National Center for Korean Traditional Performing Arts, 2007).
> Available on the KTPAC website at: http://www.gugak.go.kr/eng/about_gugak/publications/publ_viw.jsp?id=15&page=1&searchGubn=&searchValue
>
> Good introduction to all the main genres and instruments of traditional folk and professional Korean music. The focus is on genres from the south of the peninsula.

Kwon, Donna Lee (2011) *Music in Korea: Experiencing Music, Expressing Culture.* Oxford: Oxford University Press.
> An excellent survey of Korean music, encompassing traditional classical and folk music, modern composed music for Korean instruments, music of North Korea, rap and pop. There is an accompanying CD.

Li, Helie (1996) *Still Life With Rice: A Young American Woman Discovers the Life and Legacy of Her Korean Grandmother.* New York: Scribner.
> A descriptive biography that covers the era of Japanese occupation in Korea, emigration to Manchuria, the Korean war, and eventual emigration to the US.

Perris, Arnold (1983) "Music as Propaganda: Art at the command of doctrine in the P.R.C." *Ethnomusicology* 27: 1–28.
> A helpful and readable article about the political use of music in China, written just as Maoist policies were being relaxed.

Weintraub, Andrew and Yung, Bell (eds) (2009) *Music and Cultural Rights.* Champaign, IL: University of Illinois Press.
> As well as a helpful introduction, this includes two excellent and readable chapters on the impact of ICH programs on traditional Chinese music, by Bell Yung and Helen Rees.

PART 2

Music and Spirituality

Introduction

Rowan Pease and Rachel Harris

The chapters in this section move from music that is rooted in local soil to the realms of spirituality. Here we discuss five pieces of music that are used to create or maintain a relationship between humans and the divine, and we ask: "Why is music so important to religious practice in so many different cultures around the globe? Why is it an indispensable part of the rituals that forge these links between the earthly and the spiritual domain?" Music does spiritual work in many diverse ways: by expressing devotion, aiding meditation or inducing ecstasy, acting as an offering to the gods, and even creating channels through which humans and sprits can meet or commune. At a more prosaic level, music is used to teach sacred texts and myths, to regulate behavior, to draw people together and to display the richness and beauty of a religious culture or the piety of its followers. Music's key role in all these spheres may be explained in part by its special ability to enable powerful collective experiences and forge group identities. Also crucial is its affective force, its ability to transform states of mind and to transport listeners spiritually to other places, whether through the excitement of a group ritual, through solitary meditative practice, or simply listening to a piece of recorded music.

Music as Devotion

Several of the pieces in this section link music closely to text. In some cases, the text is supreme, and music merely plays a supporting role. The singer of "Sogasugā" aims to express his or her devotion and "melt the hearts of Gods" through intensely emotional poetry and music. Yorùbá culture likewise invests great transformative power in words: the text of "Ìbejì" can be sung, spoken and even reproduced on the sacred *bàtá* drums. When the drums speak with the *òrìṣà* gods and call them down to intervene in human life, they are literally beating out the words of the prayer in musical form. Note that in both these cases, the intended audience for these performances is not the people who may be present at the ritual; these performances are directed towards the spirits or the gods. Likewise in "Sudamala," a ritual myth is enacted through puppets and dance; the language of its text is incomprehensible to modern audiences, but still speaks to the gods for whom the play is offered.

Music can add otherwise inexpressible significance to text-based communications, but religious and spiritual beliefs also find expression in musical sounds alone. The *shakuhachi* piece "Tamuke" was once part of the spiritual training of Japanese Zen monks. That training is reflected in contemporary aesthetics, where performers are taught to focus intensely on each note, and conceptualize the piece as something that contains the whole universe. Spiritual meaning may even be contained in aspects of the music that cannot be heard: the inaudible grace notes of "Tamuke" embody the Buddhist philosophy of eternal striving. In the case of "Sogasugā," too, religious concepts, music, and aesthetics are integrated into a single spiritual message. The austere philosophy of the Hindu scripture Upaniṣads is reflected in its singer's striving for pure notes, which should be so simple and accessible that they can be enjoyed by the listener as effortlessly as grape juice slips down the throat.

Music and Affect

Music's power to evoke, intensify, and channel emotion is much in evidence in these pieces. In these various case studies, we see the affective power of music harnessed in practice and theorized in very different ways. The singer of "Sogasugā" evokes one or more of the nine "essences" of emotion of classical Indian aesthetic theory: love, mirth, manly vigor, compassion/sadness, anger, wonder/surprise, fear, disgust, and tranquility. The female reciters of "Subhan'Allāh" weep copiously as they chant; this emotional outpouring is regarded as essential for the success of the ritual. The *shakuhachi* player alternates breathy outbursts of emotion with moments of stillness; part of the traditional meditational practice of the *komusō* monks. In "Sudamala," the gamelan that accompanies the Balinese puppet ritual creates moods to accompany the drama on stage in order to entertain and educate human audiences, as well as pleasing the gods. If effective, a cursed child may be "freed from evil."

Scientists at McGill University have shown evidence of the effect of music on the human body: for instance the increase of the neuro-transmitter dopamine that manifests itself in shivers down the spine, a rush of pleasure or goose-bumps. But chemical analysis only confirms the easily observable effects of music on players, singers, and listeners, whether collectively shared or individually experienced. The musicians in these pieces elicit physical responses towards spiritual ends: the skilled *bàtá* drummers incite participants to lose themselves in an irresistible groove, until the *òriṣà* god responds to his calls and rhythm, and possesses, or "mounts" a dancer. Swaying together, and repeating the same phrase slightly out of sync, the swirling sound of "Subhan'Allāh" likewise reverberates overpoweringly in the women's bodies as they go into a state of trance. Part of music's ritual efficacy is surely the way it combines symbolic representation with physical experience: sometimes energizing, sometimes bringing stillness. Music itself is both bodily and immaterial, and perhaps that is why it is used in many cultures to collapse the boundaries between earthly and spiritual domains.

Another aspect of music's key role in religious practice is its ability to structure time and space. Music can slow down, speed up or subtly alter our experience of time. In "Subhan'Allāh," the assembled chanters focus intently on two simple phrases "Glory to Allah and praise him, Glory to Allah the supreme." Through their constant repetition of these words, they are enacting a Sufi spiritual technique, creating a circular experience of time to focus their whole attention on the words, thus polishing their hearts and drawing closer to God. Music can also collapse the temporal boundaries of past, present, and future through its ability to evoke memories and expectation. And so we find musicians from twenty-first-century America traveling to Japan to perform "Tamuke" at the graves of *shakuhachi*-playing forebears, forging links between their own spiritual practice and that of the thirteenth-century "monks of nothingness."

Ritual Contexts

Ritual typically takes place in special time and place outside of the everyday, creating spaces in which transformations may occur and where belief systems are enacted and validated. Music has special power to mark out acoustically the aural space and time set aside for its practice, and thus its performance is a crucial aspect of ritual. Music may not always be conceptualized in ways that link it directly to spiritual meanings, but its performance is no less indispensable to the success of the ritual. Nowhere is this clearer than in "Sudamala," which is performed as part of a ritual, accompanying a story that is itself about a ritual, and serves to structure the retelling and re-enactment of both ritual and story.

The power of music to link human and divine and alter states of consciousness also make it dangerous, and hence organized religions have often insisted that it must be regulated. Hindu devotional songs should follow the rules of poetic construction including meter and rhyme, and a singer must practice humility. In Edo-era Japan, only the *komusō* monks were given permission to play the *shakuhachi*: it was an instrument of spiritual training, not to be used for entertainment. Islamic scholars have long debated on the moral status and permissibility of different kinds of musical practice.

Musicians themselves are rarely divine or magical; they are principally enablers. Most often in ritual contexts involving altered states, it is the dancers and adepts who fall into trance; the musicians are the workers who provide the acoustic medium in which the transformation occurs. Sometimes this dangerous musical power accorded to musicians makes them feared and set apart from society; they may be low status, or confined to a special caste. Often these religious proscriptions on music have a gendered aspect; the combination of women and music is seen as particularly dangerous, but in the case of "Subhan'Allāh," the female reciters maintain their respectability because what they do is not regarded as music. In other cases, musical skill may be highly valued, and musicians themselves may be almost revered for their artistry, the beauty of their performances, their ability to move people, and enable their experiences of the divine. As the lyrics of "Sogasugā" ask, "Who has the skill and power to melt the heart of God through poetry and music?"

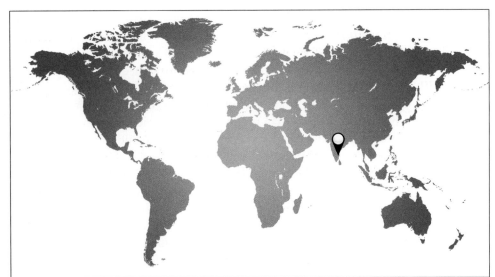

Location: Tiruvaiyaru (birthplace of Tyāgarāja), South India

"Sogasugā": A Song of Songs

Composed by Tyāgarāja; sung by M.S. Subbulakshmi, with Radha Vishwanathan; published by Saregama on the disc *M.S. Subbulakshmi Vol. 1* (2009 reissue), http://gaana.com/song/sogasuga-m-s-subbulakshmi

Chapter six

"Sogasugā"

A Song of Songs

Richard Widdess

Summary

A song by the most respected composer in the tradition of South Indian classical music, the poet-singer-saint Tyāgarāja (1767–1847), in a well-known recording by arguably the most popular South Indian classical singer of the mid-twentieth century. As well as concisely illustrating the basic structures of Indian music—*rāga*, *tāla*, song form, techniques of improvisation—the recording allows us to explore some of its deeper meanings for a South Indian listener. These include the close relationship between music and spirituality, articulated by the lyrics of the song (which refer to their own composition and musical performance) and reflected in the public image of both the composer and the performer as devotional singers. They also include the social history of the singer, M.S. Subbulakshmi, who successfully transcended negative gender stereotypes to become the favorite singer of Mahatma Gandhi and millions of other Indian listeners, a figurehead for a post-colonial India, and one of the first Indian vocalists to perform on an international platform.

> **KEY WORDS**
> - gender
> - Hinduism
> - improvisation
> - musical structure

Why this Piece?

> Who is the stalwart able to melt you, arranging an ensemble of elegant drum rhythm with truthful words full of the gist of the Upaniṣads and with great purity of notes?

So wrote the South Indian singer-composer-poet Tyāgarāja (1767–1847), in William Jackson's poetic translation of the song "Sogasugā." The poet asks, who has the skill and power to melt the heart of God through poetry and music? But as becomes clear later in the song, the poet has a deeper question: Is it I? Can *I* do this? How is this possible?

To many thousands of music lovers and musicians in South India today, the answer is strongly affirmative: Tyāgarāja, *Saint* Tyāgarāja as he is often known, could melt the hearts of God and man like no one else. His songs, handed down both in writing and through oral transmission by generations of singers, are treasured both as musical gems and as poetic outpourings of spiritual truth and emotion. They form the core of the repertoire of South Indian classical music (also called Karnatak music), and are vehicles for the performances of the most respected and popular artists in that tradition. Among such performers, the reputation of M.S. Subbulakshmi (1916–2004) stands almost as high as that of Tyāgarāja himself.

From the several hundred of Tyāgarāja's songs that have survived, and from the many recordings of them by Subbulakshmi and other artists, I have selected "Sogasugā" because it is a song about songs, about composing and singing them. It appeals to me because, through it, the poet speaks to us directly and with humility about his spiritual purposes and artistic methods. At the same time, Subbulakshmi's concise rendering, with little musical elaboration to distract us from the song itself, gives voice to a period of profound change in the social and political history of Indian music.

Musical Features

TIMED LISTENING GUIDE

Ālāpanam	0:00	A short introduction to the *rāga*, sung in free rhythm, to non-lexical vocables, without percussion accompaniment. The violinist echoes the singer's phrases
The song (*kriti*)	0:51–4:27	
Pallavi	0:51–1:49	Concluding her brief *ālāpanam*, the singer introduces Tyāgarāja's *kriti* composition. She begins with the first section, *pallavi*, which will also serve as the refrain (Music example 6.1). The *mṛdangam* player joins in to underline and embellish the rhythm
		Lyrics: *sogasugā mṛdanga tāḷamu jatagūrci ninu jokkājēyu dhīru ḍevvaḍō*
		"Who is the stalwart able to melt you, arranging an ensemble of elegant drum rhythm?"
		Music: This section is predominantly in a medium to low pitch range, but rises and falls repeatedly with increasing ornamentation. It ends with a short percussion interlude

♩ = 189

Voice

so -ga-su-gā   mṛ -dan - ga tā - ḷa - mu

clap
Time counting

count

MUSIC EXAMPLE 6.1 **Sogasugā refrain and metrical cycle**

Anupallavi	1:49–2:44	The singer sings the second line of the poem and the second section of the song
		Lyrics: *nigama śirōrthamu galgina nijavākkulato svaraśuddhamutō (Rāma . . .)*
		"... with truthful words full of the gist of the Upaniṣads and with great purity of notes? (O God. . .)"
	1:49	*Music*: The melody of this section contrasts with that of the *pallavi* by emphasizing the upper register. To underline its greater intensity, the *kanjīrā* player joins the *mṛdangam* player in accompanying this section
	2:16	The phrase *nijavākkulato svaraśuddhamutō* ascends to the upper 4, the highest note in the melody so far, and the first climax of the composition
	2:25	The whole section is then repeated. The singer uses the exclamation *Rāma*, "O God!" to link the end of the *anupallavi* with a reprise of the *pallavi*. She sings only the first phrase of the *pallavi*, *sogasugā mṛdanga tāḷamu*
	2:41	Another short percussion interlude concludes the *anupallavi*
Caraṇam	2:45–3:48	The third section, *caraṇam* is longer than the two previous sections, because it comprises two lines of poetry. Here the poet develops the basic idea stated in the *pallavi* and *anupallavi*, and personalizes it by introducing his own identity. This section is accompanied by *mṛdangam* and *ghatam*
		Lyrics: (a) *yati viśrama sadbhakti virati drākṣārasa navarasa*
		(b) *yutakṛticē bhajiyiñcē yukti Tyāgarājuni taramā (Śrīrāma!)*
		"Is it possible for Tyāgarāja to sing bhajans with *kritis* full of the nine emotions, smacking with sweetness of grape nectar, Is he able to make the rhythmic pauses in songs of loving devotion, with rhymes and in line with the lyrical rules?"
	2:45	Line (a) is set to a melody in the lower pitch register, emphasizing the lower tonic, as in the *pallavi*. This melody is sung twice
	3:00	Line (b) ascends to a higher register, as in the *anupallavi*. The *kanjīrā* joins the ensemble accompanying this section
	3:28	The climax of the whole song comes with the completion of the *caraṇam* lyrics: *yukti Tyāgarājuni taramā*. As in the *anupallavi*, the melody rises to pitch 4 in the upper register, here coinciding with the poet's name. In this phrase, we glimpse also the rarely heard note 3, in descent from 4, which adds to the emotional impact of this phrase of the composition
	3:40	The whole (b) line is repeated
	3:48	The end of the (b) line leads back into a reprise of the *pallavi*. Again the singer uses the exclamation *Śrīrāma* ("O God!") to link the end of the *caraṇam* back to the beginning of the *pallavi*

Pallavi	3:48–4:25	After the high-register climax of the *caraṇam*, the melody returns to the lower register of the *pallavi*, which is sung once in its entirety, accompanied by all the percussion instruments
	4:08	The composition ends with the words *mṛdanga āḷamu,* set to a new melody, repeated with variation. This melody highlights the note 3, which is rarely heard in this *rāga*; but it may remind us of the earlier climactic phrase of the caraṇam, one octave higher, setting the poet-composer's name (3:28)
Elaboration of the song and *rāga*	4:25–6:27	Having performed Tyāgarāja's *kriti* composition in its entirety, the musicians extend the performance with improvised elaboration based on the words of the composition, the *rāga*, and the *tāla*. The opening phrase of the *pallavi* is sung as a refrain at the beginning, during, and at the end of this elaboration
		During this section of the performance, the singer and the violinist improvise either alternately or simultaneously. The percussion instruments also alternate, with the *mṛdangam* accompanying the singer, while the *ghatam* accompanies the violin
Refrain	4:25	The first phrase of the *pallavi*
Niraval	4:31	In this style of improvised elaboration, for which Subbulakshmi was famous, she repeats parts of the lyrics of the song, but creates different melodic settings for them, within the **rāga** and *tāla*. Here she uses the words of the *pallavi*:
		sogasugā mṛdanga tāḷamu jatagūrci ninu jokkājēyu dhīru ḍevvaḍō:
		"Who is the stalwart able to melt you, arranging an ensemble of elegant drum rhythm?"
		As the improvised melody gradually rises in pitch, the violinist echoes the singer, probably thinking of the same words as he plays
Refrain	5:40	The *pallavi* refrain
Svarakalpana	5:45	A different style of improvisation, where the singer sings tone syllables (*sargam*) instead of words—like singing sol-fa. The first *svarakalpana*, between repetitions of the refrain, is shown in Music example 6.2. The improvisations gradually become longer, but each ends in the same way, with a repeat of the refrain (gradually reduced to its first word, *sogasugā*).The singer and violinist improvise in turn, and the percussionists also take turns to accompany

so -ga-su-gā mṛ - dan - ga tā-ḷa mu   sa ni dha ma dha   so-ga-   su-gā mṛ -dan - ga tā-ḷa - mu

MUSIC EXAMPLE 6.2 **Sogasugā refrain and** *svarakalpana* **(boxed)**

	6:12	Singer and violinist improvise simultaneously a longer *svarakalpana*, ending with a pre-composed *mora*—a rhythmic pattern repeated three

		times—performed together by all the musicians. The *mora* starts on beat 4 (6:23), and leads into the *pallavi* refrain
Pallavi	6:27–end	A final reprise of the whole *pallavi* melody, restating the musical and poetic theme of the song for the last time
	6:44	A brief *mora* from the percussionists makes a decisive conclusion to the whole performance

Pitch and Mode

The tonic in this performance is tuned to G. This pitch will have been selected by the singer—any pitch can be selected as the tonic—and the instruments will have retuned to match if necessary. To make comparison with other examples easier, the tonic is transposed in notated examples in this chapter to C, as in Music example 6.3, which shows the drone played by the *tambūrā* lute throughout.

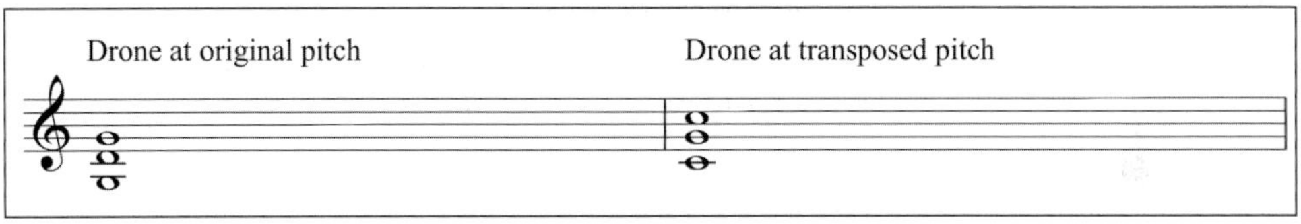

MUSIC EXAMPLE 6.3 **Drone at original pitch and transposed**

Like most Indian classical music, the main building blocks of this piece are the melodic and rhythmic modes: *rāga* and *tala*. The melodic mode or *rāga* is called Śrīranjanī. It is believed to have been created by Tyāgarāja, as most compositions in this *rāga* are attributed to him. This *rāga* makes use of the selection of melodic pitches shown in Music example 6.4. It is similar to the Western Dorian mode, but the degree 5 is missing. This gives the *rāga* a degree of instability—is the tonic 1 or 4?—that perhaps underlines the uncertainty expressed by the lyrics.

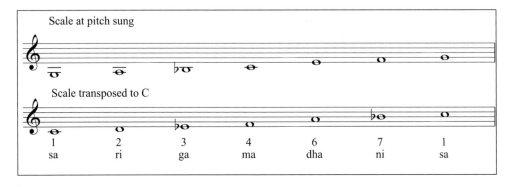

MUSIC EXAMPLE 6.4 **Scale at sung pitch and transposed**

In performance of this *rāga*, the notes 1, 2, 4 and 6 are the most important, and the most clearly articulated. Notes 3 and 7 tend to be "hidden" in ornamentation of the important notes, and are hard to identify; very occasionally they may be sung clearly, but only in descent. Music example 6.5 shows the singer's opening phrase: notice that at (a) she "skips over" 3 in moving from 2 to 4; at (b) she includes 7 in rapid ornamentation of 6, then skips over it on the way to upper 1; and at (c) she allows 7 to be heard momentarily in descending from 1 to 6. By bringing out these melodic subtleties, which distinguish *rāga* Śrīranjanī from other *rāgas* with the same scale, the artist evokes an emotional feeling or "image" unique to this *rāga*.

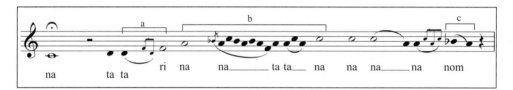

MUSIC EXAMPLE 6.5 *Ālāpanam* (beginning)

Rhythm

The musical **meter** or ***tāla*** of this song is Rūpakam, comprising a cycle of six beats. The tempo is fast, with about 89 beats per minute. In South Indian concert performances, members of the audience regularly keep time with the music with claps and silent hand gestures. To keep time in this example, count the beats as follows:

1: clap
2: touch the tip of the right-hand little finger to the left palm
3: clap
4: touch the tip of the right-hand little finger to the left palm
5: touch the tip of the right-hand ring finger to the left palm
6: touch the tip of the right-hand middle finger to the left palm
1: clap
etc.

The first beat of the cycle is the strongest; sections of the song normally end on this beat. In this example, the second syllable of the word *mṛdanga* falls on the first beat, as does the last syllable of *tāḷamu*: "*mṛDANGa tāḷaMU*."

Music example 6.1 shows the melody, rhythm, and word setting of the first phrase of the song, in relation to the time-keeping pattern of claps and finger counts. The highly **syncopated** rhythm of the melody, especially at the beginning of the phrase, adds to its intricacy and difficulty; and yet M.S. Subbulakshmi's performance seems completely effortless, unhurried, and assured, as would be expected from a musician of her caliber.

TECHNOLOGY

FIGURE 6.1 **M.S. Subbulakshmi in the recording studio, 1970, with (L to R) T.K. Murthy, *mṛdangam*; V. Nagarajan, *kanjīrā*; two *tambūrā* players (unknown); Radha Viswanathan, supporting singer; T.H. Vinayakram, *ghatam*; V.V. Subrammaniam, violin**

Source: http://msstribute.org

This photograph, taken at a recording session in 1970, shows the exact instrumental ensemble used in the recording of "Sogasugā." The names of the instrumentalists for "Sogasugā" are not recorded.

Instruments

The song is performed by a small chamber ensemble, typically used for indoor performances, staged or informal, of Karnatak music, similar to that shown in Figure 6.1. The leader of the ensemble is the singer: the voice is considered the supreme musical instrument in South India, and melodic instruments reproduce vocal style and repertoire even when they play solo. Accompanying the voice in this recording are:

Tambūrā. A long-necked lute with four strings, tuned to the tonic and fifth, which are gently plucked in constant rotation to provide a background drone.

Violin. This is the Western instrument, which was imported into South India from Europe in the eighteenth century. It has become the normal melodic instrument for accompanying the voice, and can also be played as a solo instrument. It is held in a different posture from the modern Western violin, positioned between the seated player's chest and knee or foot; this is to give sufficient stability to allow the left-hand fingers to slide along the string when necessary to achieve a smooth glissando and other ornaments, in imitation of vocal style. Thus although its outward form is that of a Western instrument, the technique and musical results are entirely Indian.

FIGURE 6.2
South Indian violin, played by Nandini Muthuswami

Photograph by Richard Widdess

Mṛdangam: This is a horizontal barrel drum (pronounced *mridúngum*) used to accompany South Indian classical music. The two heads are played with the fingers and produce a variety of pitches and sonorities. The right head is tuned to the tonic pitch chosen by the singer. The left head has a lower pitch that can be varied by pressing with the heel of the hand.

Ghatam: This is a large earthenware pot, played as a drum. The player uses both hands to strike the body of the pot in different regions to give a variety of tone colors.

Kanjīrā: A small frame drum (tambourine). A head made of lizard skin is stretched across a circular frame with one jingle. Despite striking with only one hand (the other is used to hold the instrument), the player can obtain a variety of tone colors.

Composition and Improvisation

A *kriti* is an art-song that can be either sung just as it is taught and learned, or amplified in performance by the addition of improvised elaboration of its words, rhythms, and melody. The main stages of a performance, all of which are heard briefly in "Sogasugā," are:

- *ālāpanam*: an improvised exposition of the main phrases, ornaments, and other melodic features of the melodic mode (*rāga*) in which the *kriti* is composed, sung in free rhythm without percussion accompaniment (see Music example 6.5, the first phrase of the *ālāpanam*).
- the *kriti* composition, sung in a musical meter (*tāla*) with percussion accompaniment, comprising:

   1. *pallavi*: the first section of the song
   2. *anupallavi*: the second section of the song, followed by a repeat of the *pallavi*
   3. *caranam*: the third, longest section of the song, followed by a repeat of the *pallavi*

- improvised elaboration of the composition and the *rāga*, of two kinds:

  1. *niraval*: elaboration setting the words and rhythms of the song to different melodic phrases of the *rāga*
  2. *svarakalpana*: improvised melody within the *rāga* and *tāla* structures, using tone syllables in place of words, each phrase concluding with the *pallavi*.

The *pallavi* is repeated after each section of the composition, periodically during improvisation, and at the end of the performance. Thus the words of the *pallavi*, which encapsulate the mood and meaning of the song, permeate the performance, as a reminder that this is not a purely abstract musical discourse, but an expression of religious devotion: "Who is the stalwart able to melt you, arranging an ensemble of elegant drum rhythm?"

Although this is a very concise performance, the same sequence of sections would normally also be followed in a longer performance, with more development of the improvised sections. But in Karnatak music, the main emphasis is on the words of the composition and their devotional meaning, so it is quite common for a *kriti* to be sung with relatively little improvised elaboration, as here, or none at all.

This composition has been recorded by a number of other artists beside M.S. Subbulakshmi, and some of these recordings can be accessed on iTunes, YouTube, and various Indian music websites. They illustrate a degree of variation in performance, for example, the use of instruments in place of the voice, different ways of articulating and ornamenting the composition, longer or shorter *ālāpanam*, and more or less improvised elaboration. In most cases, however, the *rāga* and the composition are clearly recognizable, and the sequence of sections given above is normally followed.

Social Context

Sound and Meaning

We can never predict exactly what a musical performance will mean to any individual on any occasion. But through careful analysis of the music and its context, we can identify meanings that are available for perception, and likely to be perceived, by listeners in the culture concerned. The perception of such meanings often takes the form of an emotional and aesthetic response rather than one that could easily be put into words, partly because much of the cultural background is well known and taken for granted. In the case of "Sogasugā," as sung by Subbulakshmi, a rich variety of meanings and associations is implied by the words of the song, the identity of their author, and the identity of the singer. Through its structure and style, the musical rendition articulates these meanings and some of its own.

The Song and its Composer

"Sogasugā" is a well-known song by the most famous poet-composer of South India, Tyāgarāja (1767–1847; sometimes spelled Thyagaraja). Its meanings inevitably include associations with the person of Tyāgarāja himself, about whom there is a rich mythology. He was the son of a learned Brahman of Tiruvaiyaru, in the modern state of Tamil Nadu (see map at the opening of the chapter). From an early age he was remarkable both for his saintly behavior and his musical gifts. Although trained in classical musical theory and practice, and renowned as the most inspiring singer of his day, he refused invitations to sing in the palaces of the rich and powerful, and performed only at his home and in the temples of the Tanjavur region where he lived, often singing his new compositions as offerings at the temples he visited. He was a devout worshipper of the god Rāma—one of the *avatār*s of Vishnu, and the hero of the epic *Rāmāyaṇa*—and his songs embody the fundamental concepts of Hindu spirituality, especially that of devotion (*bhakti*): an intensely emotional relationship with a chosen deity, a personal savior. Thus Tyāgarāja's life and work exemplify, through artistic practice, the traditional Hindu values of renunciation and devotion.

Tyāgarāja is typically depicted today as a singer of sacred songs, simply dressed in white, accompanying himself on the drone lute *tambūrā* and a pair of wooden clappers to mark the rhythm, a water pot his only other possession. He wears

Lyrics: Sogasugā mṛdanga tāḷamu
Composer: Tyāgarāja
Translation: William Jackson

Who is the stalwart able to melt you, arranging an ensemble of elegant drum rhythm, with truthful words full of the gist of the Upaniṣads and with great purity of notes?

Is it possible for Tyāgarāja to sing bhajans with kritis full of the nine emotions, smacking with sweetness of grape nectar,

Is he able to make the rhythmic pauses in songs of loving devotion, with rhymes and in line with the lyrical rules?

FIGURE 6.3 **Cover image from William Jackson's** *Tyāgarāja: Life and Lyrics*

the forehead mark of a devotee of Vishnu, the sacred thread of a high-caste Hindu, and a necklace of rosary beads; shadowy figures of Rāma and his divine companions—whom Tyāgarāja is said to have seen in a vision—may be glimpsed in the background. As William Jackson, whose book *Tyāgarāja: Life and Lyrics* bears this image on its cover, has argued, this image of the saint was to a large extent posthumously constructed, in response to a national spirit of political independence, social reform, and material prosperity in late nineteenth-century India:

> In seeking the resources which would represent the greatness of India's past and, perhaps, of its future, people seized on the indigenous genius of Tyāgarāja's appealing works, which were full of time-tested Indian values and moods.

The lyrics of "Sogasugā" are of particular interest because they are about the very act of composing and singing sacred songs for which Tyāgarāja is so famous. They are certainly full of "time-tested Indian values," but the mood is one of uncertainty rather than confidence. The poet questions whether, through the process of combining thoughts and words with music and poetic conventions, he can really persuade God to respond to his appeal. In developing this theme, he blends references to religious concepts, music, and aesthetics into an integrated spiritual message.

FIGURE 6.4 **Tyāgarāja's image decorated for the Aradhana festival in Tiruvaiyaru**
Photograph by M. Srinath

FIGURE 6.5 Saint-composer Tyāgarāja image taken in procession for the 164th Aradhana festival at Tiruvaiyaru

Photograph by M. Srinath

In the first line of the song (*pallavi*, the "growing point" of a plant or seed of an idea), he refers to the *mṛdangam* drum that accompanies vocal performances (such as the one in our recording), and to the metrical concept of *tāla*, as indispensable components of performance. The second line (*anupallavi*) adds two further requisites for a sacred song, namely melody comprised of "pure" notes— presumably he means notes sung in tune—and the philosophy of the most ancient and sacred texts (*nigama*) of Hinduism, including the Vedas and Upaniṣads.

In the third and fourth lines of the poem, which together make up the third section of the song (*caraṇam*), Tyāgarāja refers to the poetic and aesthetic requirements for a successful song. It should follow the rules of poetic construction including meter and rhyme. Going beyond the austere philosophy of the Upaniṣads referred to in the *anupallavi*, it should also express bhakti, devotion. It should evoke one or more of the nine "essences" or "flavors" (*rasa*) of emotion that are defined in classical Indian aesthetic theory, namely love, mirth, manly vigor, compassion/ sadness, anger, wonder/surprise, fear, disgust, and tranquility. But in addition, it should have the sweetness of grape juice: the grape is a fruit that can be eaten without effort, and hence it denotes poetry and music that can be immediately understood and enjoyed without difficulty.

As usual in Indian song lyrics, the poet sets his seal on his work by including his own name in the final line. But as the song returns to the opening refrain, "Who is the stalwart?," his questions remain unanswered, his self-doubt unresolved. It is perhaps left for the listener to provide an answer.

PRIMARY SOURCE

Commentary: In her early career Subbulakshmi performed as a singer–actress in four musical films, which contributed to her fame and popularity as a singer. Subbulakshmi's most famous film, the "devotional movie" *Meera* (1945), was also her last. In it she played the eponymous heroine, the sixteenth-century North Indian princess Mīrabāī, who like Tyāgarāja preferred a life as a devout singer and poetess to the pleasures of wealth and privilege (her devotional songs are still sung today). This immensely popular film established an image of Subbulakshmi as a devotional singer, and she cultivated this image ever after, never acting in films again.

FIGURE 6.6
M.S. Subbulakshmi in the title role of the Tamil film *Meera* (1945)

Source: http://dbsjeyaraj.com/dbsj/archives/26262

"Sogasugā" is but one of many hundreds of songs by Tyāgarāja, of which new performances take place every day. It is an excellent example not only of the melodic and rhythmic beauties, but also of the spiritual content of classical song in South India. The poet displays a remarkable humility in questioning how he, a mere mortal, can address and move the heart of the Divine, while at the same time setting out his tools for doing so—rhythm, well-tuned notes, meter and rhyme, ancient philosophy, heartfelt devotion, the aesthetic emotions, and, above all, ease of understanding and enjoyment. It was by performing religious devotion musically, in regional languages and styles, that M.S. Subbulakshmi melted the hearts of Indians everywhere, at a time of rebirth for the Indian nation. The poet's self-doubt was perhaps echoed in the minds of many uncertain how to forge an Indian national identity that had never previously existed. As Tyāgarāja himself had earlier been taken as the exemplar of "time-tested Indian values" in the face of social and political change—values including the rejection of material wealth, and devotion to a divine savior—so Subbulakshmi asserted those same values, through her performances of his and other devotional songs. In so doing, however, she overturned entrenched prejudices against her gender and social background (see Biography and Primary Source boxes), proving that music, while apparently promoting timeless values, can also articulate and achieve far reaching social and cultural change.

BIOGRAPHY

Madurai Shanmukhavadivu Subbulakshmi, or M.S. Subbulakshmi as she is normally known, was born in the temple town of Madurai, made her first recording in Madras at the age of 10, and went on to become the most popular singer of South Indian classical music in the twentieth century. However, she was important not only for her musical achievements but also as a significant figure in a rapidly changing society.

Subbulakshmi was a female artist in a male-dominated society. She came from a family connected to the **_devadāsī_** tradition of female temple dancers and musicians, traditionally the only context in which women were permitted to perform openly; her mother was also a singer. For other sectors of society, especially

FIGURE 6.7 **M.S. Subbulakshmi**

the high-caste urban middle classes, it was unthinkable for their women to sing, dance, or play music in public. This prejudice became even more entrenched when, in the late nineteenth and early twentieth centuries, social reformers (both European and Indian) led a successful campaign to abolish the institution of female temple dancers, on the grounds that they were sexually exploited through dedication to the temples as children and through prostitution.

Despite this prejudice against female professionalism, a few pioneer women from respectable social backgrounds took to the stage as singers or dancers, notably the singer D.K. Pattamal and the dancer Rukmini Devi. For the dancers, it was a matter of "rescuing" and "reconstructing" the ancient art of dance following the demise of the _devadāsī_ tradition, while for the singers, the challenge was to prove that they could sing the classical repertoire as well as male musicians. In becoming a professional singer, Subbulakshmi had to overcome both the disdain of male musicians and the stigma of her social background, for the _devadāsī_s were now irredeemably marginalized.

Subbulakshmi's success was indubitably due to her superb musicianship and traditional training. But her unprecedented popularity, across the whole of India, was also due to her embracing "time-tested Indian values"—principally those of spirituality, devotion, and domestic respectability (she married a senior executive in 1943, who became her trusted musical adviser). In addition to performing Karnatak classical music for the South Indian audience, she sang devotional songs (_bhajan_) in a variety of other regional languages and musical styles; she was thus able to appeal to audiences in both North and South India, and became a household name throughout the newly independent country. Her universal popularity made her a figurehead for the Republic of India (inaugurated 1947), and she was befriended by the leading spirits of the Indian independence movement. Mahatma Gandhi wrote of her: "Her voice is exceedingly sweet; she loses herself in bhajan. During prayer one must lose oneself to God. To sing a bhajan is one thing: to sing it by losing oneself in God is quite different."

Subbulakshmi performed extensively outside India, to high acclaim, and became a cultural ambassador for her country. Her first overseas concert took place at the Edinburgh Festival in 1963, and a tour of the USA, including an appearance at the United Nations on Human Rights Day, followed in 1966. The *San Francisco Chronicle* said of her singing:

"A series of miracles . . . She sings with a reedy yet dark voice and the most extraordinary flexibility. Like sleight-of-hand she throws out embellishments almost too fast to hear."

Such embellishments are an essential feature of South Indian classical vocal style and can be heard in "Sogasugā." What is often referred to as her "golden voice," described as an "unmixed chest voice and sweet tone" (A. Catlin), is considered to represent the ideal for a female classical singer in South India.

Subbulakshmi was so successful in overcoming the limitations of her social background and gender that she made a professional career respectable for other women musicians, of whatever background, and there are now many who follow in her musical footsteps. But the sound of a female voice singing his compositions is a sound Tyāgarāja himself may never have heard.

Discussion Topics

• How does the structure and style of the music convey the poet's message? Consider the contribution of the accompanists as well as that of the soloist.

• Is Indian classical music a legacy from the past, unrelated to the contemporary world? In what ways does it have contemporary relevance?

• Explore online some of the life stories of prominent Indian film actresses and singers. What challenges do they face in pursuing their careers, and how do they overcome them?

Recommended Reading

Jackson, William (1991) *Tyāgarāja: Life and Lyrics*. Madras: Oxford University Press.
A detailed study of the composer and translations of the lyrics of many of his songs. His translations are literary and poetic rather than strictly literal; a literal translation is in any case difficult because the natural word order of Telugu is different from that of English.

Jackson, William J. (2000) "'Religious and Devotional Music: Southern Area." In A. Arnold, ed. "South Asia: The Indian subcontinent." *The Garland Encyclopedia of World Music*. New York: Garland.
   An accessible overview of music and spirituality in southern India.

Viswanathan, T. and Allen, M.H. (2004) *Music in South India: Experiencing Music, Expressing Culture*. Madras: Oxford University Press.
   A useful introduction to music in South India.

Weidman, A. (2006) *Singing the Classical, Voicing the Modern: The Postcolonial Politics of Music in South India*. Durham, NC: Duke University Press.
   In-depth discussion of issues of gender and modernity.

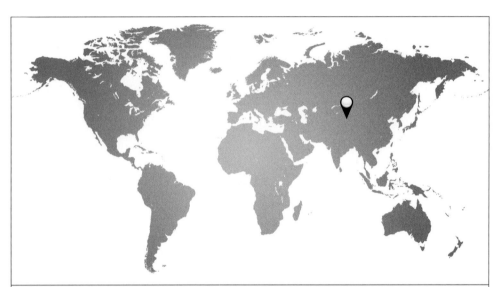

Location: Xinjiang Uyghur Autonomous Region, China/East Turkestan

Subhan'Allāh (Glory to God): Listening and Weeping in a *Dhikr* Ceremony

Sung by an anonymous group of women; recorded by Rachel Harris, August 2009, Aqsu region, China

Chapter seven
"Subhan'Allāh" (Glory to God)
Listening and Weeping in a *Dhikr* Ceremony
Rachel Harris

Summary

In a small, dusty village in Chinese Central Asia (the "Xinjiang Uyghur Autonomous Region of the People's Republic of China" to give its official title), 60 women have squeezed themselves into the guestroom of a villager's house. In a three-hour long ritual, they recite passages from the Qur'an, they sing Sufi poetry, and turn slowly in a ritual *sama* dance, and they weep copiously and demonstratively.

They are led by Bu Sarem, an elegant and charismatic woman in her sixties, who sits in the place of honor at the center of the back wall, flanked by her apprentices (*shagird*). The other women sit around her, grouped in roughly concentric semi-circles on the room's large raised platform, which is covered with brightly colored carpets. In this all-female gathering, Bu Sarem draws back her sequinned face veil and conducts the proceedings, almost as an orchestral conductor directs an orchestra. She also leads the performance, giving a long opening solo section of recitation herself then leading the other women in repeated rhythmic chants (**dhikr**), which include short phrases from the Qur'an and Arabic language prayers. She points to her apprentices to perform longer sections of individual recitation, and guides the whole group through emotional peaks and troughs towards the climax of the ritual. After around an hour she leads into a new chanted *dhikr*: *Subhan'Allāh wa bihamdihi, subhan'Allāh il adhīm* (Glory to Allah and praise him, Glory to Allah the supreme).

KEY WORDS
• body
• emotion
• gender
• Islam

Why this Piece?

I spent the first 10 years of my research in Xinjiang studying the masculine world of Uyghur music as it is conventionally understood. I wrote about the "classical" Uyghur Muqam repertoire, the Uyghur pop industry, and issues of nationalism and representation, but I rarely thought about gender. I worked with male colleagues, whose wives appeared from the kitchen with food but rarely joined us to eat. I openly smoked and drank, laughed at the—frankly very dirty—jokes told by male

FIGURE 7.1   Women gather around a traditional tablecloth (*dastkhan*) for food and tea
before beginning their ritual

Photograph by Rachel Harris

musicians, and generally enjoyed my outsider status which enabled me, if not to
be entirely gender neutral, at least to flout some of the rules. Then I got married
to a Uyghur man, and my view of Uyghur culture and society was turned inside
out. We spent a long summer in my mother-in-law's village in central Xinjiang,
and I took my place in the heart of the women's sphere, with my own small child
in tow, helping with the work of home-keeping and hospitality: fetching the water
from the well, gathering wood and lighting the fire, nursing babies, feeding animals,
baking bread in the *tonur* brick ovens, preparing dough for noodles and dumplings.
Now it was the men who appeared as shadowy and inconsequential figures on the
periphery of a woman-centric world.

In this conservative Muslim village, women who played the **dutar**, a long-necked
lute, or sang folk songs were somehow not quite respectable; people made snide
jokes when they spoke about them. My mother-in-law would not have been happy
if I had decided to work with them. But another kind of music-making (although
it was certainly not locally understood as "music") was the province of highly
respected, even powerful women in the community. And so I became interested
in the **büwi**: women who had memorized the Qur'an, who washed the bodies of
the dead, and performed rituals for funerals, to heal the sick, and to cast out
bad luck.

Musical Features

TIMED LISTENING GUIDE

0:00–1:45	Bu Sarem leads into this new *dhikr*. Most of the women follow her three-note melody, which rises and falls within the range of a minor 3rd on a four-square rhythm. One woman, a *büwi* from a neighboring village, obstinately sticks to her own slightly different melody and rhythm, which overlaps with the main group: this is an oral tradition, there is no prescribed melody, and each teacher may transmit it slightly differently to her pupils
1:45–1:50	Bu Sarem calls out in Uyghur, "Come close, hold hands! Recite at the same time together, as if with one voice." The women shuffle forwards on their knees and form tighter concentric circles around her
1:50–2:30	The *dhikr* is now more unified, and begins to grow in intensity
2:30–3:00	One woman begins to rock from side to side and to cry out rhythmically, "Woy Allah!" while the others maintain the *dhikr*
3:00–4:00	The trancing woman gives high-pitched rhythmic cries, "Woy Allah!," jerking her body back and forth. Some of the women try to calm her while the others maintain the *dhikr*, which is now becoming very scattered rhythmically while the voices are more strained and emotionally heightened. Another woman is weeping loudly. This is the high point of the whole ritual

FIGURE 7.2 Seventeenth-century Iranian representation of the phrase *bismillāhi raḥmāni raḥīm*, in the form of a bird

Courtesy of the Pergamon Museum

4:00–5:50	The trancing woman settles into a rhythmic repeated "Woy, woy, woy," continuing to jerk her body. Her rhythm is distinct from the rhythm of the chant
5:50–7:10	The pace of the chanting slows slightly and the intensity drops, the trancing woman is calmer and the chanting voices are more relaxed, and now more unified
7:10–7:18	This section of the ritual is concluded with the slow, falling well-known Arabic phrase, *Bismillāhi raḥmāni raḥīm* (In the name of God, the most gracious, the most merciful), which opens the recitation of every surah of the Qur'an, and opens and closes every new *dhikr* in these rituals

Experiencing this ritual live was almost overwhelming for me. It was the first ritual I had attended as well as the largest and most powerful, and I was quite unprepared for the extreme heat and claustrophobia and the waves of emotion that washed over me. Be warned! Even listening to this short audio excerpt can be an intense experience.

It is a "piece" only in the loosest sense: a piece of *dhikr*, one phrase of Arabic recited rhythmically over 80 times: *Subhan'Allāh wa bihamdihi, subhan'Allāh il adhīm* (Glory to Allah and praise him, Glory to Allah the supreme). It comes over an hour into this long ritual, and forms the emotional climax of a complicated sequence of repeated prayers and longer solo sections of the Qur'an. The women gradually settle into a rhythmic four-square beat which grows in intensity to a peak where several women weep noisily and one woman falls into a trance.

Sixty voices overlapped, reciting the same phrase slightly out of sync and slightly off pitch, forming a wash of sound. As the women chanted their *dhikr* they swayed from side to side or backwards and forwards, some more actively than others, physically locking into the rhythm. A simple transcription on the stave would express too little of the experience of this repetitive chant. It began weak and scattered and gradually built in intensity as the assembled women latched onto the rhythm, together but never in perfect unison, their voices always slightly overlapping, slightly out of sync, until—as I felt, sitting in the room with them—the sound was palpably reverberating inside me, drawing me along. It is striking that getting into the groove here does not mean perfect unison—this is not at all like a marching band—as they approached the climax each woman swirled off into her own rhythm and pitch, nonetheless maintaining the chant, and falling back into a more steady togetherness as the emotional intensity subsided.

Social Context

Healing Rituals

Muslim women in many parts of the world gather in groups to perform rituals related to healing and spiritual benefits. Many of these gatherings are emotionally saturated. They typically involve reciting the Qur'an, prayers, group singing of religious songs, and a kind of circling or whirling *sama* dance: a less formalized version of the dance of the Mevlevi "Whirling Dervishes" in Turkey. The specific form and meanings of the rituals vary considerably in different societies and different contexts around the world. Women's rituals do not form an exclusive tradition; they are related to mainstream male practices: *dhikr* is historically associated with the (male-dominated) Sufi orders, and women often learn to recite the Qur'an from male religious clerics (*mullah*) who have been educated in religious institutions (*madrassah*).

In Uyghur society, women are not allowed to enter the mosques, and when they pray at home they must do so silently in case the sound of their voices leads men to sinful thoughts. *Büwi* are thus the main providers of religious teaching for village women, and their gatherings—which men may not attend—provide the main channel for women's religious (and indeed musical) expression. In addition, they provide religious services for the community, performing rituals for the sick, the unlucky, and at funerals. They also perform large-scale rituals at specific points on the Islamic calendar. Bu Sarem explains:

> We seek for blessings on the night of Barat and during Ramadan (the month of fasting), and on the day of the call to prayer (Fridays). On Thursdays or Mondays we recite for people who request it. If you hold a ritual in your home it will dispel the danger that comes from the seven sides, and your wishes will come true. We ask Allah to forgive the sins of that family, and we pray with weeping. If there is an illness in the family we recite and blow into a bowl of water and have them drink the water, and then the illness will be cured.

These informal women's gatherings probably constitute the most widespread and significant aspect of Islamic practice in the region: hundreds of women's groups across Xinjiang meet regularly for rituals like the one we heard. They are particularly important in keeping religious practice alive in a society where government policy is often hostile towards Islam. Some of the older women performing these rituals have lived through extraordinary social upheavals brought about by the attempts of the Chinese Communist Party to revolutionize, modernize, and reform society. During the disastrous "Great Leap Forward" of the 1950s, they scavenged for grains of wheat and boiled them with nettles so their children would not starve. They continued to perform their rituals, out of sight of the village authorities, right through the chaos of the Cultural Revolution in the 1960s and 1970s when the mosques were closed down and the mullahs beaten and humiliated. In the 1980s life became easier for them and they were able to practice their religion more openly. More recently, after 2001, the political situation took another downturn: the authorities became increasingly afraid of Islamic extremism, and police crackdowns on all kinds of religious practice once again drove them underground. Right through this complicated history, the *büwi* have continued their rituals: their crucial role in the life and death of the community, and their informal nature—there are no dedicated schools or meeting houses for *büwi*—means that they are hard to track down and hard to eradicate.

Listening to the Qur'an

The sense of the holiness, and the blessings (*baraka*) imparted by the sounded Qur'an—as the word of God—pervades every part of the Muslim world. Its power and spiritual function are quite apart from the understanding of every word of the Arabic text. Memorizing the Qur'an has long been fundamental to raising children in Muslim societies. It is an integral part of socialization and it provides the basis of a shared Islamic heritage. Listening to the Qur'an is an aesthetic experience, a spine-tingling auditory experience, and a cathartic process that mediates listeners' relationship with God.

In this *dhikr*, it is evident that all the women are active participants: listening, vocalizing and embodying the sounded Qur'anic phrases, but whenever Muslims listen to the Qur'an, they are actively performing a religious act. Proper listening involves making themselves into a suitable host for the presence of divine words by embodying the correct responses and attitudes, and making the words resonate in their bodies and hearts.

The importance of listening, and the affective power of the Qur'an is mentioned within several of its verses:

> [A]nd when they hear what has been sent down to the Messenger, thou seest their eyes overflow with tears because of the truth they recognize. (Qur'an, Surah 5:83)

> Allah has sent down the most beautiful words: a scripture consistent in its repetition. At which the skins of those who fear their Lord crawl, but then their skins and their hearts are softened for the remembrance of God. (Qur'an, Surah 39:23)

The *büwi* expressed this same sense of emotional engagement with their faith, although the metaphors they drew on to convey the experience and the meaning of the ritual were much more down to earth. Turaysem explained their excitement to me thus:

> The oil is sizzling in the pot. Their love for Allah is so strong, they can't stop themselves crying, just like the pot on the stove. When the oil is hot you must throw in the meat otherwise the oil will catch fire. It's just like that. Then you must put in the vegetables otherwise the meat will burn. So just like that the women cry a lot . . . Allah's passion is like the hot oil in the pot, their passion for Allah is so strong.

PRIMARY SOURCE

Dhikr

In Sufi traditions of Islam, any part of the Qur'an can become the focus of intense mystical engagement, to the point of ecstatic arousal. For such engagement to actually take place requires dwelling on the particular phrase so that the full impact of its meaning can be allowed to unfold. This is achieved through repetition, so that the "audible" present is filled with the single meaning of its message as in *dhikr*. (Regula Burckhardt Qureshi 2006: 507)

Dhikr is most commonly associated with Sufism, a mystical branch of Islam that emphasizes striving towards union with God, and whose adherents, who are found across the Islamic world, adhere to orders (*tariqa*) founded by revered saints.

FIGURE 7.3 From the Ihya 'Ulm ad-Din of Al-Ghazālī (c. 1058–1111)
Held in the Tunisian National Archive

Dhikr ("remembrance, reminder, evocation") is both a concept and a meditative practice for Muslims around the globe. It involves the repeated chanting of the names of God or Arabic phrases from the Qur'an accompanied by ritualized body movements and rhythmic breathing. *Dhikr* is thought to aid Sufis along their mystical journey towards the passing away of the ego and its unity with the divine. The medieval Muslim philosopher al-Ghazālī wrote that *dhikr* polishes the heart, allowing it to serve as a mirror reflecting the divine attributes. Performing *dhikr* is thought to bring the believer to a realization of divine truths such as the unity of God and the unity of existence. Performing *dhikr* brings the faithful to a state of mindfulness of God. It is thus a form of ritual remembering, and an unveiling of eternal truths.

Some of the classic writings on *dhikr* express well the links between sound, emotion and body which ethnomusicology tries to understand:

> Know that the listening comes first, and that it bears as fruit a state in the heart that is called ecstasy; and ecstasy bears as fruit a moving of the extremities of the body, either with a motion that is not measured and is called agitation or with a measured motion which is called clapping of the hands and swaying of the members.

Al-Ghazālī was a Muslim theologian, philosopher, and mystic of Persian descent. Sometimes described by historians as the single most influential Muslim after the Prophet Muhammad, he wrote more than 70 books on the sciences and Islamic philosophy, and is credited with bringing the orthodox Islam of his time into closer contact with Sufism.

Emotional Work

While the form and sounds of the women's ritual may be similar to, even derived from, Sufi practice, the purpose of their rituals is quite different. While Sufis seek to polish their own hearts, *büwi* weep in order to bring spiritual benefits to their community. Their practice is part of what we often call popular Islam, a web of distinctively local practices which are often as much about creating and maintaining social ties as they are about individual faith. Bu Sarem explains:

> When we recite, our passions come to the boil. Because in our lives in this world we can't always stick to doing good deeds. We live, and we don't know if we are doing good. We fear Allah. Allah created us, and when we die we go to him, so we ask for mercy. We are sinful beings, so we cry to ask [forgiveness] for our sins.

The *dhikr* that we are discussing in this chapter is performed during the festival of Barat, the "Night of Forgiveness." This is the night when the contemporary *büwi* hold their largest and most significant rituals, reciting and weeping right through the night. In popular belief in Muslim Central Asia, Barat—the night of the fourteenth of the month of Shabaan—is when the Tree of Life is shaken. Each person has their name written on a leaf of this tree, and the leaves of those who are going to die in the coming year would fall to the ground.

FIGURE 7.4 **The Tree of Life represented in a carved window in Sidi Saiyid mosque, Ahmedabad, northwest India**

Photograph by Vrajesh Jani

The fourteenth is also termed the Night of Forgiveness. This reflects the belief that two angels sit on the shoulders of every person, the angel on the right recording good deeds, and the angel on the left recording sins. On the Night of Forgiveness the angels enter into the individual's book the amount of merit she or he has accumulated during the year. When the *büwi* perform their *dhikr* on this night, they are trying to intercede on behalf of those in their community who will die, asking that their souls be admitted to Paradise. One young woman in our household said: "They weep for our sins; when we die we don't know if we will go into water or fire."

What distinguishes the practice of these women most clearly from Sufi traditions is that their purpose is not only to accrue individual spiritual benefits: this is also a form of communal emotional work. Weeping, the embodied emotional response that demonstrates their passion for Allah, is what makes the ritual effective, and listening to the repeated sound of the *dhikr*—"Glory to God"—is what provokes the weeping.

Technologies of the Body: Music and Emotion

Musicologists writing about Western classical music have generally begun by asking: "How does music evoke emotion?" Putting the question in this way gives a central role to "the music," usually as represented by a notated score, thus according an odd form of agency to these notes on a page. They suggest that we can identify a particular set of musical qualities—related to intensity, contour and movement—that produce affective responses in listeners. According to music psychologists, these "affective responses" are not the same as full-blown emotions. They are immediate, bodily responses to what is being heard, like goose-bumps or a hot flush. A further layer of psychological processing is needed for listeners to decide what this response emotion means to them emotionally, and that depends on external factors. Are they listening to a tragic opera in which the desperate heroine is about to leap to her death? Are they remembering that they heard this piece once before while speeding down an empty desert road?

Some musicologists suggest that these affective responses are produced through the way that a piece of music moves towards or moves away from a "home." This might be a tonic (thinking in terms of mode or key) or a strong beat of the bar (thinking in terms of rhythm and meter). When the music moves away (such as syncopated, non-diatonic notes) listeners feel an increase in tension; when it moves towards this "home" (as on a perfect **cadence**) listeners experience a reduction of tension. This kind of explanation works well if we are thinking about certain kinds of Western classical score—what we might call **linear** compositions—but it doesn't fit at all well with the piece we are talking about here: a repeated short phrase. Here the structure is better understood as circular, or perhaps in three-dimensions: a spiral or a vortex within which affective responses are spun.

Ethnomusicologists who have written about music and emotion have shifted the emphasis away from "the music" as represented by notes on a page. Human minds and bodies are central in this approach; the focus is on the embodied experience of musical sound. In this way of thinking, human bodies are not bounded and discrete; they are reflexively linked to the material and cultural environment. This active view of emotional engagement places the participants at the heart of the analysis, as agents who makes emotion happen by their "musicking." When we listen to music, when we dance or sing or play music, we have the sensation of synchronizing with the physical movements of others. We "fall into phase" or "get into the groove." We feel this as a physical sensation of coordinated motion and as an emotional connection. You might have had this kind of experience while singing in a choir, out clubbing, at a drumming session, or even in an aerobics class where the leader carefully tailors the beats per minute of the tracks she plays in order to encourage and enable the maximum physical exertion from her class.

But beyond these embodied, affective responses, the way that people experience and understand emotional events like this also depends on the social context and their cultural background. As the anthropologist Michelle Rosaldo has argued, "Just as thought does not exist in isolation from affective life, so affect is culturally ordered and does not exist apart from thought." For me, a white British woman sitting in the room, experiencing the affective force of the *dhikr*, my primary feeling was of bewilderment. I could not experience the same emotions that the participants were experiencing because I did not understand what they were experiencing. In order to understand something of what they felt, we need to explore the social context.

It may Sound like a Form of Music to Outsiders, but is it OK to Treat this Kind of Ritual Practice as Music?

Ethnomusicologists have long concerned themselves with a wide array of sounded practices, including ritual practices, which are not regarded as "music" by their practitioners; indeed the idea of "music" may hardly be recognized in some societies, or it might refer to some very specific imported style: Christian missionary hymns, for example.

Across the Islamic world, the Arabic term **musiqa** shares the ancient Greek roots of the contemporary English term "music," but the history of its meanings and interpretation is quite different. A debate has raged for centuries about the permissibility of listening to *musiqa*: the so-called '**sama debate**'. Since the Qur'an itself has nothing to say on this subject, it is all about interpretation. Does listening to music lead to sin, and should therefore be avoided by the pious? The medieval Islamic philosopher al-Ghazālī made an early, and still influential, intervention into the debate, arguing that "Music and singing do not produce in the heart that which is not in it, but they stir up what is in it." In Central Asian popular thought, both sides of the debate are represented. One folk tale recounts that the tail of the donkey ridden by the Devil is made from the strings of musical instruments, and they will entice people to follow him on the Day of Judgement. Central Asian musicians have defended themselves by arguing that the revered Prophet Dawut (he of the tale of David and Goliath in the Christian Old Testament) was the inventor of music.

The debate also revolves around the problem of what constitutes music. Does it include singing or just instrumental music? Is a frame drum a musical instrument? In practice, it is almost impossible to separate out the rich musical traditions of the Islamic world from its diverse ritual practices. As the directly transmitted word of God, the Qur'an should not be associated with the ambivalent category of music, yet Qur'anic recitation draws directly on the musical rules of **maqām**, the modal system of Arabic classical music. In most Muslim societies, musicians are also employed as *muezzin* (one who gives the call to prayer) or as Qur'anic reciters. The most famous of all Egyptian singers, Umm Kulthum, learned as a child to recite the Qur'an and sang **qasida** poems about the Prophet. The contemporary musicologist Lois Al Faruqi describes a hierarchy of sounded practices, ranging from the sacred word of God (the Qur'an) right down to the widely condemned music associated with pleasure and sexuality.

There are particular problems associated with women performing music in many Muslim societies. In conservative societies, such behavior is often seen as shameful for the woman's family, unless it is within a specific context such as a wedding. Professional female performers have historically often belonged to designated, low-class groups and were regarded as little better than prostitutes. In many cases, modernity has brought greater opportunities for Muslim women to pursue careers as musicians without fear of bringing shame on their families. In contemporary Xinjiang, female musicians, singers and dancers are on TV every day, but still in this conservative village it is not respectable for local women to sing in public. In other cases the liberating trends of the twentith century have provoked a twenty-first-century backlash. The contemporary Egyptian Islamist al-Qaradawi has written that women exist to provoke the sexual instinct, and should therefore be hidden away from sight, while art exists to provoke sexuality and thus is an evil that requires repentance. Women in contemporary Uyghur society, as in other parts of the Islamic world, must negotiate these debates as part of their daily lives.

BIOGRAPHY

Bu Sarem, the senior *büwi* in the area, was a person of great charisma, still beautiful under a black and gold embroidered veil. Her recitation had almost instant power to provoke weeping. She herself was reticent about her past, but the women in our family were quick to fill in the details. "Bu Sarem became a *büwi* after seeing ghosts," they said, "She is a true healer, a shaman. When she was young she was wild, she had a lover. Even now she likes to talk and laugh."

This kind of gossip echoed a saying which several people quoted for me when I told them I was doing research with *büwi*, "When a 'slag' gets old she becomes a *büwi*." Even though these women were not performing "music" as such, clearly some stigma still attached to them. But such gossip was muted and, within village society, *büwi* were widely respected and even feared for the role they play in dealing with sickness and death. "Do your husbands support what you do?" I asked another *büwi*. "Of course they do . . . if they don't want to go to Hell!" she said. Sometimes I thought that these women had found the perfect way to get around social restrictions imposed on them so that they could get together and have a good time making music. At other times it seemed that theirs was a deep spiritual calling: like shamans, they had been forced to become healers in order to heal themselves; the practice of their faith fulfilled a deep physical need. Turaysem told me:

After I had my second child I was not well, and I had no time for my prayers for a few years. Then early one morning I had a dream. A fine old man with a handsome beard sitting on a carpet came towards me from the sky. I was in a graveyard, and he lectured me about the Qur'an. I was very afraid. I had developed a liver illness, and I thought I would die. At that time my youngest child was only six months old, I was so scared. After that dream I woke up, and I understood myself. This was twelve years ago. Since then I have been praying and reading the Qur'an.

Turaysem was a young woman when I first met her but she was already regarded as a *büwi* of considerable power. She was unusually tall and with a manner of exceptional authority. She spoke to me at length about her background and training

FIGURE 7.5 **Turaysem**
Photograph by Rachel Harris

in the art of Qur'anic recitation, and offered to teach me this art. This was a generous
offer, made at some personal risk: teaching Islam to children was banned by the Xinjiang
government during this period, and Turaysem had already been in trouble for teaching
local girls to recite the Qur'an. Associating with a foreigner in this closely controlled
society ran the risk of bringing her into conflict with the local authorities again.

Conducting fieldwork was often a nail-biting business. Some of the women were
understandably reluctant to meet with me, but many others actively pushed me to get
more involved with their activities. They wanted to teach me, to explain about what they
did, they wanted copies of my videos of their rituals, and they wanted to know more
about Islam in other parts of the world.

Discussion Topics

- What do you think is most important in producing emotion and altered states? Is it the
sound of the music? Is it the experience of reciting together in a group? Or is it the belief
system? If you like, you can experiment by recording your responses after listening to
this track alone, and after reciting along with it as a group. Did anyone fall into a trance?

- What do you think about the ethics involved in this fieldwork? Should I have let them
take the risk of being caught associating with a foreign researcher? Should I have
published this research?

Recommended Reading

Becker, Judith (2001) "Anthropological Perspectives." In Patrik N. Juslin and John A. Sloboda, eds. *Music and Emotion: Theory and Research*. New York: Oxford University Press.
> Becker argues that musicologists should pay attention to anthropology when they study music and emotion.

Burckhardt Qureshi, Regula (2006) *Sufi Music of India and Pakistan: Sound, Context, and Meaning in Qawwali*. Oxford and New York: Oxford University Press.
> A rich ethnographic study of a type of Sufi ritual in Pakistan.

Harris, Rachel (2013) "'Doing Satan's Business': Negotiating gendered concepts of music and ritual in rural Xinjiang." In Rachel Harris, Rowan Pease, and Shzr EeTan, eds. *Gender in Chinese Music*. Rochester, NY: University of Rochester Press.
> A fuller treatment of the material introduced in this chapter.

Kapchan, Deborah (2009) "Singing Community/Remembering Common: Sufi liturgy and North African identity in southern France." *International Journal of Community Music* 2(1): 9–23.
> Evocative first-hand description of women's *dhikr*.

Nelson, Kristina (2001) *The Art of Reciting the Qur'an*. Cairo: American University in Cairo Press.
> The seminal work on Qur'anic recitation, based on work with top Egyptian reciters in the 1980s, including an overview of the *sama* debate, and the musicality of recitation.

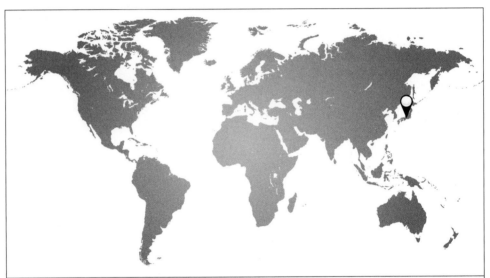

Location: Suzuka, Mie Prefecture, Japan

"Tamuke" (手向): A *Shakuhachi* Requiem

[Tamuke 手向 (literally: hands facing [each other in prayer]): to offer; to sacrifice; to pray.]

Played by Okuda Atsuya on *shakuhachi*, Sound of Zen, Son Tech D00EM04802; recorded 11 June 2002 in Izumi Hall, Nishi Kokubunji, Tokyo, Japan, and 2 July 2002 in Asao Shimin Kaikan, Kawasaki, Japan

Chapter eight
"Tamuke" (手向)

A *Shakuhachi* Requiem

Kiku Day

Summary

This chapter is concerned with the reinterpretation and appropriation of traditional music across cultures. The focus here is on "Tamuke," a **honkyoku** piece for the Japanese vertical bamboo flute *shakuhachi*. *Honkyoku* were the repertoire of Zen Buddhist *komusō* monks of the **Fuke** sect during the Edo period (1603–1867). These "monks of nothingness" had exclusive rights to play the *shakuhachi*, which they used for their spiritual training and for begging. Today, "Tamuke," as popularized through the performance of Watamzumi Doso and later by his student, Yokoyama Katsuya, has become a favorite piece for *shakuhachi* players around the world, especially in the West. The title refers to an offering to a deity or to a person about to depart, but is often translated as "**requiem**"—a term describing a particular ritual and a musical genre within Western classical music. As a result, "Tamuke" is now heard at funerals in the United States, Europe, and Australia as a requiem. Western *shakuhachi* players also play "Tamuke" at important and holy places for *shakuhachi* in Japan as a requiem for the *shakuhachi* ancestors. This chapter examines these new uses of a piece from a musical genre that originally served as spiritual training for monks, and explores the appropriation and act of cultural translation of non-Western music into terms drawn from Western classical music and serving new eclectic forms of cross-cultural spirituality.

KEY WORDS

- cultural translation
- emotion
- style
- timbre
- transnational flows
- Zen Buddhism

Why this Piece?

"Tamuke" was the first piece I learned when I began studying the *shakuhachi* with master player Okuda Atsuya in Japan; the first piece in a master–pupil relationship that was to last for 11 years of intense study and still continues today. There are no beginners' pieces in *honkyoku*; furthermore, "Tamuke" is an unusually difficult piece to begin with as a player new to not only a new instrument but also a whole musical tradition. During my first 18 months as a *shakuhachi* novice, I went once a week to Okuda's studio Zensabō and worked exclusively on "Tamuke." I quickly learned how different the teaching methods of *shakuhachi* were to what I had encountered learning Western classical music in Denmark. No études, no scales to practice, no pedagogical methodology such as I had experienced when studying the piano and flute. The most common way to learn was simply to play along with your teacher. This method taught me many aspects of *honkyoku*, including aesthetic values, the flow, and the pace of the pieces. Okuda would tell me that not only did this one piece contain the world of *honkyoku*, but also that each note was to be played as if it contained the whole universe. The complexity within the simplicity surprised and startled me, and I discovered something new in the piece each time I played it. Okuda also told me that this piece could be played to wish a newly departed soul safe passage on its way. "Tamuke" is a melodic and beautiful piece and has now become perhaps one of the most popular *shakuhachi* pieces among non-Japanese players.

Musical Features

TIMED LISTENING GUIDE

Played on a 2.55 *shakuhachi* (approximately 77.30 cm). Opening the finger holes will create the following notes: G♯; B; C♯; E♭; F♯ (ro; tsu; re; chi; ha)

Line 1 = the whole of line 1 in the score (see Figure 8.3). Each line can be divided into phrases, which are the length of one breath

0:00–0:16	A1, line 1	*Introduction of mode*: The first phrase opens with one of the
0:16–0:22	A1, line 1	**nuclear notes** (G♯) being approached by the auxiliary note below (F♯), which is produced by bending the G♯ a whole tone down. Then the melody moves on to the other note (A) that is
0:23–0:32	A, line 1	closed related to the nucleus. The second phrase takes us via B to C♯, the perfect 4th above the nuclear note and down to G♯ again
0.33–0:43	B, line 1	*Introduction of melody*: The melody and all the main notes are
0:43–0:52	B, line 2	introduced including the E♭ and E. When the melody climbs to
0:52–1:01	B, line 2	G♯ an octave above, an alternative fingering is used to soften
1:01–1:12	B, line 2	the top note (an "enharmonic" note)
1:13–1:29	C1, line 3	Part of main melody. At 1.18 you can hear a clear example of a
1:30–1:42	C1, line 4	"growl" on the first C♯ and then at G♯, a non-pitched effect
1:43–1:56	C2, line 5	Part of main melody with variations of C. The closing of C and
1:57–2:08	C2, line 5	C1 are closely related. This section builds up tension towards
2:09–2:24	C2, line 6	a peak
2:25–2:38	D1, line 7	Small peak 1. According to Okuda, the proper playing of this phrase has been surrounded by secrecy and can vary according to school. At 2:25 you can hear a "***muraiki***," which is a breathy sound
2:39–2:42	D1, line 7	Continuation of section D, these two phrases are used first as a
2:42–2:59	D1, line 8	"landing" after the preceding peak, an emotional fragile point in

		the melody. It is a short moment where you can breathe and be safe again. There is then a build-up to the even larger peak
3:00–3:16	E1, line 9	Large peak 1. This is the first of two emotional peaks. It is an important part of the expressiveness of "Tamuke." The phrase arrives at a beautiful release into stillness. You can hear a high whistling sound, a non-pitched effect, above the main tone at 3:00 and another *muraiki* breathy sound at 3:04
3:16–3:29 3:29–3:40	E1, line 10 E1, line 10	Continuation of section E. Variation of D line 7 and has the role of both landing the peak and building towards the next
3:41–3:51	D2, line 11	Small peak 2. A fast ascending movement. This is the phrase where Yokoyama Katsuya in his version quotes Itsuki no Komoriuta. The abrupt ending anticipates the second large peak
3:51–4:08	E2, line 12	Large peak 2. Again an emotional and dramatic peak, which arrives at stillness. Basically the same as E1 line 9
4:09–4:26	E2, lines 12–13	Continuation of section E2. Variation of E1 line 10. The final note in the second phrase of E2 (top of line 13) is the same as the final note in line 2 of E1, which ends on an A, but fingered differently (an "enharmonic" note). Again, as in E1, it leads up to a smaller peak
4:27–4.44	D3, line 14	Small peak 3. A variation of D1 but instead of ending on G♯—the nuclear note, it ends on C♯, the perfect 4th above, which gives the peak an open-ended feeling. This leads into the final stages of the piece
4:46–5:10	D3, line 15	Continuation of section D3. The most important feature of this phrase is the notes E and E♭—both with a type of vibrato (*yuri*) called *takeyuri* (lit: bamboo shaking) produced by gently shaking the *shakuhachi*. It is meant to be reminiscent of the handbell of the Zen master Fuke and through this imitation it references the supposed 1000-year-old origins of the *shakuhachi* in Tang Dynasty China
5:10–5:42	A2, line 16	The two phrases ending the piece, which move from the nuclear note to a 4th above and then back to the nuclear note, are a variation of the introduction

Honkyoku and the *Shakuhachi*

Honkyoku are the solo repertoire left by the *shakuhachi*-playing *komusō* monks (monks of nothingness) of the Fuke sect of Zen Buddhism. The name *honkyoku* literally means "original pieces" and is used to refer to the religious music played by the monks as part of their spiritual training. After their sect was abolished in 1871 by the modernizing Meiji government (see later), the *shakuhachi* players formed different "schools" of playing, which are described later, and took part in ensembles playing music for entertainment, rather than for religious purposes. They continued to play the *honkyoku* as solo repertoire.

The *shakuhachi* is tuned to a pentatonic scale (D, F, G, A, C on standard instruments, which are 1.8 *shaku* or ca. 54.5 cm in length, but G♯; B; C♯; E♭; F♯ on the longer *shakuhachi* used on this recording), but these notes can be altered using techniques described below to give different modes. The majority of pieces are in *miyako-bushi* mode (on the standard instrument D, E♭, G A♭, C, or in our example G♯; A; C♯; D; F♯), which is the mode used in "Tamuke." One of the main features of *shakuhachi* music is the formalization of different head positions when playing. The standard head position is called *kari* and is the position for straight open holes and chin raised. The other position is called *meri* and is played with the chin

TECHNOLOGY

The *Shakuhachi*

The *shakuhachi* is a Japanese vertical notched oblique bamboo flute with four finger holes on the front and one thumbhole on the back. The *shakuhachi* of the Edo period consisted only of the bamboo and perhaps a mouthpiece inlay made of buffalo horn and a thin layer of Japanese lacquer made from the sap of the *urushi* tree. When ensemble playing became the main means of income for *shakuhachi* players, the need for well-tuned instruments increased and the modern *shakuhachi* was born. It is cut into two attachable halves. The length of the bamboo and thereby the pitch of the tube can thus be regulated, while retaining a node at the top and one at the bottom of the finished instrument. The bore is furthermore coated with *ji*, a paste made of *urushi* and *tonoko* (powder from ground stone). The application of *ji* to the bore is the reason for names that separate the older type of *shakuhachi* (*jinashi shakuhachi*) from the modern (*jinuri shakuhachi*)—the former literally meaning without *ji*, while the latter means *ji* applied. The application of *ji* means that the shape of the bore can be carefully calculated, modified, and thereby controlled, by the maker, in contrast to that of the older *jinashi shakuhachi*, which, as noted above, consists of only the natural bamboo and at times a thin layer of lacquer applied for protection against wear (nodes and other irregularities may, however, be filed down). While the *jinuri shakuhachi* has dominated since Meiji times, during the past 10 to 15 years the *jinashi shakuhachi* has become increasingly popular, particularly among non-Japanese players.

FIGURE 8.1 *Jinashi shakuhachi*
Photograph by Kiku Day

FIGURE 8.2 *Jinuri shakuhachi*
Photograph by Kiku Day

withdrawn towards the chest. This head position decreases the blowing angle and brings the lips closer to the mouthpiece. This lowers the pitch compared to those blown in the *kari* position and, combined with partially closed finger holes, gives rise to pitches not represented in the **anhemitonic** pentatonic scale (that is, a pentatonic scale without **semitones**). The *kari* and *meri* notes also differ greatly in timbre (sound quality). *Kari* notes are strong and bright, while the *meri* notes are softer and less loud. These timbral differences are used as building blocks in *honkyoku* music and therefore constitute essential features of the genre. Imitation of natural sounds, such as wind, movements of water, and bird sounds are also typical of this music. These sounds are called *zatsu-on* or "noise," such as the "growl" at 1.18, or the high whistling sounds around 3:00 and 3:04. *Honkyoku* music is characterized by small leaps centerd on nuclear notes. Often the principal nuclear note changes within a piece to the note a perfect 4th above and moves back again before the end.

Most *honkyoku* are in free meter, although this depends on the school of playing. This does not mean that there is no sense of pulse, but that the pulse can slow down and speed up several times in a single piece. The role of the teacher becomes even more important in the transmission of pieces in free meter, as it is by following the teacher, playing in unison with him or her, that the pupil learns the flow of the piece. My teacher spoke often about "flow"—he even said it in English many times to be sure I understood him.

"Tamuke"

"Tamuke" originates from the Fusaiji temple, but several "schools" of *shakuhachi* play it today. Two musical features that are worth exploring further in this piece are its ornamentation and sound qualities. For a piece from the *honkyoku* tradition, "Tamuke" is rather heavily ornamented, although the degree of ornamentation depends again on the school of playing. Many of the notes in the melody are ornamented with a grace note. For example when the piece moves from the introduction into the main piece at 0:33 in the recording, the C♯ and A are both ornamented with a grace note above the main notes. This is done by covering finger hole 4 (the top hole in the front) just before playing the C♯ and covering holes 2 and 4 just before playing the A. The practice of closing a hole the moment the player begins to play a note, or of opening a finger hole the moment the player stops blowing into the *shakuhachi*, is typical of ornamentation for this instrument and also typical of the Buddhist philosophy surrounding it. It is the striving for the grace notes that is important; in some cases it does not matter if the grace notes cannot themselves be heard, the attention paid to playing them and the aim of doing it are of a greater importance than the audible grace notes themselves. At other times, however, it is important that the grace notes are heard: you can hear it twice in a row at 2:08 and 2:11 in the recording. In the phrase from 1:30 to 1:41, several ornaments can be heard where the main notes in the melody are re-articulated by just lifting a finger and thereby opening and closing a finger hole very quickly. The notes immediately above are also heard, although they have no particular role in the melody and are just regarded as ornaments.

PRIMARY SOURCE

Notation

Today, the notation used by the majority of *shakuhachi ryūha* or guilds is the *ro tsu re* system including the largest groups Kinko, Tozan and most Myoan schools. *Ro tsu re* are the first three notes:

Ro (ロ): with all holes closed
Tsu (ツ): the lowest hole open
Re (レ): the two lowest holes open
Chi (チ): thumb hole and top hole closed
Ha (ハ): thumb home and the two lowest holes closed

As you can see, these symbols are a representation of the fingering only. They do not indicate the pitch produced, the rhythm, or whether a note is to be played in *meri* or *kari* position. Although most schools use the *ro tsu re* system, each school has its own version of the notation with slight variations between them. Also, each school has its own set of musical features or styles, and the notation will represent this. This means that the notation is not easily accessible for all *shakuhachi* players. Indeed, it serves as an aide memoire rather than as a prescriptive musical score. Contemporary composers often prefer to write music for *shakuhachi* in Western notation, as it appears more "neutral" to them. They fear that if a piece is written using notation of one school (for example, the Kinko) then it will inhibit players from another school (for example, the Tozan) from playing it.

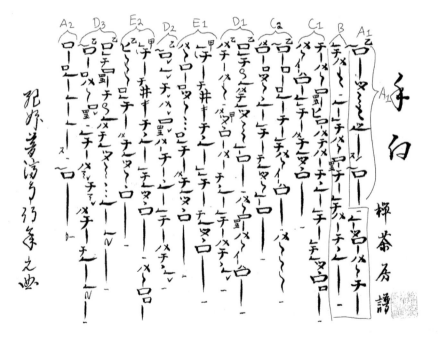

Note: The score is read top to bottom, right to left.

FIGURE 8.3 Tamuke score, with structure

Courtesy of Okuda Atsuya

Many contemporary players play "Tamuke" very emotionally due to its connotations of death and its use as a requiem. "Tamuke" contains peaks that can be played as emotional outbursts, which involves the use of the technique *muraiki* (lit: "uneven breath" but sometimes translated as a "breath including the sound of wind"), where you can hear a blast of air. You can hear a soft *muraiki* at 2:25, where Okuda blows softly so the note can still be heard, and a hard *muraiki* at 3:04, where the note cannot be heard.

Timbre

As explained in the section on *honkyoku* and the *shakuhachi*, the two main different sound qualities are **meri** and **kari** notes. In this particular recording of "Tamuke" by Okuda Atsuya, there are several examples of the timbral qualities of these notes. In the phrase that begins at 4:30, with only a short breath after the previous phrase, the first four notes are E E♭ E E♭ with various durations. The E is a *meri* note (i.e., flattened from the F♯ *ha*) called *ha-no-meri*, and is repeated. The next note is *chi* (E♭), a *kari* note. You can hear that the *meri* notes have a softer timbre than the brighter *kari* notes. Then the phrase continues with E E♭ and C♯. The softness of the *meri* E is again very clear in contrast to the *kari notes* E♭ and C♯. The phrase ends with A and C♯. The *meri* A (a flattened *tsu* B; hence called *tsu-no-meri*), is a long note played with a vibrato created by moving the head and bending the note between A and A♭ (a technique called *yuri*). The C♯ comes as a release to the phrase. But as the phrase is descending, one would expect it to continue the descent to G♯, the nuclear note as the almost identical phrase in the first half of line 8 in the score did. However, the C♯ gives the phrase a very open ending— open for possibilities, open to the unknown. And with this open feeling, the piece can then move toward the end. A *honkyoku* typically ends a phrase on the softer *meri* notes, creating a tension that leads to a taut silence; the next phrase will pick up this tension with a *meri* note. In this way, phrases are connected to one another. Thus, ending a phrase with *kari* notes can signify a compositional technique used in order to create feelings other than those conveyed by the average phrase.

Social Context: From Unemployed Warriors to World Stage

Honkyoku is a repertoire with roots from the Edo period (1603–1868), when it was played by the *shakuhachi*-playing *komusō* monks (monks of nothingness) of the Zen Buddhist sect Fuke. Fuke was recognized as a sect under Rinzai Zen—one of the main branches of Zen Buddhism in Japan. The sect only admitted men of the *samurai* class, formerly warriors, as members of the order. The first decree granting special privileges to *komusō* monks was enacted in 1614 by the Shōgun (feudal leader) Tokugawa Ieyasu (1543–1616). When the Tokugawa family gained power over Japan as the *shōgun*, there was a long period of peace. Many *samurai* warriors were no longer needed and they became unemployed. Japanese society at the time was made up of distinct class divisions and people took up work according

FIGURE 8.4 Woodblock print by Koryūsai Isoda (1735–1790), showing two women
disclosing the face of a *komusō* monk using a mirror
Courtesy of John Singer

to their class. For a *samurai*—that is, a man born into a *samurai* family—it would
be dishonorable to take up farming or other work of lower ranking classes. Instead,
religious begging was a way for the *samurai* to make a living with their honour
intact. The special privileges granted the *komusō* included monopoly rights over
the use of the *shakuhachi* (laymen were officially prohibited from playing the
shakuhachi from 1677) and travel passes that allowed them to travel to any part
of Japan. The *shakuhachi* was used as tool for spiritual training by the mendicant
komusō monks, who dressed in Buddhist garb with a woven basket covering the
entire face when begging for alms. Each temple developed its own body of music,
which taken all together comprise a repertoire of approximately 150 *honkyoku*
from the Edo period known today.

The Edo government was overthrown in 1868 and in October 1871 the new
Meiji government (1868–1912), intent on modernizing Japan, abolished the Fuke
sect and the following year prohibited begging (although it was again made legal
in 1881). These events, along with the Meiji government's decision to teach only
Western music in the compulsory education system, naturally had a strong impact
on the *shakuhachi*, its music and environment, and led to major changes. From the

FIGURE 8.5 *Shakuhachi* players dressed as *komusō* conducting *takuhatsu* (religious mendicancy) at festivities in Okayama City, 2013

Photograph by Tanaka Takafumi

abolition of the Fuke sect, players of the *shakuhachi*, hitherto exclusively a tool for religious training, were to take two distinct paths: secular and religious. The secular path, that of professional musicians who played for paying audiences, became the mainstream in the realm of **hōgaku** ("national," i.e. Japanese, music), while religious players were generally disdained as mere amateurs and eccentrics.

Secular *shakuhachi* players began to earn a living playing ensemble music for entertainment; the *komusō* called these "outside" pieces (**gaikyoku**) or "disorderly" pieces (*rankyoku*). In particular, the *shakuhachi* gained a place alongside the **koto** (zither) and **shamisen** (long/necked lute) in an ensemble called *sankyoku* (lit: "three pieces"). Some talented *shakuhachi* players founded their own schools using the Japanese guilds system. This system, known as **ryū** (for the style) or *ryūha* (for the school) is characteristic of all Japanese art forms. These schools ensure the transmission of the various regional styles and styles of certain masters, and have endured to the present day. As well as these new schools, during the late nineteenth and early twentieth centuries new pieces for mass performance were composed. These changes probably saved the *shakuhachi* from falling into oblivion in the late nineteenth century; instead, it became widespread and popular among the general

B I O G R A P H Y

Okuda Atsuya (b. 1945; as with all the Japanese names in this chapter, his family name, Okuda, comes first) initially made his name as a professional jazz trumpet player, although he had studied *shakuhachi* since he was young, among others briefly with Yokoyama Katsuya, who disseminated *shakuhachi* through his performances of Takemitsu Tōru's orchestral piece *November Steps* and for three years with Okamoto Chikugai, an important amateur *shakuhachi* researcher and player, who collected many old pieces. Okamoto gave Okuda various *honkyoku* scores, including older ones from different *ryūha*. Okuda considers himself as being mainly self-taught. In 1985 he gave up his career as a trumpet player in order to focus on *shakuhachi* playing and opened a *shakuhachi* teaching studio named Zensabō. Okuda is one of the pre-eminent masters of the *jinashi shakuhachi*, built without smoothing out the bore, who carries on playing the old style *jinashi shakuhachi*. Okuda continues to teach his style of *honkyoku* playing, which is a very refined and subtle way of playing the large *shakuhachi* with raw untreated bores he is inclined to play. Okuda's playing is not loud in volume but it is rich in complexity. He has recorded three CDs with *honkyoku*: *Sound of Zen*, *Bamboo Zen*, and *Sō-Zen*.

FIGURE 8.6 Okuda Atsuya
Photograph by Kiku Day

public. The period can be seen as the first *shakuhachi* "boom," in which the instrument became a part of a new Japan—renewed, democratized, and free from feudal restrictions.

The second *shakuhachi* boom began when top players from three different schools, namely Yamamoto Hōzan from the Tozan school, Aoki Reibo from the

Kinko school and Yokoyama Katsuya from the Kokusai Shakuhachi Kenshūkan (International Shakuhachi Study Group), formed the trio Sanbonkai in 1966 and transcended strict rules on guild systems. The *shakuhachi* then broke through internationally when *November Steps* for *shakuhachi*, **biwa** (lute) and orchestra, composed by Takemitsu Tōru, was played around the world in the late 1960s and 1970s. From the 1970s onward non-Japanese players—mostly from the United States—went to Japan to study with Japanese *shakuhachi* masters. They brought back the *shakuhachi* to countries such as the United States, Australia, and Switzerland. Today, the *shakuhachi* is, together with the *taiko* drum, the most popular Japanese instrument outside Japan.

Is "Tamuke" a Requiem?

"Ise district origin. Combines the elements of requiem and elegy of the Western music." (Yokoyama Katsuya, *Japanese Traditional Shakuhachi I* (OCD-0940) 1985)

"The meaning of 'Tamuke' is an offering to the gods or to the Buddha. This piece is played during the Buddhist service for the dead." (Yokoyama Katsuya *Shika no Toune: Shakuhachi Koten Meikyoku Shūsei—1* (Victor JRZ-2563) 1976)

"From Ise region, 'Tamuke' has meanings of requiem or elegy of Western music and I experience the calm graciousness of abundant forgiveness." (Kakizakai Kaoru (a student of Yokoyama), *Koten Shakuhachi* (Classical Shakuhachi) Victor—VZCG-304 2003)

"Prayer for Safe Passage. The term *tamuke* refers to making spiritual offerings to the Buddha. Originating from the Ise district of Japan, 'Tamuke' combines the elements of the requiem and the elegy of Western music. It is a prayer for safe passage through life and through death." (Riley Lee, *Breath Sight, Yearning for the Bell, vol. 1, Tall Poppies* TP015 1992)

In sleeve notes such as these that accompany popular recordings of "Tamuke," and in daily speech, *shakuhachi* players often describe "Tamuke" as being a requiem. How suitable is this categorization? The *New Oxford Companion to Music* defines a requiem as follows:

The Mass for the Dead, which begins with the Introit "Requiem aeternam dona eis Domine" ("Give then eternal rest, O Lord"). The text is basically the same as that for the normal Latin Mass, but with the more joyful parts (such as the Alleluia, which is replaced by the Tract) . . . The first more or less complete setting of music to a requiem Mass, a piece by Ockeghem, dates from the late 15th century. By the 17th century composers had become more adventurous and composed more dramatic music for this mass. Liturgically the Requiem Mass is played at funerals and memorial services and on All Soul's Day (2 November), when it is celebrated in memory of the faithful departed.

Historically, then, a requiem was set to a particular text in the Latin mass and its form was more or less fixed. That said, it is possible today to encounter many different music pieces or works from other art forms such as poetry, or painting, which have been described as requiems, in examples of cultural translations across time. The *honkyoku* canon developed at about the same time that such mature requiems as Mozart's (1791) and Haydn's (1771) were composed, and Brahms completed his requiem between 1865 and 1868, just when the Edo era came to a close.

"Tamuke," a piece belonging to the Zen *honkyoku* genre, which originated in a very different cultural setting and which bears radically different cultural connotations from those of the Roman Catholic Church, has been translated and reframed as a requiem in the twentieth century. Music generates meaning in many different simultaneous forms, not all of which are immediately obvious. Meaning arises not only from the sound, notation, and performance practices but also from the language used to describe it, and the conceptual and knowledge systems in which it is placed. Translating the word "*tamuke*" as a requiem immediately places it within a certain context, with a reference of meanings and emotions already attached. At the same time, the meaning and use of the word "requiem" has been translated across time and place in the West, and continues to be open to negotiations and new connotations of a new spirituality. Music is intensely involved in negotiating and generating new meaning. When musicians—either Japanese or non-Japanese—define "Tamuke" as a requiem they are performing an act of cultural translation.

Like "requiem," the meaning of the word *tamuke* has shifted far since its first attested appearance over 1000 years ago in the *Man'yōshū*, the oldest existing collection of poems from Japan (first published in 759). Here, "Tamuke no Kami," the god of Tamuke, is referred to as the god of travel. In one of the poems, *tamuke gusa*, ropes made from plants tied to trees as an offering, is offered to Buddhist and Shintō gods. Another poem mentions a place to pray for the safety of a voyage by boat after embarkation. The Tamuke god is also mentioned as living at mountain passes or at the top of hills. We learn that travellers would pray to the Tamuke god for safety during their journeys when passing these places. Certain mountains, such as Nara Yama, where the god of Tamuke is enshrined, are referred to as Tamuke mountain (Tamuke Yama). And so we find that, in literature, *tamuke* is described as the action of offering or sacrificing or dedicating things to the gods, in particular a traveller's guardian deity, and/or the Buddha or the spirit of a deceased person in order to ensure safe passage. It is often used when a person passes from one state to another, not only through death, but also through rites of passage such as coming of age or graduating from school. Indeed, no historical documents confirm the use of *tamuke* as a piece to be played at funerals. It might be that the meaning of *tamuke* as found in the *honkyoku* repertoire has changed over the centuries, from denoting an offering to the gods to remembrance of a deceased person. The only *shakuhachi* scholar, however, to put forward such a claim in sleeve notes is Tsukitani Tsuneko, and she provides no evidence for this claim, neither does she suggest when this change might have occurred.

Unlike the visual and literary arts, music lacks denotative (literal or explicit) meaning, which perhaps explains why it is particularly powerful in creating connotative meaning, which is more suggestive or associative. This *hyperconnotative* character of music, its intense power to create cognitive, cultural, and emotional associations, is perhaps what gives it a unique role in the way that we imagine and desire other cultures, in our fantasies of exotic distant times or places. Many non-Japanese players believe they play *honkyoku* the way *komusō* monks played during the Edo period without taking into account the changes that occur to oral traditions over time. Several members of the European Shakuhachi Society's Facebook group have recently been engaged in a discussion about the *komusō* monks playing "Tamuke" at funerals. One of the arguments stresses the fact that "Tamuke" (as it is often played today) cites a phrase from the folk tune "Itsuki no Komoriuta" (Lullaby of Itsuki); for most Japanese this tune connotes sentiments such as injustice, sadness, and a wish to die. It includes the following words: "I am no better than a beggar . . . Who will cry for me when I die? . . . When I am dead, bury me by the roadside." This is used to bolster the argument that "Tamuke" is a requiem. "Lullaby of Itsuki" *is* cited in "Tamuke" as transmitted by Yokoyama Katsuya, whose style of *shakuhachi* playing is one of the most popular among non-Japanese players, but it is not found in the versions played by the various Myōan schools, who strive to maintain the Fuke sect's way of playing; this suggests that its inclusion is a new phenomenon. And so the "Tamuke" that has now been widely disseminated to the world is a newer version in which the process of translating meaning had already begun in Japan. As a requiem sets the listener immediately in a context of emotions of sadness and loss at funerals, "Lullaby of Itsuki" fits well. It also makes musical sense, as the melody shares the same mode as "Tamuke." Among the Japanese, however, the word *tamuke* connotes not so much sadness at irrevocable loss, but rather hope for a favorable outcome during a passage from one stage to another in life including but not exclusively death.

Does this new notion of "Tamuke" as a requiem change the way in which players nowadays approach the piece? It is in free meter and rather open to interpretation. The *shakuhachi* researcher Kanda Kayū describes the piece as being played rather quickly. However, as a requiem it is played slowly and with solemnity. "Tamuke" is now played in front of graves or statues of *komusō* monks as a requiem and as remembrance of these *shakuhachi* ancestors—a phenomenon seen for example in the Shakuhachi Roots Pilgrimage—a tour to Japan for *shakuhachi* players led by Alcvin Romos. Ramos wrote in his 2005 blog: "We offered shakuhachi honkyoku within the inner sanctuary of the Honden [main temple] after offering tamagushi [sacred branch offering of the Yu tree] to connect more with the Kamisama [God]." If "Tamuke" is a piece played as a requiem for persons who were close to the player, the act of playing for the *shakuhachi* ancestors becomes an efficient way of claiming one's lineage in the *shakuhachi* tradition, whether Japanese or non-Japanese.

In this chapter, we have explored how the spiritual meanings of a piece of music have changed as it has moved across time and across continents, in what I call acts of "cultural translation." "Tamuke," once a piece played for Zen Buddhist spiritual training, referring to a prayer for safe passage, has been recast using a term borrowed from the Roman Catholic liturgy and Western art music tradition as a ritual for the dead. In this new context of meaning, players from across the world use "Tamuke" to assert a cultural link to their *shakuhachi* playing forebears, the Edo-era monks of nothingness.

Discussion Topics

- Acts of cultural translation, such as the one described in this chapter, are an increasingly common phenomenon in the globalized world in which we live. How much does the way we perceive a piece of music depend on the words or images to which it is attached? Consider other examples you may know where similar processes have taken place (e.g. Nusrat Ali Khan's "Alaap" in *The Last Temptation of Christ*, or Samuel Barber's Adagio for Strings in *Platoon* and remixed as a trance track by *Tiesto*). Listen to these pieces first without video images, and then again with the video. How does your perception of the music change? Do some research on the original contexts of these pieces. Do you find it problematic that they have been used in these new ways?

Further Listening

Okuda Atsuya. *Zen no oto (The Sound of Zen) OKUDA Atsuya plays Jinashi-nobe Shakuhachi* (D00EM04802, Son Tech, 2002).

Walzenaufnahmen Japanischer Musik (Staatliche Museen zu Berlin, 1901–1913).
Historical wax cylinder recordings from the early 20th century, including a few rare *shakuhachi honkyoku*.

Watazumi Dōso *Yuri-Sashi: Shakuhachi hotchiku of Watazumi Humon/Itcho Humon* (COCJ-36281, Columbia, 2010 (original recording 1952)).
This recording contains a version of "Tamuke," played by Watazumi, the teacher of Yokoyama Katsuya.

Yokoyama Katsuya *Zen: Katsuya Yokoyama plays classical shakuhachi masterworks* (SM 1033/34–50, Wego, 1988).
This recording contains a version of "Tamuke," where "Itsuki no Komoriuta" (Lullaby of Itsuki) is quoted.

Recommended Reading

Berger, Donald P. and David W. Hughes (2000) "East Asia: Japan: Shakuhachi." In *New Grove Dictionaries of Music and Musicians*.
A somewhat technical overview of the instrument.

Blasdel, Christopher Y. Snapshot (2000) "*Syakuhati* 'Walking on its Own'." In *The Garland Encyclopedia of World Music*, vol. 7, East Asia. New York: Garland.
Evocative contextualization.

Simura, Satoshi (2000) "Chamber Music for *Syakuhati.*" In *The Garland Encyclopedia of World Music*, vol. 7, East Asia. New York: Garland.
>Introduction to *shakuhachi* in ensembles.

Tsukitani Tsuneko (2008) "The *Shakuhachi* and its Music," translated by Charles Rowe. In Alison M. Tokita and David W. Hughes, eds. *The Ashgate Research Companion to Japanese Music*. Aldershot: Ashgate.
>A useful overview.

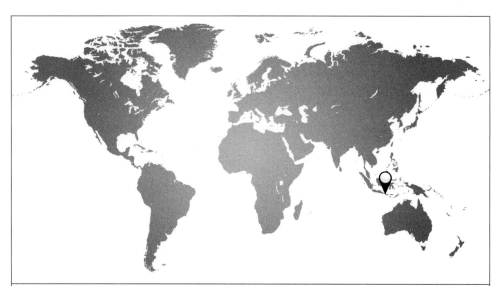

Location: Sukawati village, Bali, Indonesia

"Sudamala" (Freed from Evil): Exploring a Ritual Piece for Balinese *Gendér Wayang*

Transmitted by I. Wayan Locéng; played by Segara Madu *gendér wayang* group (Paula Friar, Emily Garland, Nicholas Gray, Rachel Hewitt) 19 March 2012, at a concert in SOAS, University of London

Chapter nine

"Sudamala" (Freed from Evil)

Exploring a Ritual Piece for Balinese *Gendér Wayang*

Nicholas Gray

Summary

Gendér wayang is the name given to a small quartet of bronze **metallophone**s, used in Bali to accompany the shadow play (*wayang kulit*), a sacred drama based on stories from the ancient Indian epics *Mahabharata* and *Ramayana*. The piece "Sudamala" (Freed from Evil) is played at the end of a special ritual shadow play while the puppeteer prepares a purificatory holy water that will be used to lift the curse on a child born in inauspicious circumstances. The piece itself is unusual in structure, and its special ritual function can best be understood in connection with legends surrounding the demonic figure of Kala and the threat he poses to humanity, legends that are fundamental to the structure and role of the *gendér wayang* instruments themselves. Web resources include links to a concert performance that includes legends of Kala, "Sudamala," and other *gendér* pieces as well as a new composition, which reflects on and explores this web of meaning.

> **KEY WORDS**
> - Hinduism
> - musical structure
> - ritual
> - theatre, variation

Why this Piece?

I became fascinated with the sound of Balinese **gamelan** when I was quite young, about 12 years old, after being taken to a concert in London by my parents. A gamelan, which is now familiar to many students studying music in universities in Europe and America, is an ensemble from Bali or Java in Indonesia, whose instruments are mostly made of bronze: gongs, rows of small gong kettles, and instruments with metal keys in rows like xylophones. The gamelan I first heard was a modern type called *gong kebyar*: a loud, fast style with incredibly intricate **interlocking patterns** on the metallophones. I felt blown away by the look of the instruments, the strangeness of the tuning, and the ringing quality of the sound.

I later learned there were several different kinds of gamelan in Bali: some for temple festivals and dance, with many instruments playing interlocking patterns together, and other, smaller types for specific occasions. When, much later, I got the chance to go to study the music in Bali, I chose to learn a special type of gamelan called *gendér wayang*. *Gendér* is the name of the instrument and *wayang* means shadow puppet, so this is the gamelan that accompanies shadow puppet plays. The shadow plays tell important stories for the Balinese Hindu religion. The stories are usually taken from one of the ancient Indian epics *Mahabharata* or *Ramayana*. A puppeteer, called a **dalang**, sits behind the screen, in front of a lamp and the puppets' shadows show through the screen on the other side.

Most of the music is fast and features complex patterns that interlock between the instruments. Half the group plays *polos*, or the basic part, and the other half plays the *sangsih* part that interlocks with it. The fast pieces are used when there is action in the puppet show, such as warriors going off to battle. Some other pieces are slow and accompany the puppeteer's singing: these are often pieces that paint a mood or emotion, such as sadness or love, according to what is happening in the play.

The *dalang* shadow puppeteer is more than just an entertainer—he (or she, although most *dalang* are men) is a person of great knowledge and skill, having to tell the long stories in the characters' different voices in an ancient language called *kawi*. Some *dalang* become priests and are then allowed to hold a special ceremony called Sudamala, which is a kind of protection or healing ceremony for children who have been born in dangerous circumstances, especially if they are born in a particularly unlucky week in the Balinese calendar. This is believed to make the child vulnerable to attack from a fierce demon called Kala (see "The Story of Kala").

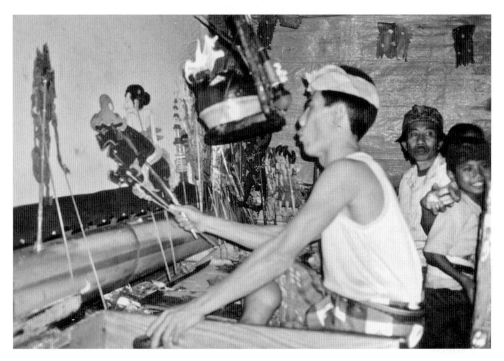

FIGURE 9.1 A *dalang* puppet master

Photograph by Nicholas Gray

The name of the piece I have chosen, "Sudamala," is so called because it is played while the puppeteer conducts the ceremony of the same name to lift this curse, creating holy water that is given to the child's family.

Musical Features

TIMED LISTENING GUIDE	
0.00 (26.10 on video)	The piece "Tabuh Gari" is used to end performances of *wayang*. Here, it runs straight into the piece "Sudamala." Note the winding, restless theme that finally settles on a **chord** that repeats over and over, getting faster (a typical ending signal in *gendér wayang*)
1.55 (28.04 on video)	*Introduction to "Sudamala"*: "Sudamala" can be thought of either as an extension of "Tabuh Gari," or as a separate piece. Pieces often have an introduction section that is different in style from their main "body." This introduction is slow, with many pauses, and the music doesn't seem to settle until it leads directly into the "body," *pengawak*, that follows

3.54 (30.03 on video)	*"Sudamala" Part 1*: This is the main theme or body of the piece "Sudamala." The final phrase of the introduction leads into this main section, which starts when the players' left hands are on the bottom note. There is a slow, basic melody played by all the players' left hands together which gradually rises in pitch before returning to the start, when it repeats. This type of simple, repeating cycle of melody is very common in most types of gamelan.
	    Meanwhile, the players' right hands play something different: a faster pattern that fits in above the basic melody. There are two interlocking parts: *polos* (basic) and *sangsih* (different). The *sangsih* part adds some higher notes to the *polos* part. These higher notes fit with the *polos* because they are at an interval four keys apart, which is felt to be harmonious. As the intervals are not exactly equal, this two-note chord actually varies in size.
	    The theme of "Sudamala" repeats several times and then is followed by two variations

6.08 (32.15)	*"Sudamala" Part 2*: Here, the first variation, the right hands keep to the same sort of patterning as in the theme, but the left hands begin to join in with quaver patterns (which also interlock or interweave with each other), so the overall effect is of a dense web of sound as four parts move against one another in **polyphony**
7.55 (34.04)	*"Sudamala" Part 3*: In this last section, which is yet another variation on the theme, the right-hand patterns keep up their momentum, although the note patterns have changed. The left hands play a gently oscillating melodic phrase that is repeated in sequence at descending note levels before repeating. All that is left of the theme now is its general shape and mood. My teacher Locéng said of the relationship between the theme and the two variations that "the road is the same"

TECHNOLOGY

FIGURE 9.2 *Gendér wayang*

Photograph by Nicholas Gray

The *gendér wayang* group is much smaller than other types of gamelan: it consists of just four instruments with bronze keys hanging over bamboo tubes cut to just the right length to make the note sound louder and longer. Two instruments are large, while two smaller instruments play an octave higher. These higher instruments double the music played on the larger ones, though sometimes only the two large ones are used.

The five-note scale, called *sléndro*, used by this type of gamelan is tuned differently from Western music: the distances between the notes are slightly larger than a tone, and the instruments are tuned very slightly apart in pairs, which creates a special acoustic effect making the sound "shimmer."

Interlocking Patterns: Variation

A performance of the piece "Sudamala" can be heard on the following link to a concert, featuring our group in London (http://www.youtube.com/watch?v=l-a8BQ en5LI) as well as a track on the accompanying CD. "Sudamala" was the last piece played in the concert that mixed traditional Balinese music, new compositions, and storytelling. This video link is the second half of the concert; I will discuss the first half and the storytelling later.

In our concert, "Sudamala" followed straight on after another piece, "Tabuh Gari," which is used to end *wayang* plays. These two pieces are often connected in this way, because the Sudamala ceremony takes place just after the end of a *wayang.* After the final chord of "Tabuh Gari," a rather long, winding introduction to "Sudamala" eventually leads into the main theme at 30:00.

Although the five-note scale used for *gendér wayang* (the scale is called **sléndro**) is tuned differently from a Western scale, it is possible to give an approximate notation using Western music notation. Here, I have transcribed the basic theme (referred to as Part 1 in the Timed listening guide), which starts at 30:00 on the video.

Each staff in Music example 9.1 shows a single instrument: the top staff shows the *sangsih* part, while the lower staff shows the *polos* part. The left hands of both parts play nearly the same slow melody, notated in minims, while the two right-hand parts play in quavers.

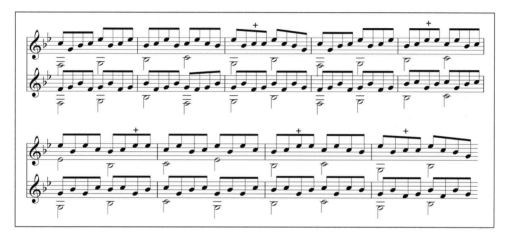

MUSIC EXAMPLE 9.1   Theme of "Sudamala"

Transcription by Nicholas Gray

These two right-hand parts interweave or interlock, sharing some notes but diverging at times to produce two-note chords (often at an interval four keys apart), as represented in Table 9.1, in which each box represents a key of the 10-keyed *gendér*, from the lowest note on the left to the highest note on the right (see below).

F	G	B♭	C	E♭	F	G	B♭	C	E♭

TABLE 9.1

From this table, it is clear that the instruments have two octaves of a five-note (pentatonic) scale. Also, the common interval used as a chord—four notes apart—is sometimes notated as a Western 5th (F–C) and sometimes as a minor 6th (G–E♭). In the actual tuning used, *sléndro*, the difference between these is not so great, because the small intervals between keys are larger than a tone and the large intervals between keys are smaller than a minor 3rd. In the example just given, some other intervals occur as well, for instance, in the last bar.

In Bali, this kind of interlocking pattern is known as *kotékan*, and in faster pieces, each part is more likely to have rests while the other part fills in with notes, as in this example (perhaps "interweaving" might be a better description than "interlocking," here). *Kotékan telu* means that a pattern is created with just three notes (F, G, and B♭ in the example below), while *kotékan pat* means using four notes, adding a C in the example below to coincide with the F to create a two-note chord (see Music example 9.2).

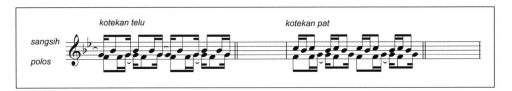

MUSIC EXAMPLE 9.2 *Kotékan*

Transcription by Nicholas Gray

Much of the *gendér* repertory is in variation form like this piece. Almost all the fast pieces are based on a thematic section followed by one or more variations, which are called *runtutan* in Sukawati, and *peniba* in other parts of Bali. The first, thematic section is usually called *pengawak*, meaning "body."

A simple example is the fast piece "Pangkat Grebeg," in which the first section consists of a left-hand ostinato figure with a right-hand interlocking *kotékan* that is repeated several times before a bridge passage leads to the same passage being repeated one note higher and then another transition leads down to the original level. The one variation section features the same left-hand ostinato but with different, more complex *kotékan*.

Such variation sections also occur in other Balinese gamelan forms. But in these, the structure usually consists of the main theme being repeated several times and the single variation only once, whereas in *gendér* theme and sometimes several variants are often repeated a number of times. I have heard of pieces in East Bali that had up to 13 variation sections. It is often the case that each variation gets more complex than the last.

Social Context: Stories, Rituals, Music

As I mentioned earlier, this piece is used to accompany the ritual called Sudamala that gives the piece its name. The legendary background to this ritual tells of a terrifying demon called Kala, born accidentally from the sperm of the god Siwa (the Indian god Shiva). This legend explaining the Sudamala ritual also hints at a special power in the *gendér* instruments themselves. The demonic entity Kala

PRIMARY SOURCE

The Story of Kala

FIGURE 9.3 The demon Kala on the entrance to a medieval meditation cave in Bali called Goa Gajah

Photography courtesy of Judith Gray

One of the stories in the concert tells how the god Siwa had two sons: Raré Kumara, a beautiful child, and Kala, a terrible demon. Kala realizes that because Raré Kumara was born in a vulnerable week, itself called *wayang*, he is permitted prey, and so the demon begins to pursue him. Siwa tries to protect Raré Kumara, as does the earthly king Mayasura, but Kala is relentless in his pursuit. Raré Kumara hides in the following places: a clump of untied *lalang* grass (a reed used for thatching), under a rice granary, among tied up bundles of wood, and in the uncovered hole in an oven. Kala discovers him in each of these places and curses humans who in future leave these items as they had been left. Finally, Raré Kumara finds a *wayang* performance in progress and the *dalang* hides him inside one of the bamboo resonators of the *gendér wayang* instruments. Kala appears, furious, and starts devouring the offerings for the performance. The *dalang* points out that by doing this, Kala is now in his debt and refuses to surrender Raré Kumara. The *dalang* states that, in future, puppeteers will be able to save anyone threatened by Kala through performing *wayang sudamala* (a purificatory shadow play), followed by the *sudamala* ritual to create a protective holy water. This story explains how the *dalang* is given a priest-like, healing power.

is allowed by his father, the god Siwa, to eat all those moving about at noon or dusk. Wanting to eat his younger brother, Panca Kumara or Raré Kumara, he pursues him. Panca Kumara hides in various places, such as a bundle of *lalang* grass, then a bundle of firewood under a granary, then an oven but, each time, he is discovered by Kala. Finally, he takes refuge in the bamboo resonator of a *gendér* during a *wayang* performance. Panca Kumara receives the protection of the *dalang* and from this point on, the curse on those born in the week *tumpek wayang* may be lifted by a *wayang* performance. The story illustrates both the purificatory power of the *dalang* and the perception of *gendér* as sacred instruments. There is another story in Bali, also called "Sudamala," which tells of how one of the heroes of the *Mahabharata* epic, Sadewa, lifts a curse and transforms the fearful goddess Durga into a more benign and friendly form. This story too reflects the meaning and purpose of "Sudamala," which means "freed from evil."

The first half of our concert, which featured the story telling, can be found at http://www.youtube.com/watch?v=0EH87ay_f8c. In this, storyteller Tim Jones tells several stories about Kala and how he was born. The last story, which tells of Kala's pursuit of Raré Kumara, can be found on this video from 31:55 (see Textbox 9.2). Some of the symbolism may seem very specific to Balinese culture (for instance, the exact structure of a Balinese oven), but the underlying theme of the power of the storyteller as an artist and the power of music to heal, seems quite clear. The *dalang* is given permission to call the gods, speak in their voices, speak freely of current events, and carry out purification ceremonies. Often, the terrifying aspects of some gods and goddesses in Bali turn out to be keys to understanding spiritual aspects of ourselves and have the ability to make us think not only of forces of good and evil in the world around us, but also help us to turn inwards towards understanding.

The Course of a *Wayang*

So, how is the piece normally used in performance? A booth is set up outside, either in the outer courtyard of a temple (if the *wayang* is part of a temple ceremony) or in the courtyard of the house compound (if it is for a more personal ceremony such as cremation, tooth filing or other lifecycle ritual). A green banana trunk is used as the base (the puppets can be inserted using their sharp handles when still), and the white screen and lamp set up. The play will go on for several hours so members of the audience come and go. Children sometimes go to sleep, only waking up for the battle scenes and the comedy scenes of the clowns. Older people follow the *dalang's* dialogue more closely, relishing the use of the ancient *kawi* language, and the subtle references to philosophy and religious ideas.

The use of music is integral to the structure of a *wayang* performance, providing a kind of framework for the drama. A piece is usually played before the play begins, which helps to draw the audience and gives the *dalang* time to prepare the offerings. Then follows the "Pemungkah": a lengthy overture containing many sections. It begins with the dance of the *kayon* puppet, which represents the Tree of Life. While the overture continues, the *dalang* brings out all the puppets and arranges them on

TECHNOLOGY

FIGURE 9.4 **The *kayon* and other puppets assembled on the screen**
Photograph by Nicholas Gray

The *kayon* and other puppets are assembled on the screen. Note the green banana trunk that is used as a base in which to insert the sharp puppet handles. This enables the *dalang* to rest some puppets while moving others. Human figures have moveable arms, and the clowns also have moveable jaws. Also note the special coconut oil lamp that makes the puppets appear as intricate shadows on the other side of the screen.

The choice of these puppets varies slightly from place to place, but often includes the following figures: *kayon* (Tree of Life), *tunggal* (used to represent the abstract figure of God), *bayu* (god of wind/energy), *tualén* (the main clown), Siwa (the god Shiva), Wisnumurti (fierce aspect of the god Vishnu), Ludramerti (fierce aspect of Shiva), Durga (fierce aspect of the goddess Uma), Sungsang/Kepuh (tree growing in graveyards, sacred to Durga).

the appropriate side: gods and *alus* (refined) characters to the *dalang's* right and *keras* (coarse) characters to the left. These are then taken off the screen again and handed to the assistants on either side, leaving just the *kayon* puppet in the middle of the screen. The *kayon* dances again and leaves the screen, after which the *dalang* sings an introductory song, usually "Alas Harum" ("The Scented Forest"). During this song, the *dalang* brings in the puppets who will take part in the first scene: usually a combination of royal characters from the good, Pandawa side, together with their servants, the clowns Tualén and Mredah. These servants (alongside two other servants for the bad, Korawa, side) are among the most important characters because they translate the medieval Javanese poetic language spoken by the royal characters into everyday Balinese. The audience understands the play through the clowns.

The *gendér* are silent during the subsequent meeting scene but start playing again with a fast piece as the characters move to depart. During the course of the play, any of the following mood-setting pieces may be performed, depending on the action: "Rébong" for romantic scenes or the appearance of a beautiful woman, "Mesém" for refined characters crying, "Bendu Semara" for coarse characters crying, "Lagu Délem" for the appearance of the clown Délem, or "Tunjang" for witches and the goddess Durga. Some of these pieces (the sad pieces and "Rébong") are in a slow, highly ornamented style that accompanies the *dalang's* vocal melody. However, the commonest instrumental pieces are semi-improvised "Batél," based on loud repeated melodic phrases that follow the fighting action and increase in strength and intensity towards the end. Finally, the piece "Tabuh Gari" is used to signal the end of the performance, when the *dalang* places the *kayon* in the middle of the screen.

If the performance is being held for the Sudamala ritual, it is only at this moment that the offerings for this are brought to the *dalang*, who starts to carry out the ritual as the piece "Sudamala" is played. Often, just the first part of the piece, the main theme is played, over and over throughout the entire ritual. In the ritual, the *dalang* picks some of the most holy puppets and places them against the screen. The *dalang* prepares offerings and, saying prayers, takes each puppet and waves the handle through the flame of the lamp, and dips it into a container of water. The puppets are replaced on the screen and the *dalang* fixes flowers to them while saying further prayers. Flowers are also sprinkled in the water container that is given to the family of the child who drinks and is sprinkled with the now holy water.

There is another type of special shadow play that is itself a ritual, and takes place during temple festivals and other religious occasions. This is called *wayang lemah*, which means "daytime *wayang*." This can only be performed by a *dalang* who has also been initiated as a priest (*mangku dalang*). Instead of a screen, a thread is stretched between two branches of the sacred *dapdap* tree. This performance is ritual rather than entertainment and it is often half-lost in the hubbub of the surrounding temple ceremony. Usually no one actually watches this special ritual shadow play, because the intended audience is the gods rather than human beings.

Sometimes the *gendér* instruments are used on their own without the puppets and *dalang*, as an accompaniment to the lifecycle ritual of tooth filing. This (very gentle!) filing of the canines is carried out at adolescence and symbolizes being able to control our selfish desires. *Gendér* players can sometimes be seen playing on either side of the cremation towers as they are carried to the death temple during the very elaborate Balinese funeral ceremonies.

BIOGRAPHY

FIGURE 9.5 I Wayan Locéng c.1930–2006
Photograph by Nicholas Gray

My *gendér* teacher, I. Wayan Locéng, whom I first met in 1987 and who passed away in 2006, taught me the piece "Sudamala" and told me many of these stories. Locéng lived in Sukawati, a large village in south Bali, about halfway between the capital, Denpasar, and Ubud, where many tourists stay. Sukawati is rapidly becoming part of the suburban sprawl that surrounds Denpasar. It has many *banjar*, village districts or hamlets that organize ritual and social events of which one, Babakan, has become a renowned centre for *wayang* and its music. This is due to the old royal court of Sukawati, which was once an important patron of the arts but which has now all but faded away. The family of shadow puppeteers who served this court are today known as "the family of Sukawati *dalang*." The prestige of this family of puppeteers and musicians has led to them developing a very fast, virtuoso, flashy style of playing *gender*, with very complex interlocking patterns.

Locéng was born around 1930 (he was never too sure of the exact year) and he witnessed many of the events of Indonesia's turbulent history: the Dutch colonial period, the Japanese occupation (1942–1945), and the struggle for Indonesian independence that followed. Locéng, although not himself a *dalang*, accompanied and trained many of the most famous puppeteers on the island. He was renowned for his deep knowledge of the shadow play and its music. He was continually creating new and evermore complex versions of the pieces and was widely regarded as the finest player on Bali. From the late 1970s he began to teach pupils from America, Europe, and Japan and by the end of his life, he had taught around 100 foreign pupils. He often talked about why he made changes to the pieces he had inherited, saying that he felt obliged to develop them creatively:

> I thought it's as if you're given 10 coins; if, later, you still only have 10, it means it's not useful—it's very bad. So, I was given 10 pieces in basic versions. It's like capital. It's right that eventually it should give interest.

"Sudamala" is one of the simpler pieces in the Sukawati repertoire. Probably, because of its use in ritual, it was felt more appropriate to maintain its calm, empty, meditative atmosphere. Another version of the piece I know, from Abang village in East Bali, is quite different melodically but shares the same style and atmosphere. In Sukawati, Locéng did rework this piece, but instead of changing the first section (the theme), he simply added the two variation sections. In other pieces, he and other members of his old group not only added variation sections but also reworked the themes as well. So, this piece, "Sudamala," illustrates neatly his way of working from the simple towards the more complex.

Discussion Topics and Activities

- What is a ritual? How does it differ from theatre? Why is music often used in both?

- In Europe and America, puppets are usually thought of as appropriate only for children, but in this context we find puppets being used in a ritual performance for adults. Can you think of other examples in which puppets are used in rituals? Why do you think puppets are used in this way?

- Indonesia is a huge, diverse country in which major world religions (especially Islam, but also Hinduism in Bali and Christianity elsewhere) have taken root but often have often adopted a particular local flavor or style. Find out more about the use of music in these different traditions in Indonesia.

- Can you make your own interlocking patterns inspired by Balinese music?

Further Listening

Bali: Gender Wayang of Sukawati (B0017GSGD7, The World Roots Music Library, 2008).

Music for the Balinese Shadowplay—the Mahabharata (Gender Wayang Pemarwan) (B000008NN5, CMP, 1994).

Recommended Reading

Gray, Nicholas (2011) *Improvisation and Composition in Balinese* Gendér Wayang: *Music of the Moving Shadows*. Farnham: Ashgate Publishing Limited (SOAS Musicology Series).
     This book includes some of the examples in this chapter, and more in-depth discussion of *gendér wayang*.

Hobart, Angela (1987) *Dancing Shadows of Bali: Theatre and Myth*. London and New York: KPI.
     Further information on the Balinese shadow play.

McPhee, Colin (1966) *Music in Bali: A study in Form and Instrumental Organization in Balinese Orchestral Music*. New Haven, NJ, and London: Yale University Press.

McPhee, Colin (1979) *A House in Bali*. Oxford: Oxford University Press.

Tenzer, Michael (1991) *Balinese Music*. Singapore: Periplus Editions.
     More useful introductory sources on Balinese gamelan.

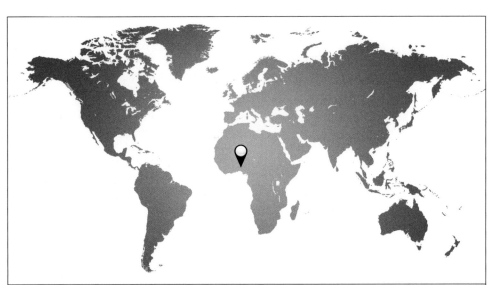

Location: Òsogbo and Ẹrìn-Òsun, Nigeria

"Orin Ìbejì" (Song of the Twins): Sounding the Sacred Twins of the Yorùbá

Sung by Doyin 'Fáníyì; recorded by Amanda Villepastour, August 1999, Òsogbo

Chapter ten
"Orin Ìbejì" (Song for the Twins)

Sounding the Sacred Twins of the Yorùbá

Amanda Villepastour

Summary

The Yorùbá people of southwest Nigeria have the highest twinning rate in the world, which largely explains why they have an **òrìṣà** (deity) known as Ìbejì (the Yorùbá word for twin). By studying a sample of the music dedicated to the Ìbejì, which is employed by devotees to communicate with *òrìṣà* in the metaphysical world, the reader will get a general insight into Yorùbá *òrìṣà* worship, as well as gain an understanding of how chant, song, and drumming are constructed and performed. By examining the uttered and drummed praise poetry (*oríkì*) for Ìbejì as performed in song and drumming, I demonstrate how the Yorùbá language adjusts to various musical forms in order to communicate with the divine, as well as entertain the living.

KEY WORDS
- devotion
- genre
- language and music
- ritual
- surrogate speech

Why this Piece?

On my first fieldtrip to Ọ̀yọ́, Nigeria in 1999, I often walked around the town with my friend and research collaborator, divining priest (*babaláwo*) Táíwò Abímbọ́lá. His name identifies him as a twin, as all first-born Yorùbá twins are called Táíwò or Táyé and the second-born is called Kẹ́hìndé. I quickly lost count of how many people I had been introduced to called Táíwò or Kẹ́hìndé in Ọ̀yọ́. Táíwò Abímbọ́lá's late mother, whom I only knew as Ìyábejì (mother of twins), had given birth to two sets of twins, and told me that there was a woman in Ọ̀yọ́ who had five sets of living twins.

Táíwò and I travelled to Òṣogbo, a Yorùbá town in southwest Nigeria famous for its artwork and its annual festival to celebrate Ọ̀ṣun, a river goddess of fertility and motherhood. He introduced me to his childhood friend, traditional priestess Doyin 'Fáníyì (see Figure 10.5). As we waited to be picked up for a ceremony in the palace Ọ̀ṣun shrine, Doyin and I started chatting about the devotional music of the *òrìṣà*, the sacred deities of traditional Yorùbá religion. She allowed me to video her singing some *òrìṣà* songs, including this song for Ìbejì, until our taxi arrived.

FIGURE 10.1
Tones in Yorùbá

Transcription
by Amanda
Villepastour

Ọ̀sun's central town shrine is situated in the walled palace of Òṣogbo's king, the Atáója. As Doyin and I disembarked from the taxi, a small group of drummers surrounded the car and greeted Doyin and me with drum language. Doyin placed paper money on their foreheads and shoulders and encouraged me to do the same. The drummers followed us into the shrine; these priests are accustomed to foreigners, as the Ọ̀sun festival attracts devotees and tourists from around the world every August. We were welcomed by the priests sitting around the sacred vessels and accoutrements of the goddess, including lavishly cast brass bells, decorated brass fans, and cutlasses, as well as a large, elaborate wood sculpture of Ṣọ̀pọ̀nnọ́, the powerful òrìṣà of smallpox.

As I was ushered to the altar, I was handed some kola nuts by the highest Ọ̀sun priestess, the Ìyá Ọ̀sun, and was instructed by Doyin to cradle them inside some banknotes and "pray into them." Doyin beckoned, "Ask for what you want. Pray for your family, your health, and don't forget your work. Pray for your research!" She instructed me to put my forehead to the ground and then hand the money and kola nuts to the Ìyá Ọ̀sun, a blind woman whose daughter sat beside her and reported the configurations of the kola nut pieces that were dropped onto the mat. Repeated throws were interpolated with declamatory utterances that were

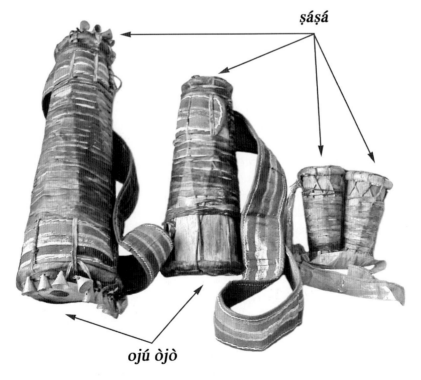

FIGURE 10.2 *Bàtá* drums

Photograph by Amanda Villepastour

neither speech nor song, but praise poetry called *oríkì*, as well as the divination verses unlocked by each configuration of the pinkish vegetable fragments falling in front of me. On the final throw, onlookers declared in spoken unison, "*Ó yàn!*" (It's favorable!) The Ìyá Ọ̀ṣun divined all afternoon for those entering the space. As the room filled with people and gained intensity, the priests chanted, sang, danced, and tranced through the night.

After the public climax of the festival, which lasts several days, I travelled to the neighbouring town of Ẹ̀rìn-Ọ̀ṣun and first met Rábíù Àyándòkun (see Figure 10.6), the master drummer with whom I went on to study for many years. Also known as Bàbábejì (Father of Twins), Rábíù taught me a devotional rhythm for Ìbejì on the sacred **bàtá** drums. He later taught me how to play Ìbejì's *oríkì* on the lead *bàtá* drum. Some years later, we worked together in London to produce the recordings discussed in this chapter, and to conduct collaborative research on how the drums actually "speak."

Having personally experienced how common twins are among the Yorùbá (45 in 1000 Yorùbá births result in twins, as opposed to just four in 1000 world-wide), and how revered the Ìbejì are across the sacred and secular boundaries of Muslims, Christians, and the minority *òrìṣà* worshippers who keep old customs alive, in this chapter I set out to share my fascination with a spiritual tradition that links the sacred to the scientific.

Musical Features

TIMED LISTENING GUIDE

First statement (A section)

0:03	(See Music example 10.1) The first two lines of the song are rendered in call-and-response style with Doyin singing the lead line accompanied by a friend responding with the chorus:
0:07	*Kere kere yàn* This part of the song is immediately recognizable by its rhythm as much as its text and melodic contour

Text:

Mo wá 'bejì	I am looking for the twins
Mo wá 'bejì relé	I am looking for them to take them home
Kere kere yàn	They are favored with goodness

Using the same, recognizable rhythm, common variations of "*Mo wá 'bejì*" are "*Ọmọ 'bejì*" (twin children) or "*Mo mú 'bejì*" (I will take the twins). The words "*Kere kere*" are purely musical with no real meaning, and are likely derived from drum **vocables**. "*Yàn*" is a declamatory word that can be interpreted in a range of ways, including "chosen" and "favored." In the context of twins, whose infant mortality is high, "*yàn*" can indicate "survival." The word "*yàn*" is also used for a favorable divination; "*Ó yàn!*" declares that all is positive when the four kola nuts fall in the most desired configuration with two sides up and two sides down

Music: Each musical phrase closely follows the pitch contour of Yorùbá speech. The second phrase, "*Mo wá 'bejì relé*," has a lower start note than the first, and the third phrase (the chorus) has an even lower start note, so the melody "terraces" down and slides off a half-spoken "*yàn*" exaggerating ordinary speech in Yorùbá. The man singing the chorus chooses a note comfortable to his range and sings in loose parallel to Doyin

Some of the phrases—such as "*Kere kere*" where performance of the crotchets is not as evenly spaced as shown in the transcription—might sound more like 6/8 than 2/4 to some listeners. In fact, the shifting between binary and ternary **grooves** with microrhythms that are hard to notate with staff notation is one of the features of Yorùbá and other African musics

Listeners unfamiliar with this type of music may find it hard to locate the main beat of the song. "*Wá*" might sound like it is stressed because *a* is the loudest vowel in any language and this syllable also hits the highest pitch in this phrase, but in fact it is the quieter, lower-pitched sound *i* in '*bejì*" that falls on the strongest beat in the phrase. The best way to find the beat is to see how the dancers' feet fit with the song

Naming text (B section)

0:15   This section, which I have named B for our purposes, moves into the sequential naming conventions of families with multiple births starting with the first- and second-born twins

Text:

0:15	*Táyé yàn*	Táyé (the first-born twin) survives
	Kéhìndé yàn lóònìí	Kéhìndé (the second-born twin) will survive today
	Kere kere yàn	Chosen!
0:21	*Ìdòwú yàn*	Ìdòwú (born after twins) is favored
	Àlàbá yàn lóònìí	Àlàbá (born after Ìdòwú) is favored today
	Kere kere yàn	They are favored
0:27	*Ìdògbé yàn*	Ìdògbé (born after Ìdòwú) is favored
	Apàpá yàn lóònìí	Apàpá (born after Ìdòhọ) is favored today
	Kere kere yàn	Chosen!
0:32	*Ìdòhọ yàn lóònìí*	Ìdòhọ (born after Ìdògbé) is favored today
	Kere kere yàn	Chosen!

Táyé is a nickname for Táíwò, and derives from "*tọ́-ayé-wò*" (the one who tasted the world) while the second-born name, Kéhìndé, comes from "*kó-ẹ̀hìndé*" (the one who came last). Ìdòwú may be the third child of triplets (Ìbẹ́ta) or a single birth after twins, and so forth. All of these names are loaded with cultural assumptions; for example, Kéhìndé is considered to be troublesome, while Ìdòwú children are expected to be stubborn

Music:
This section of the song moves into a chant-like style (bars 9–22) somewhere between song and speech. Doyin exaggerates the glides of natural speech, marked in the transcription as *glissandi*, but the melodic notes always follow the contours of natural Yorùbá speech within a phrase, although may terrace up or down to a new set of notes from phrase to phrase. The chorus builds in intensity and rises in pitch slightly, marked by the small arrows above the staff (bar 12)

Return to main lyric (Section A)

Text:

0:36	*Mo wá 'bejì*	I am looking for the twins
0:51	*Mo wá 'bejì relé*	I am looking for them to take them home
	Kere kere yàn	They are favored with goodness
	Mo wá 'bejì	I am looking for the twins
	Mo wá 'bejì relé	I am looking for them to take them home
	Kere kere yàn	They are favored with goodness
	Ẹdúnjọbí	Ẹdúnjọbí! (Praise name for twins, lit: "The colobus monkeys are born together")

> *Music:* When the main text re-enters in bar 24, it has crept up a semi-tone, which adds intensity. The song can be thought of as ternary form where the opening section (A) introduces the main text, the next part (B), which might vary in length or word order, names the children born after the twins, and the (A) section returns to mark the approach of the end of the song, usually identified by a slight *ritardando*
>
> Bringing the song to a joyful cadence, Doyin declaims one of the Ìbejì's praise names, "Edúnjọbí." The "*o*" after this name adds emphasis and emotion by exaggerating Yorùbá speech, where utterances are often extended with this falling sound

Text and Music

In order to understand how the text of Ìbejì relates to chanted speech, sung melody, or talking drums, it is essential to understand the basics of the Yorùbá language, for musicians must obey the rules of the language otherwise the text becomes unintelligible (as European missionaries found when they first set Yorùbá texts to well-known hymn tunes). The rhythmic organization must respect these linguistic rules, while also moving listeners to dance, sing, and fully participate in ceremonies where the whole community is called upon for a common sense of purpose. Musical performances of devotional texts also delight and entertain their listeners as master musicians demonstrate their musical prowess and imagination.

The song and drum examples I present in this chapter fall within the Ọ̀yọ́ dialect group (known as "Yorùbá proper"). Yorùbá is a true tone language with three pitch bands, meaning that the relative pitch of syllables determines the meaning of words. The word "Yorùbá" employs all three tone bands (see Figure 10.1). The high tones are marked with an acute accent (*á*), mid tones have no diacritical marking (*o*), and low tones are marked with a grave accent (*ù*). Changing the relative tone of a syllable usually changes the meaning of a word, as in the following example:

A màá lọ   "we will definitely go"—*mà* indicates "definitely"

A máa lọ   "we will go"—*máa* indicates the future

Máà lọ   "don't go"—*máà* denotes the imperative negative

Spoken Yorùbá frequently glides between vowels, which may be embedded within or between words. Indeed song, chant, and drummed **surrogate speech** can exaggerate these glides, which are very fast in natural speech and may not be obvious even to native speakers.

Yorùbá is a very elided language: syllables are left out in natural speech, just as in English we write "do not" but usually say "don't." Most Yorùbá verbs end in a vowel while most nouns start with a vowel, so verbs and nouns are frequently merged into a single word. For example, in musical texts, the first syllable of Ìbejì disappears, as it might in ordinary speech where two consecutive vowels are usually elided (marked by an apostrophe as in "'bejì"). So for instance, in bar 1 of Music example 10.1, "*wá*" (look for) + "*Ìbejì*" becomes "*wá 'bejì*."

MUSIC EXAMPLE 10.1 Melody of Orin Ìbejì, sung by Doyin 'Fáníyì

Transcription by Amanda Villepastour

Aside from the technicalities of how speech is realized in music, the words of this song for Ìbejì offer some insight into Yorùbá family culture. Given the prevalence of twins among the Yorùbá, there is a large repertoire of songs for the Ìbejì. I have chosen this particular song as one hears it in many areas of Yorùbáland (as well as Cuba, where the song was passed down through slavery). Although the text can vary, and some words are commonly substituted, the song is melodically and rhythmically stable and is easily recognizable.

Ìyáàlù notation and strokes

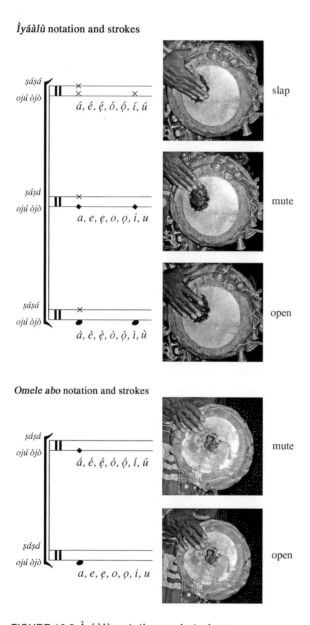

Omele abo notation and strokes

FIGURE 10.3 *Ìyáàlù* notation and strokes

Diagram by Amanda Villepastour

The generic lyrics give us insight into the naming conventions of Yorùbá people; from bar 9, we hear a sequence of appellations that list the actual names of children who are born into families with twins. Yorùbá children are frequently named according to the circumstance of their birth. For example, Tòkunbò denotes a child born overseas, so one often hears this name in Europe and North America. Àìná indicates a female baby born with the umbilical cord around her neck, while Babátúndé marks a birth of a boy that closely follows the death of his father or grandfather. Ìbejì praise texts list the naming conventions not only for twins, but for the children after their arrival. The child born after Táíwò and Kẹ́hìndé is always called Ìdòwú, while the child born after Ìdòwú is called Àlàbá, and so forth.

As I have explained, Yorùbá music is largely determined by the intrinsic structure of its text. The major rule of song, chant, and drummed speech is that the musical melody must follow the melodic contours of natural speech, otherwise the words would become unintelligible. Generally speaking, Yorùbá songs are pentatonic (with the approximate major scale degrees of *do re mi so la* or *do re fa so la*). The absence of semitones helps to disambiguate the speech tones and maintain the clarity and meaning of the text. Yorùbá songs are almost totally syllabic, due to the demand that the pitch contour of the Yorùbá language follows the melodic contour of ordinary speech. Doyin's song performance of Ìbejì praise poetry illustrates most of the features just discussed; the piece is syllabic, pentatonic, and closely follows

---

TECHNOLOGY

Bàtá ensembles comprise at least three drums (see Figure 10.2) which may be duplicated, or even include drums from other kinds of ensembles. Like many traditions around the world, Yorùbá drummers think of their instruments as if they were human, so routinely ascribe family relationships between instruments and genders to each drum, although they are almost always played by boys and men. The *iyáàlù* (mother drum) is the leader of the ensemble, reflecting the authority Yorùbá women wield in the home and the marketplace, while the *omele abo* (the female accompanying drum) is imagined by some as the *iyáàlù*'s co-wife, harking back to polygamy, still common throughout Yorùbáland. The *omele akọ* (the male accompanying drum), which is sometimes said to be the husband of the *iyáàlù* and *omele abo*, comprises two small drums and is the easiest to play so has the lowest status, explaining why it is often played by a boy. The *iyáàlù* can "talk" on its own in dance rhythm or the free speech rhythm of *oríkì*, while the *omele abo* reinforces the *iyáàlù* when it is playing in dance rhythm, helping to make the text very clear (as in Music example 10.2). Although the *omele akọ* plays only a rhythmic role, a twentieth-century innovation is to tie three of these small drums together into a configuration known as *omele mẹ́ta* (three accompanying drums) to emulate the three tones of Yorùbá speech.

As you can see in Figure 10.2, each *bàtá* drum has two heads. The larger skins, the *ojú òjò* (lit: "face of rain," but can also be translated as "face that talks a lot") of the *iyáàlù* and *omele abo* are the primary "talking" skins, while their small skins, with the onomatopoeic name *ṣáṣá*, play both a linguistic and purely rhythmic role and are struck with rawhide beaters that produce a sharp, cracking sound.

The largest two drums are held horizontally with the strong hand playing the larger skin and the rawhide beater (*bílálà*) playing the smaller skin. The larger skins of the *omele akọ* are also known as *ṣáṣá* while their small skins face down in playing position and are not struck. Various hand positions and striking techniques on the large skins of the *ìyáàlù* and *omele abo* produce distinct sonorities that reflect the speech tones of Yorùbá (see Figure 10.3). An open tone (the lowest-pitched sound) on the *ìyáàlù* articulates a low speech tone, while a mute on the same drum reflects a mid-speech tone, and a slap in the middle of the skin reflects a high speech tone. The *omele abo* only produces two distinct sounds: an open, ringing tone indicates a spoken mid tone, while the mute tone is played for high speech tones. The interlocking open tones on the *ìyáàlù* and *omele abo* create melodies that articulate low and mid speech tones and render the chants to be easily identifiable. For example, bars 2 and 3 of the rhythm of Ìbejì ring out the following melody (shown in Music example 10.2).

Apart from copying the rise and fall of Yorùbá speech, the drums also imitate the rhythms of speech in free speech rhythm, as shown in Music example 10.3. The commas above the staff indicate a pause or breath in the utterance.

MUSIC EXAMPLE 10.2 Open-tone melody played on the *ìyáàlù* and *omele abo*
Transcription by Amanda Villepastour

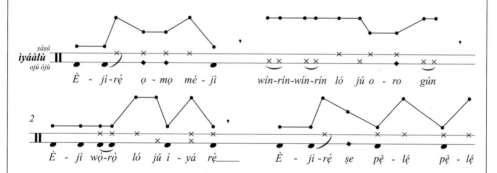

MUSIC EXAMPLE 10.3 Demonstration of drummed *oríkì Ìbejì* with voice
Transcription by Amanda Villepastour

Èjìrẹ́ ọmọ méjì	The two of them, two children
Wírínwírín ló jú orogún	They are tiny in the presence of co-wives
Èjì wọ̀rọ̀ ló jú ìtá rẹ̀	But they look large in the eyes of their own mother
Èjìrẹ́ ṣe pẹ̀lẹ́ pẹ̀lẹ́	Both, go gently.

the contours of spoken speech tones. Priestesses like Doyin (as well as their song repertoires) have not been impacted by colonial forms, most powerfully exerted by the church. While a novice listener may simply jump to the ethnocentric assumption that she is singing "out of tune," one is hearing the microtonal shifts of traditional Yorùbá performance, where exact pitch is less important than the stylistic and emotional performance of what is really an incantation (ọfọ̀). For òrìṣà devotees, an admirable performance is one that demonstrates a mastery of text, intoned with spiritual authority, or "àṣẹ," a Yorùbá concept that encompasses verbal authority and transformative power. This particular song performance is not dissimilar from what one would expect to hear in an òrìṣà ritual, apart from the fact that there would be more people chanting the chorus, rather than just the one young man heard in the recording.

Sacred texts move between different musical genres with ease. A chanted text may be spoken in a prayer (àdúrà), chanted as oríkì, appear in a song, or can be imbedded (although not uttered) within drummed, surrogate speech performance where the melody of spoken words is mimicked by the rising and falling pitch of the drum or may be coded with special drum strokes to resemble natural or heightened speech.

Drumming as Surrogate Speech

A very similar text for Ìbejì is also commonly drummed. The rhythm of the drums (the iyáàlù and omele abo) that renders the text in Music example 10.4 is very similar to the rhythm of the song (Music example 10.1) and is instantly recognizable even to musically inclined cultural outsiders. Indeed, in both sacred rituals and the secular settings of lifecycle parties such as weddings and funerals, participants often start singing along with the drums when they hear this rhythm, while any twins present will dance in front of the drums and "dash" the drummers with money in exchange for their praises.

The transfer of speech into bàtá drumming is a complex process. The Yorùbá have many different kinds of drum ensembles, the most popular being the dùndún variable-pitch pressure drums. Yorùbá speakers find the dùndún the easiest to understand when text is played by drummers, as it faithfully mimics natural speech by following the contour of spoken or sung words. The dùndún has a pitch range larger than that of a piano, and can also render the glissandi of Yorùbá speech (as exaggerated in Doyin's sung performance). Bàtá drums, however, have fixed-pitch heads, so cannot mimic the sliding contours of Yorùbá speech. Instead, bàtá drummers use an elaborate system to encode speech into drum language (see Figure 10.3).

In the first few seconds of the recorded excerpt (although not notated in Music example 10.4), the iyáàlù (lead) drummer plays the oríkì for Ìbejì in free speech time (see the Music example 10.3 for a transcription of Ìbejì's drummed oríkì). Like speech, the oríkì is always slightly different with each performance, but many Yorùbá listeners, especially twins, will recognize this drummed praise poetry, while the other drummers in the ensemble listen for the metrical part of the rhythm that gets going at eight seconds. When the *omele abo* player hears the first "*Mo mú 'bejì*" in metrical rhythm played on the *ìyáàlù* lead drum (bars 1 and 2), he joins in with the special strokes on his own drum that make the texts even clearer (entering in bar 2) while the *omele akọ* player joins in with his rhythmic part as soon as he can (bar 3).

The accuracy of text rendition is the most important, and most difficult challenge of Yorùbá drumming. Not only must the drummer have an enormous repertoire of sacred text and his performance techniques internalized, but he requires social and sacred knowledge to be able to sound the appropriate *oríkì* or rhythm in the correct moment. His livelihood also depends on this, for drumming the appropriate praises for a person motivates the recipient to respond by dashing the drummers with cash. One often sees an elegant woman dance towards a drummer while peeling notes from her purse then pressing them one by one against his sweaty forehead. The notes momentarily stick, then cascade to the ground where a small boy or young man diligently collects the currency for later distribution within the ensemble. The woman may continue to dash and make an ostentatious display of her wealth as the drummer launches into further drummed flattery to ensure the flow of cash as long as he can. Such is the skill of the drummer; knowledge of her full name, husband, town, ancestors, and famous deeds and generosity will feed into this public celebration of community belonging, as well as ensure that the drummers get paid!

The *bàtá* drummer's efficacy to elicit spirit possession in rituals will also ensure that he is repeatedly hired. His skill to bring the spirits into the bodies of devotees depends largely on his knowledge of sacred texts, which are believed to speak directly to the spirits and invite them into the ceremony. If the *òrìṣà* are slow to "mount" their worshippers, the drummer may even insult the spirits to anger them enough to possess a devotee. But the drummers must also make people dance with their irresistible grooves, for it is believed that the movement itself creates a "framework" that the *òrìṣà* recognize, for they too, it is believed, like to dance in front of the drums.

Social Context: Òrìṣà Worship

The homeland of the Yorùbá people straddles contemporary southwest Nigeria and southern Benin to its west. The ethno-linguistic term Yorùbá has been employed since the 1890s to encompass peoples who speak some 20 dialects across the region. There are said to be 20 to 30 million speakers of Yorùbá dialects. Only around five percent of contemporary Yorùbá people are dedicated *òrìṣà* devotees, while the remaining majority are around half Muslim and half Christian. Many modern-day Christian and Muslim Yorùbá people condemn *òrìṣà* worship, viewing it as a dark, backward survival from the past. Some denounce the traditional ways publicly and engage with traditional priests secretly, while others may have more respect for *òrìṣà* worship, particularly as the volume of international scholarship about its diverse global manifestations continues to grow. Despite condemnation of the

MUSIC EXAMPLE 10.4 *Bàtá* drumming for Ìbejì, performed by Rábíù Àyándòkun

Transcription by Amanda Villepastour

Text for Music example 10.4: *Bàtá* **drum language for Ìbejì**

Mo mú 'bejì	I will take the twins
Mo mú 'bejì relé	I will take the twins home
Tere tere yàn	*Tere tere* (non-lexical vocables) Chosen!
Mo mú 'bejì	I will take the twins
Mo mú 'bejì relé	I will take the twins home
Tere tere yàn	*Tere tere* favoured with goodness
Kẹ́hìndé yàn	Kẹ́hìndé is favoured
Èjìrẹ́ yàn lóònìí	The two of them will survive today
Tere tere yàn	*Tere tere* survived
Kẹ́hìndé (yàn)	Kẹ́hìndé is favoured

old ways, some *òrìṣà* beliefs and practices have been absorbed by Christians and Muslims and pervade contemporary life. Reverence for twin births, high social status for the parents of multiple births, and old naming customs within the families of twins are modern-day cultural practices that bridge the religious differences among the Yorùbá. One may hear a spiritual song for the *òrìṣà* of twins at the naming ceremony parties of Christians and Muslims, while the same repertoire can emerge in traditional rituals involving animal sacrifice and spirit possession, where a deity may take over the body of a devotee for a time. The Ìbejì's capacity to reach across these contrasting social and spiritual worlds is unique, for religious conversion to Christianity and Islam had no impact on the world's highest incidence of twins among the Yorùbá people.

Òrìṣà worship is commonly framed as a "religion," and is increasingly claimed as a world religion by its global devotees in the Americas and the Caribbean. However, *òrìṣà* worship is diverse from place to place, and may differ substantially even between neighboring house temples. Yet there are core beliefs that tie the various practices together. Most obvious is the belief in the *òrìṣà* themselves, (transliterated as *oricha* in Cuba, *orixá* in Brazil, and *orisha* in English-speaking regions). The *òrìṣà* are deities that may derive from forces of nature, such as the goddess of tornados Ọya, or historical figures, exemplified by the very popular *òrìṣà* Ṣàngó, recorded in oral literature as a fifteenth-century king. Some may simultaneously manifest in natural phenomena and be remembered as historical personalities, just as Ọya was also Ṣàngó's mythological wife and Ṣàngó is also the god of lightning. Most *òrìṣà* appeal to human desires and needs; Ọ̀ṣun is a river goddess of femininity and fertility to whom the barren may beg for a child, while

PRIMARY SOURCE

Ère Ìbejì (sculptor unknown)

As I walked through Les Puces de Saint-Ouen (a flea market in the north of Paris) in December 2012, I spotted a pair of Ìbejì (see Figure 10.4). More recently, I saw a similar pair in one of the upmarket African art galleries on the Left Bank of the Seine, valued at 3800 euros. During the twentieth century, there were said to be some 40,000 Ìbejì sculptures flooding the "primitive" art market in the global north as Christian and Muslim Yorùbá sold or discarded their *òrìṣà* sacred objects. Unethical dealers also extracted such objects from *òrìṣà* devotees within questionable circumstances; indeed many Ìbejì have been repatriated to Nigeria following legal cases.

Purchased at under 100 euros, my own Ìbejì are unlikely to be very old, or may even have been produced for the tourist art industry using artificial ageing techniques. Notwithstanding, this pair of Ìbejì are typical in design with large heads that emphasize the *òrìṣà* of destiny, Ori (literally "head"). They display wide-open eyes, the elaborately raised coiffure of priests, Ọ̀yọ́ tribal marks on the cheeks, and beaded vests that obscure the male and female genitals underneath.

In cases where one or both twins die during childbirth or during their infancy, Yorùbá women traditionally commission wood carvings (*ère*) of one or two twins,

FIGURE 10.4 *Ère Ìbejì*

Photograph by Amanda Villepastour

which are prepared with medicines and incantations by diviners. Where one twin has died, the mother feeds the *ère* Ìbejì, dresses it in a beaded vest like those worn by my figurines, and wears it in the front of her wrapper. She may also give it to the living twin for play.

Although twins are revered by all Yorùbá today and worshipped by *òrìṣà* devotees, it was not always so. Early writings of missionaries report that the infanticide of twins was common in the mid-nineteenth century due to their association with multiple births of animals, particularly the colobus monkey (*ẹdun*), which usually bears twins. Multiple births were also believed to cause sterility of crops and people. Horrendous stories of executioners plundering houses and seizing infant twins appear in the Church Missionary Society archives, and as late as the 1930s, the American anthropologist William Bascom, who conducted years of research in Nigeria, was told that twins were ominous, especially if they were both of the same sex, since it was feared they had come to kill the father in the case of twin boys, or the mother if twin girls were born. The parents, Bascom was told, would choose their favorite twin and not feed the other, leaving it to die.

Although the movement from twin infanticide to worship may be partly explained by Christian influence, the Yorùbá reverence of twins is often attributed to a past king (Aláàfin) of the town of Ọ̀yọ́, Àjàká, who himself fathered twins so reformed earlier customs. Rather than have the twins killed, oral literature tells us that Àjàká sent their mother into exile with her children, relatives, friends, and servants. The twin children then became kings in two other Yorùbá towns, Èpé and Oǹdó.

Ọbàtálá is the *òrìṣà* of creativity and is believed to mould the foetus inside the womb. Children born with disabilities are believed to be Ọbàtálá's responsibility. Functioning like an indigenous social service, Ọbàtálá compounds (walled clusters of family houses) traditionally cared for the disabled. Some *òrìṣà* are also associated with inherited craft lineages, such as Ògún, the deity of iron, blacksmiths and hunters, Ọbàlùfọ̀n, the *òrìṣà* of weaving, Òrìṣà Oko, the deity of farming and agriculture, and Àyàn, the Yorùbá god of drumming. Because of the prevalence of twins among the Yorùbá, Ìbejì is one of the deities found across Yorùbáland.

Making offerings to the *òrìṣà* of food, cloth, and other valuable objects, as well as the occasion humane sacrifice of animals (almost always eaten by devotees), is an important spiritual exchange with the *òrìṣà* as they are petitioned for protection against calamity and for success in life's endeavours. The Ìbejì are petitioned to protect twins in particular (where infant mortality may be an increased risk), and to protect children generally. Spirit possession is also a mainstay of *òrìṣà* worship, where some *òrìṣà* may possess the bodies of devotees (who are often amnesiac after the experience) and speak directly to the congregants in a ceremony. However, Ìbejì is not a spirit that possesses its devotees. Rather, the Ìbejì may "speak" to worshippers through one of the various methods of divination; the most common methods use cowrie shells or palm nuts to access significant corpuses of divination oral texts. Attached to these Yorùbá trance and divination technologies is an elaborate system of herbal medicine.

Chief Priestess, Doyin 'Fáníyì

BIOGRAPHY

Doyin 'Fáníyì (see Figure 10.5) was born into a long line of *òrìṣà* priests in Òṣogbo. Her father was the Chief Priest of Òṣun in the town and died when Doyin was a child. She was adopted by Austrian artist, Susanne Wenger, who was initiated into the *òrìṣà* priesthood in the 1950s and became instrumental in protecting *òrìṣà* devotion from colonial and Christian oppression. Emerging from this remarkable heritage, Doyin has herself become a chief and leading priestess internationally, frequently travelling to Europe, the USA, and Brazil. She holds an MA in linguistics from Ìlọrin University and is a PhD candidate at the University of Ìbàdàn.

Doyin's musical performance is that of an authoritative priestess and sounds different from the polished songs of professional folkloric performers. Singing for Ìbejì is an act of devotion for Doyin, rather than a product for entertainment. Her style of performance resembles what one would expect to hear in a ritual. Doyin learned her repertoire of prayers, praise poetry and songs while a child during *òrìṣà* ceremonies. Resisting formalized learning of this sacred repertoire, Doyin once said, "You learn with your body; it's not like going to school." Doyin typically teaches songs with gesture and dance.

FIGURE 10.5
Chief Priestess, Doyin 'Fáníyì, Òṣogbo 2010
Photograph by Amanda Villepastour

Regardless of their religious persuasion, many Yorùbá believe that uttered words have transformative power, and that incantations and prayers have the facility to change the physical world and life's outcomes. This belief in the efficacy of language transcends religious categories so the power of the spoken word is culturally pervasive. Given the high mortality rate of twins, the musical renditions of Ìbejì poetry not only celebrate the wealth associated with multiple births, but constitute a plea to spare the twins from death. Indeed the word "*yàn*," which appears in the songs and drum texts for Ìbejì, may be interpreted as "survival" or "meaningful existence" as devotees, parents, and musicians chant, sing, dance, and drum the twins into continued life. Other Ìbejì lyrics, such as, "*Èjìrẹ́ alákíṣà di aláṣọ,*

BIOGRAPHY

Rábíù Àyándòkun

Like most contemporary Yorùbá drummers, Rábíù Àyándòkun (b. 1958) is a Muslim (see Figure 10.6). His father, Yusuf Ìgè Àyánsínà, initiated Rábíù's musical training when he was six and on reaching adolescence, his father took him out of school to complete his training as a master drummer. At times humiliated by his peers in a modernizing and colonial Nigeria, Rábíù has risen not only to be one of Nigeria's most famous drummers, but he has made an international name through two decades of touring in Europe and the USA, as well as recording with Nobel Literature Prize winner Wọ́lé Ṣoyínká and legendary jazz drummer Billy Cobham. In recognition of his international work to promote the largely endangered *bàtá* drumming tradition, as well as the fame his work has brought to his town, its king awarded Rábíù a chieftancy title, Agbáṣà Ẹ̀rìn-Ọ̀ṣun (the cultural ambassador of Ẹ̀rìn-Ọ̀ṣun) in 2004.

FIGURE 10.6 **Master drummer Rábíù Àyándòkun, London 2007**
Photograph by Amanda Villepastour

o so alagbe di olóúnję" (Twins turned the poor into the rich, you turned the beggar into somebody with food to eat) speak not only of spiritual exchange, but mobilize communities to offer support to the *ìyá 'bejì* (mother of twins).

Discussion Topics

- Listen carefully to the song "Orin Ìbejì" and try to find the beat. Can you place your feet to the beat?

- In these Yorùbá songs and chants, the intelligibility of the text is of paramount importance. Think about music in religions with which you are familiar. Are the texts audible? Can they be understood by most followers?

- In the drumming piece, language is rendered in a purely instrumental form. Can you think of any other musical traditions that can do this?

Further Listening

Adedayo Ologundudu. *Orin Orisa: Yoruba Traditional Songs of Praises for Orisa* (mp3 album, 2009).
> This is a collection of 16 òrìṣà songs by an Atlanta-based babaláwo (divining priest). Songs are performed by male and female lead singers with a vocal chorus and a percussion ensemble. There is one song for Ìbejì in the collection.

Bascom, William Russell. *Drums of the Yoruba of Nigeria* (CD FE 4441, Folkways Records, New York, 2007 [1953]).
> This re-mastered recording includes òrìṣà rhythms played on igbin, dùndún, and bàtá drums and 21 photographs with detailed notes.

Branda-Lacerda, Marcos. *Yoruba Drums from Benin, West Africa* (CD SF 40440, Smithsonian/Folkways, Washington, DC, 1996).
> Nineteen tracks illustrate various regional Yorùbá drumming ensembles in neighboring Benin. The accompanying booklet includes cultural information with photographs of drumming ensembles and musical transcriptions.

G. Odukwe Sackeyfio. *Yoruba Bata Drums—Elewe Music and Dance* (CD FE 4294, Smithsonian Folkways Recordings, Washington, DC, 2001 [1980]).
> This recording includes various genres of bàtá drumming. The accompanying notes include lyrics to two Egúngún (ancestral) songs.

Recommended Reading

Chappel, T.J.H. (1974) "The Yoruba Cult of Twins in Historical Perspective." *Africa* 44: 250–265.
> The author is an art historian who has specialized in wood sculptors. Bearing twins was often associated with female promiscuity and the belief that women had consorted with spirits, and so mothers of twins were formerly persecuted or even killed. The author discusses when and how the practice of infanticide developed into twin worship among the Yorùbá.

Chemeche, G., J. Pemberton, and J. Picton (2003) *Ibeji: The Cult of Yoruba Twins.* Milan, 5 Continents.
> This book contains dozens of photographs of Ìbejì wood sculptures, as well as articles from prominent art historians and Yorùbá wood carvers. The text offers insight into traditional Ìbejì practices, cultural and technical information about the woodcarvers, and numerous song, poetry, and divination texts in praise of the Ìbejì.

PLATE 1
A stone street in
Jerusalem's Old City.
Photograph by
Abigail Wood.
(Chapter 1)

PLATE 2 Christian pilgrims in the Old City, Jerusalem. Photograph by Abigail Wood.
      (Chapter 1)

PLATE 3 Babani Kone at a wedding party in Bamako, 2008. Photograph by Lucy Duran.
(Chapter 2)

PLATE 4
Raushan Orazbaeva.
Photograph by
Saida Daukeyeva.
(Chapter 3)

PLATE 5 A training class at the International Capoeira Angola Foundation, Bahia.
Photograph by Hugh Marriage. (Chapter 4)

PLATE 6 Korean drumming and dancing in a Yanbian park. Photograph by Rowan
Pease. (Chapter 5)

PLATE 7
Korean woman playing a *puk* at a party, Northeast China, 1999. Photograph by Rowan Pease. (Chapter 5)

PLATE 8 A village woman in Chinese Central Asia attending a ritual gathering. Photograph by Rachel Harris. (Chapter 7)

PLATE 9
Kiku Day playing
shakuhachi dressed as a
komusō monk. Music
Academy Concert Hall,
Copenhagen, February
2013. Photograph by
Britt Lindemann.
(Chapter 8)

PLATE 10 *Wayang Kulit*, shadow puppet theatre, Tejakula, Bali. Photograph by Hans Lemmens/The Image Bank/Getty Images. (Chapter 9)

PLATE 11 Master drummer, Rábíù Àyándòkun in London, 2007.
Photograph by Amanda Villepastour. (Chapter 10)

PLATE 12 *T'ungso* player statue, Yanbian Korean Folk Culture Village. Photograph by
Rowan Pease. (Chapter 5)

PLATE 13 A man wearing bull horns and a robe with the South Sudanese flag blows a horn during celebrations marking three years of independence, Juba, July 9, 2014. Photograph by Charles Lomodong/AFP/Getty Images. (Chapter 11)

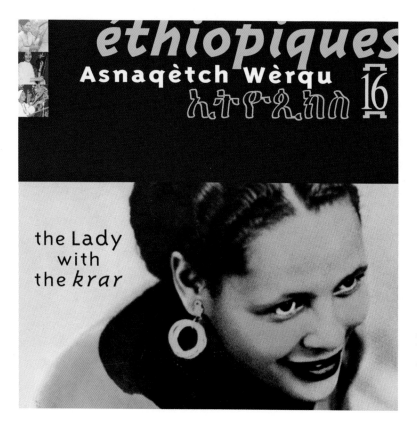

PLATE 14
Asnaqetch Werqu, the Lady with the *Krar*. Photograph courtesy of Buda Musique. (Chapter 13)

PLATE 15 The Krar Collective playing a modernized *krar*. Photograph by Thomas Raggam. (Chapter 13)

PLATE 16 Mati Zundel. Photograph by Mark van der Aa. (Chapter 14)

Lawal, Babatunde (2011) "Sustaining the Oneness in Their Twoness: Poetics of twin figures (ère ìbejì) among the Yoruba." In Philip M. Peek, ed. *Twins in African and Diaspora Cultures: Double Trouble, Twice Blessed*. Bloomington: Indiana University Press.

> This chapter contextualizes the cosmology of Ìbejì within Yorùbá traditional culture and òrìṣà worship. The author also focusses on the material culture of twin figures (*ère*) and recent cultural and artistic developments such as a new tradition of photographs of twins.

Villepastour, Amanda (2010) *Ancient Text Messages of the Yorùbá Bàtá Drum: Cracking the Code*. Aldershot: Ashgate.

> A technical study of how the natural speech of Yorùbá language is played on the *bàtá* drums. The author explains how Yorùbá is translated into a coded drum language, spoken and understood only by *bàtá* drummers. The book includes a 42-track CD, dozens of transcriptions, and translated drum texts.

Villepastour, Amanda (2014) "Talking Tones and Singing Speech among the Yorùbá of Southwest Nigeria." *Jahrbuch des Phonogrammarchivs der Österrechischen Akademie der Wissenschaften* 4: 29–46.

> This article builds on previous scholarship and explains the technicalities of how Yorùbá text is set to melody. The author argues that song is exaggerated speech, making the text even easier to understand.

PART 3

Music and Movement

Introduction

Rowan Pease and Rachel Harris

The last four chapters of our book explore music that has been in one way or another uprooted and set on the move across the world. Music is and has always been supremely portable: long before the advent of file sharing, a musical idea carried in somebody's head could be reconstituted with new materials in a new land. Musical ideas can be virulent, easily spread from person to person, but today the internet makes these phenomena far more spectacular, enabling a much swifter dissemination and far wider reach. Think, for example, of the extraordinary success of Korean rapper Psy's 2012 release "Gangnam Style" and the thousands of globally dispersed parodies it spawned, each one with its own peculiarly local meanings, from the all-American values of "Farmer Style" from Kansas to the slightly crazed "Uyghur Style" from Kazakhstan (at the time of writing it was easy to find them both on YouTube). Musical sound and style may be transformed in the course of these global journeys, but, even more notably, the meanings attached to music can become detached and new ones attached.

These chapters consider several overarching and intertwined types of movement, of peoples, and of sound: migration, diaspora, the spread of Western culture through imperialism and globalization, and the technological advances that are changing the way that music is circulated and even constituted. There have been few chapters in our book that have not touched on the movement of people and the ways it shapes music: such as the resignification of the Zen musical offering "Tamuke" as it spread to the global *shakuhachi* community, or the traces of an ancient migration in the Malian call to the horses, "Soliyo."

Music and Diaspora

Music is a highly effective, if not *the* most effective, way of forging the communal links that bind diaspora communities in their new lands, and maintaining the sentimental links to their homeland across many generations. We have already encountered the musical remembering of forced migration in the Capoeira Angola of Brazil; the musical impact of the Atlantic slave trade routes arises again in chapters in this section on Latin American digital cumbia and African-American soul.

A more recent, traumatic movement of people has been the dispersal of the Dinka people across the globe as a result of violent civil war in Sudan. A pastoral people, the Dinka have a tradition of personal songs, which include clan genealogies, individual biographies, and actual events in people's lives. These songs have taken on even greater importance in maintaining personal ties as the Dinka have been forced to flee their homeland, and their families have been torn apart. Angela Impey writes about the "Song of Akuac," a sung letter sent in the form of a cassette recording from Sudan to London in the 1980s. In this most intimate of songs, a man tells his relatives abroad about his wife's shameful infidelity. "Song of Akuac" not only elicits their sympathy but also admiration for the eloquence of his words and sweetness of voice. The medium of song transforms his anger into an aesthetic, expressive form through which he can invite his relatives to share his pain across many thousands of miles.

A more symbolic attachment to homeland is explored by Ilana Webster Kogen, who has chosen the piece "Tezeta" (Nostalgia), a song of lost love that instantly evokes a longing among Ethiopians for their homeland. Even among those living still in Ethiopia, the song conjures up an imagined and irretrievable golden past viewed from an imperfect present. As it travels abroad, "Tezeta," just like Ethiopian food, is adapted to the tastes of new homelands and audiences—in jazz, gospel, soul, or rap versions—without losing its bittersweet melodic contours or its potency. In Addis Ababa itself, global trends are evidenced by the use of drum machines and synthesizers rather than traditional instruments to accompany the song. But music's power to bind and represent the Ethiopian community is nowhere more evident than in the pride expressed in Aster Aweke, a singer who has triumphed on the world music scene while retaining the unmistakable high-pitched vocal style and ululations of Ethiopian music. Musical creativity in the diaspora often feeds back into the homeland and in turn sparks new transformations in music-making at home.

Global audiences

"Tezeta," like all music, can carry multiple meanings. Ostensibly, the song expresses yearning for a lost love, but its lyrics can also contain oblique political criticism, a technique known as "wax and gold." These subtle messages are only audible to listeners attuned to the language and politics of Ethiopia. Aweke's world music audiences will doubtless find their own, no less valid, meanings in the song. Terry Callier's song "Dancing Girl," the topic of Caspar Melville's chapter, likewise uses lyrics about love and sexuality to voice social criticism of the racial and economic politics of 1970s' America. Arising out of the musical melting pot of Chicago, a decade later the album it came from, *What Color is Love*, found resonance among a completely different community of London clubbers, who found that it spoke to their own sense of dissatisfaction with the racial politics of 1980s' Britain.

Unlike "Tezeta," "Dancing Girl" was not remixed and adopted to local musical styles; instead, its authenticity as a product of African-American music rooted in a specific time and place was highly prized in London. Terry Callier's track was inherently hybrid, mixing jazz, funk, progressive rock, country and western, and classical orchestral sounds. Rather than stressing a particular ethnic or national identity, Callier's musical and cultural mix could be taken as a symbol of the possibility of collaboration and sympathy across lines of race and nation. In 1970s' America, this mix made him unmarketable in a music industry that was divided along racial lines. It came as a total surprise to Callier when his career was revived through the interest of 1980s' London DJs.

Music Uprooted

Among both the Dinka and the "rare groove" DJs, the physical medium that carries their music—cassette and vinyl—is highly prized, despite the availability of digital alternatives. But our last chapter, by Geoffrey Baker, is about a piece of music that is thoroughly immaterial and deterritorialized: "El Alto de La Paz." The very scene it belongs to is rootless: digital cumbia was invented as a cyberspace joke by a Dutch conceptual artist, and has since grown; it is attributed to the "Buenos Aires underground," yet the scene exists more clearly in the marketing realm than in the physical city. A cosmopolitan duo, Argentinian producer Mati Zundel and Canadian rapper Boogat, created "El Alto de La Paz" together over the internet, using file swapping to share ideas and sounds picked up by Zundel on his travels around South America. Through music-mixing software, Zundel was able to layer and refashion these sounds, thus liberating them from their former associations and infusing them with new meanings. Although the roots of cumbia itself are in the movement of people from Africa to Latin America—as slaves and later as impoverished economic migrants—this piece is part of a more privileged trans-national culture of circulation that feeds on itself as it traverses the globe. It was only through leaving Argentina that Zundel learned to become a Latin American musician. A music that had been disparaged as tacky and parochial by the upper classes in Buenos Aires gained legitimation through overseas approval, to the extent that the genre is becoming a symbol of national identity. Nevertheless, as with the singers of "Tezeta," Zundel compromised to increase his music's circulation overseas: conforming to international copyright laws, and changing his name to something pronounceable by foreigners. He signed to a hip cosmopolitan label with a strong Buenos Aires identity, which evokes a sense of authenticity. Even in this most rootless of musical cultures, there is a desire to link music to place. These chapters are, as Melville writes, testament to "the strange routes that culture can travel and the surprising ways in which popular art produced in one context can, through the unanticipated flows of global cultural transmission, find value, meaning and a new audience in very different times and places."

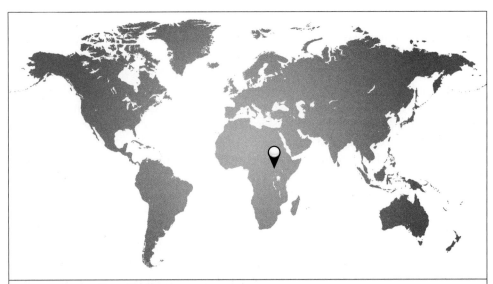

Location: South Sudan

"Song of Akuac": Audio-letters from South Sudan: Tracing Dinka Networks, Connections, and Intimacies beyond the War Zone

Performed by two anonymous male singers with a single drum; recorded by the singers c.1983, in South Sudan

Chapter eleven

"Song of Akuac": Audio-letters from South Sudan

Tracing Dinka Networks, Connections, and Intimacies beyond the War Zone

Angela Impey

Summary

KEY WORDS
- cassettes
- circulation
- conflict
- migration
- pastoralism

This chapter explores the practice of song-making and sharing in the culture of the Dinka people of South Sudan. It focuses in particular on the global circulation of songs in the form of cassette audio-letters which pass between South Sudan and the global Dinka diaspora. This phenomenon of personal song-making has its roots in a culture of seasonal nomadic pastoralism. However, against the recent historical background of civil war and the forced migration of many millions from their homes, this tradition has been repackaged to accommodate extended geographies and to address a multitude of new concerns. Cassette audio-letters infuse old song structures with new concerns. They are also progressively replacing face-to-face interaction and live performance as ways of communicating and mediating private information. In this way, they have enabled clan groups who are scattered across the globe to retain intimate connections with one another and with their cultural identities. The chapter concludes with a reflection on the "affiliative" power of the cassette tape itself, suggesting that the object has become inextricably implicated in the complexity of networks, connections, and intimacies of this contemporary global cultural practice.

Why this Piece?

My story begins with an old cassette tape belonging to a Dinka friend in London. Although barely audible due to almost 30 years of play, the cassette contained what appeared at first to be a mild-mannered song rendered by two men in unison to the accompaniment of a single drum. I was surprised to discover that it was in fact a "shaming" or "insult" song, composed by my friend's relative in South Sudan to publicly chastise his wife for her involvement in a number of extra-marital affairs. Rather than inform his relatives about the dissolution of his marital home in a letter, he had produced a cassette audio-letter, using a culturally defined song style that permitted him the freedom to share his story as fervently as he saw fit.

The Cassette

The portable cassette player became the standard home audio-technology in the mid-1970s, offering opportunities to ordinary people to record, replicate, and distribute their own music to whomever they chose. However, whereas cassette technology in most parts of the world offered the opportunity for the experimentation with, and redirection of musical products, it appears to have assumed a different function in Dinka culture. Introduced into the southern Sudan region at the outset of the second civil war, and at a time when vast numbers of people were fleeing their homes, the cassette appears to have been adopted specifically in order to preserve and reinforce existing cultural practices, and thus to secure them in time, place, and memory.

FIGURE 11.1 Akuac's cassette
Photograph by Angela Impey

Given that cassette tapes and their players are typically robust and resistant to dust, heat, and shocks than their digital competitors (e.g. CDs, mp3 players, or laptops), it would be simple to attribute the ongoing use of cassette players in a country such as South Sudan to practical considerations. Equally, they are more affordable, portable, and considered to last longer. I would argue, however, that, in this context, cassettes are not merely functional items of recording technology, but have come to serve as active partners in the global network of Dinka social relationships.

Recording a cassette allows for the inclusion of interferences and everyday sounds of one's environment, thus bringing the listeners into an intimate, sensory space of communication. Recording a song on a cassette is a decisive act and the product is a tangible result of that act that cannot easily be replicated in the digital world. Sending a song as an mp3 file over the internet lacks the physical presence of a cassette and cannot be kept as a memento, as one would a box of letters or postcards that can be touched and exchanged. But a cassette can be endlessly rewound and replayed, thus creating an active space for listening that is more immersive and intense than the internalized practice of reading.

This is not to say that Dinka do not use digital technology and many young people will use several types of technology concurrently. For instance, while on a recording trip in the region of Bor town, I met an important elderly composer of war songs who insisted that his compositions be recorded on cassette. Young men would therefore use analogue/cassette technology to create a primary recording of his songs, but they would then convert the track to mp3 file and sell it in the local market as a digital download onto mobile phones. Such a process would only be allowed to occur with songs that are considered to be public property and many war songs, such as those composed by the elderly man in Bor town, were "donated" to the common cause.

Such frankness, my friend informed me, would not be tolerated in any other form of communication; however, certain songs offer cultural license for the candid disclosure of painful, shameful, or otherwise undesirable experiences, thus enabling individuals to reclaim their personal dignity and secure the respect of their clan and community. The ultimate purpose of such "fighting with song" is the reinstatement of social harmony; an idealized order that is referred to in Dinka as *cieng*, which is loosely translated as "to live together" or "to respect."

In this chapter, I will explore the practice of song-making and sharing among the Dinka of South Sudan, focusing in particular on the circulation of songs in the form of cassette audio-letters between clan members in South Sudan and the global Dinka diaspora. More specifically, I will examine how this tradition of personal song-making that is rooted in a culture of nomadic pastoralism, i.e., shaped by seasonal movements between specific water points and "cattle camps," has been adapted to accommodate population dispersal across continents and cultures. Focusing on the song on the cassette tape—to which I have given the title "Song of Akuac"—this chapter will examine how the intimacy communicated through its poetic conventions helps to nurture and sustain Dinka clan relations. This practice of exchanging cassette audio-letters has become all the more crucial in light of the extreme social fragmentation experienced by the Dinka as a result of protracted civil war in South Sudan. The chapter will conclude with a reflection on the significance of the cassette tape as an object that continues to be the carrier of choice for certain kinds of personal song in spite of the greater ease of access and widespread use of new digital technologies. I argue that the object itself has become a culturally significant part of the complex connections, identifications, and intimacies of this contemporary global cultural practice.

Musical Features

TIMED LISTENING GUIDE	
0.01	Muffled speech, possibly introducing the song and two singers, which is characteristic of many recordings of this nature
	The poor quality of the audio reflects the condition of the cassette tape, which is damaged from several decades of play, but singers do not generally aspire to high-quality recordings for such performances. Quality is judged on the composition itself, and rated according to its melodic and poetic interest, and the integrity of the message
0.14 singing starts	The song starts in an upper register and follows a descending contour, although appears to have no tonal center. One singer plays what might be a small drum (*lor*) or taps the table, producing a regular four beat that provides the rhythmic underpinning of the entire song. Note the use of standard pentatonic (five-tone) scale and the linear nature of the melody, which appears not to adhere to any predictable structure
0:23	At this point, the listener becomes aware of a second singer who either sings in unison or shadows the first voice closely

0.48	Background thud. There is little effort made to keep recordings of this nature clear of background sounds; on the contrary, the intimacy of the recording is enhanced by such spontaneous and unrehearsed sound spillages, which help to bridge the distances in time and space between performers and listeners. This is part of the reason why audio-letters of this nature provide a sense of grounding and proximity beyond that of a written letter, by capturing the affective soundscape of the performer's home
	The meandering linear contour of the melody adds to the conversational quality of this genre of personal song. The singers make little use of melodic repetition other than to occasionally emphasize an important point in the narrative. Far from being structurally fluid, however, the musical phrasing is determined by the tonal inflections of Dinka language, by text-rhythm (e.g., short and long vowel sounds), and by the constant rhythmic accompaniment
1:17–1:25	Note here the rare repetition of a phrase
1:57 2:17 2:24 2:33 2:43	At this point, the melodic phrases begin to be delivered in call-and-response style, characterized by the performance of a solo phrase, which is followed by two or more phrases by both singers in unison. This occurs several times. The time settings in the left column refer to the start of the solo phrases
4:00	The song reverts to continuous unison singing, much of which hovers around a low pitch and produces the expectation of a final resolution

The population of South Sudan comprises some 63 language groups, the largest of whom is the Dinka (*Muonyjieng*), a Nilotic pastoralist people who share close ethno-linguistic features with a number of smaller groups such as the Nuer and the Shilluk. Nilotic pastoralists are renowned for their intimate association with cattle, which are integral to every aspect of social, political and religious life. Images of, and references to cattle permeate their performances, from the images that are invoked in lyrics that reference the colors, sizes, and mannerisms of their favorite bulls, to the stylized impersonation of the shape of their horns in dance.

Dinka song culture is highly idiosyncratic and builds on the narrative documentation of actual events and autobiographical information. Songs are categorized according to genre. Each genre is identified by specific musical distinctions and by the times and places of their performance, and classified according to their expressive purpose. These include narrating genealogical histories, praising particular clan members, or, as in the case of the song on the cassette, shaming someone who has offended you. Most personal songs are performed solo or, when performed in a group, are sung either in unison or in simple call-and-response format.

Dinka songs follow a standard pentatonic scale and build on an extended series of linear, interconnected song segments. They are accompanied only by clapping sticks (**atuel**) or a single drum (**lor**). The aesthetic canon of personal songs is based largely on the creative interaction between language and melody, and the specific arrangements between them differ somewhat across Dinka dialect groups. For the Dinka "Bor" dialect group, for instance, a good song is one that contains large intervallic leaps; their aim is to stimulate public interest and encourage a lively response. A good lyricist should make use of judicious language, which is achieved

FIGURE 11.2 **Dinka man singing with his young bullock, South Sudan**
Photograph courtesy of Robin Denselow

through the imaginative use of metaphors, metonyms, and similes that normally invoke finely observed mannerisms and images of cattle. The following lyrics serve as examples:

> Majok (black and white bull), shining like the evening star
> I bought a colorful bull with a white tail for my clan
> Like an ostrich (black and white bird), I bought a bull for my clan . . .

> The color of my bull is as bright as the rainbow in summer, and always makes me sing . . .
> Marumjok is adorned with many things

> He shines as if he is wearing all the lights of Ethiopia
> He is beautiful like a woman with pretty hair
> Majok's black spots are as black as a herd of sheep

All men and women aim to accumulate a repertoire of personal songs during their lifetime. A person who lacks the ability to create good songs may commission a piece from a respected composer in his or her community in exchange for a cow or a cash fee. Occasionally that composer will be talented lyricist only, in which case a second individual, who has an aptitude for good melody-making, will be approached to complete the process. Once achieved, the song will be taught to its

FIGURE 11.3 Dinka cattle camp, South Sudan
Photograph courtesy of Robin Denselow

"owner," who will commit it to memory. People sometimes accumulate a repertoire of several hundred songs through the course of their lifetime.

Dinka songs are entirely orally transmitted and while they may change over time, most remain both lyrically and melodically stable during the life of the performer. In oral cultures, such as that of Nilotic pastoralists, people employ a range of memory prompts to remember the finer details of their songs and poetic recitations. Although no research has yet been conducted on how these techniques are constructed in Dinka songs, we can assume that structural elements such as text-rhythm, melody, and rhythmic accompaniment serve as aides for proper recall.

Given that songs are used to transmit information and to inspire admiration, the manner in which they are performed, and the localities in which performances take place, are considered as meaningful as their lyrical content. Many of the more respected song styles (e.g., ox songs) are customarily performed in cattle camps, which are located near to strategic grazing areas and water points, and where many thousands of cattle will be accommodated during designated seasons of the year. Cattle camps are considered sacred in Dinka culture and are the sites where special songs are performed to affirm the social and spiritual values of the clan. Ox songs are generally performed by young men either while preening their favorite bulls and decorating them with bells and tassels, or leading their bull around the camp in order to make public their exceptional prowess.

Other song types will be performed in a dancing ground beside a village or a group of homesteads, where people will congregate to socialize or to celebrate family rituals. On these occasions, songs are performed in groups of men and women to the accompaniment of a small drum. Dinka dancing is energetic and forceful, and is characterized by jumping as high as possible while holding the arms in the air in imitation of the horns of one's personal bull.

Social Context

"Song of Akuac" was composed in the mid-1980s at the onset of the second civil war. At this time, the song's composer had become a soldier in the Sudan People's Liberation Army (SPLA) and most of his relatives had fled to Egypt, Canada, and the United States. "Song of Akuac" illustrates the tragic circumstances that many families found themselves in as a result of war: an absentee husband, a disillusioned wife who abandons him in favor of other men, and a family home that is all but destroyed as a result.

As marriage is a core institution in Dinka society, and is formalized through the exchange of cattle belonging to various clan members, a large number of people are involved in the networks and obligations of the marital relationship. Accordingly, the dissolution of a marriage does not only impact the nuclear family, but has consequences for the clan in general. This might account for why the composer felt compelled to share the details of his circumstances with his clan members across the world, and why he chose to do so via a culturally legitimate performance practice. The depth of the sympathy that he elicited from his "shaming song" may be measured by the long period that his cassette audio-letter had been in circulation, and, indeed, why it was offered to me as a prime example of how songs are used to maintain intimate familial relationships across extended times and spaces. From this we can see that this cassette tape has played a vital role in mediating these family and clan relationships, effectively standing in as a social partner in the transmission of deeply personal information.

Analysis of the Song Lyrics

As I mentioned earlier, Dinka songs provide an important platform for the public enunciation of a range of subjects and sentiments. Candid pronouncement on the transgressions of others is permitted within the confines of certain song types, their objective being to facilitate emotional catharsis and to restore social harmony. Individuals implicated in another's songs are protected by the employment of poetic language, whose deeper meanings and inferences are understood only by an inner circle of family or clan.

Two contradictions become apparent when listening to "Song of Akuac." First, despite its deeply personal content, the composer does not deliver his message alone but sings in unison with another man. It is not unusual for two friends to perform one another's songs throughout their lives. This often represents a lifelong bond between friends of the same age that will likely have had its origin in the seasonal residencies in the cattle camps. Singing another person's songs, and in unison with

PRIMARY SOURCE

The Song Text

The names in the song have been changed to protect the identities of the people involved. The English translation can only approximate the poetic depth and cultural nuances of the Dinka lyrics:

This is the Song of Akuac
I have stopped milking the cow [I am now an adult man]
I met with the nonsense of the town
But the talk of the town is sticky [morally degenerate]
Akuac has joined this stickiness together with Deng, Biar, and Niyeer
[names of her three lovers]
Deng, Biar, and Niyeer: it is you who put that sickness in her throat
    If you dive deep into the river, you will find black fish
I will dive after you and shame you!
You [Akuac] are a nobody
You walk around with a swagger
Even a chicken has more purpose than you!
    Akuac once loved me
When we married we became well respected
You used to call me Head of the House
Mother of X and Y [two sons, names withheld]
I was recognized in the town of Abi
But you humiliated me
You made me homeless and everybody wondered why
    When these men came to visit, you introduced them as relatives
I sacrificed a sheep for them
After they ate, Yor ['cousin'] left and you followed
I was unaware of what was happening
When I found out, you left me broken
    When war breaks out, conflict is a great equalizer
But still the people of Gogrial know who is who
It is those men who destroyed her.

Deng [generic for 'man'] is a fisherman who sells charcoal in the market
How is he better than me? [referring to his own status as a keeper of cattle, which is considered 'clean' or respectable]
Deng doughnut! [i.e., he cooks like a woman]
Deng fish! [i.e., he smells like a fish]
Deng charcoal! [i.e., he is dirty]
How is Deng better than me?

them, is a deeply empathetic gesture, and in this case represents the friend's profound identification with the pain and humiliation of the composer. Such a performative gesture speaks to the widespread belief in Dinka culture that individuals can only be fully recognized in the context of their clan or community.

The second paradox lies in the contrast between the apparent sweetness of the vocal style and the hard-hitting nature of the lyrics. This mirrors a more fundamental tension between what is often described as the inherently violent disposition of Dinka youth, which is displayed in particular when a young man's dignity has been offended, and the more idealized condition of social harmony and self-control, which is encapsulated in the concept of *cieng*. While Akuac's romantic liaisons may be a fundamental affront to her husband's self-respect, custom dictates that his rage must be contained within the aesthetically circumscribed expressive medium of the song.

A general analysis of the lyrics reveals that the song is presented in narrative fragments, each one addressed to a different audience: to Akuac, her three suitors, and to the composer's clan members, from whom he seeks affirmation. More generally, however, the song is a reflexive meditation aimed at facilitating emotional release and at reinstating the personal dignity of the composer.

Close inspection of the lyrics reveals the discriminating use of rhetorical devices that both reinforce the sentiments of the message and astutely weave his listeners—exclusively clan members—into the singer's "inner world." The first device is the use of metaphors and similes, whose meanings are specifically culturally situated. In the following examples, for instance, the composer comments on certain qualities that are considered damaging to masculine pride in Dinka culture, accusing his wife's suitors of indulging in demeaning work practices that transgress desirable standards of the body and of personal hygiene:

> Deng doughnut! [i.e., he cooks like a woman]
> Deng fish! [i.e., he smells like a fish]
> Deng charcoal! [i.e., he is dirty]

Second, by invoking references to specific smells, touches, and tastes, listeners are intimately woven into the singer's sensory world. The associations of these sensory references are deeply culturally determined, however, and understanding their meanings lends assurance to his audience of the intimacy of their social connection.

Third, the song not only draws diasporic subjects into the composer's experiences of people and places, but makes reference also to actual members of his family. It identifies the places that have significance to them, for example, the region of Gogrial, the town of Ai, and it alludes to the clan's history, for example, the wife, her suitors, and the boy's clan names (which I have not included in the translation). People's identities are signified via their relationships to their maternal and paternal grandparents. By identifying their own personal relationships to these sites and senses, therefore, listeners who have resettled in distant localities of the world are offered visceral claim to the actual places, relationships, and experiences recited in the song. Additionally, by recounting only fragments of his personal experience, the composer invites his listeners to fill in the details of his story, thus summoning their participation in an empathetic co-construction of his narrative.

As we have seen, cassette audio-letters like this infuse old song structures with contemporary concerns that are a product of displacement and migration. They are also increasingly replacing face-to-face interaction as ways of communicating and mediating private information. In this way, they have enabled clan groups who are scattered across the globe to retain intimate connections both with one another and also with their cultural identities.

BIOGRAPHY

The Story of a New Nation

South Sudan is a landlocked country located in the Sahel region of northeastern Africa, and is bordered by six countries, namely Ethiopia, Kenya, Uganda, the Democratic Republic of Congo, the Central African Republic, and Sudan. It is the newest country in the world, having achieved its independence only on 10 July 2011, following almost half a century of civil war against Sudan.

The separation between the nation-states of Sudan and the Republic of South Sudan has a long historical precedent. As with much of pre-colonial Africa, the Sudan region had been home to hundreds of small, discrete kingdoms and city-states. Centuries of trade and migration resulted in the establishment of strong cultural alliances between northern Sudan and the Arab Middle East, while the south became more closely identified with pastoralist groups of East Africa and with Christianity. While its geographical features—its deserts, major rivers and mountains—may originally have been responsible for forging a regional separation between north and south, over time the rift has become deeply inscribed as cultural, linguistic, and religious. This schism was intensified when the British assumed administrative control of Sudan under an Anglo-Egyptian Condominium in 1899, placing the civil service almost exclusively in the hands of northern "Arabs," and largely depriving the south of all rights and benefits from the government. Despite the commitment made to greater equality between regions at the time of Sudan's independence in 1956, the ongoing sense of disenfranchisement in the south led to the development of a low-intensity civil war. By the early 1960s the war had escalated into a full-scale insurgency, causing the death of half a million southerners and forcing many hundreds of thousands into refugee camps in neighboring countries.

Following the accession to power of an apparently moderate government in the north in the early 1970s, a peace agreement was brokered between the two regions, and the country enjoyed 10 years of relative peace and prosperity. Although the peace accord stated that the south would be able to develop its cultures and religions within a united socialist Sudan, commitment to these aims was short-lived. By the early 1980s, the government had embarked on a systematic campaign to "Arabize" the entire country, pronouncing Arabic the official national language, and instituting an authoritarian interpretation of Islamic law. These, and a range of other alleged violations, prompted the resumption of civil war, this time far more brutal than the last and resulting in the death of some 2 million southerners.

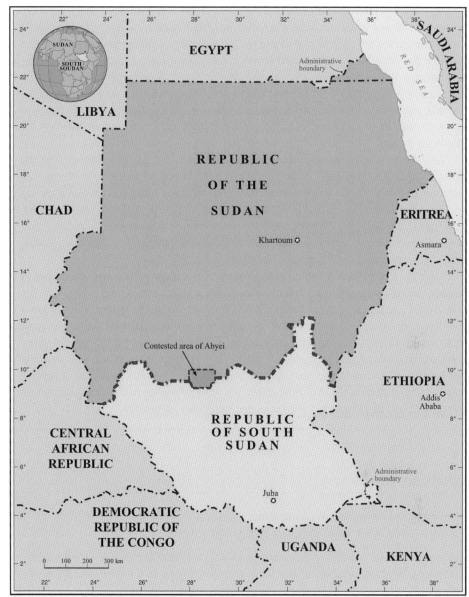

Map compiled from United Nations data, for information purposes only. Borders are approximate.

FIGURE 11.4 Republic of South Sudan

In 2005, a Comprehensive Peace Agreement was signed between the Sudan People's Liberation Army in the south and the government of Sudan. The agreement provided for a six-year interim period of autonomy for South Sudan, and was followed by a referendum that allowed the people of the south to determine their future status. In January 2011, the south voted overwhelmingly in favor of secession, and in July that year they formally celebrated their independent sovereignty as the Republic of South Sudan.

The wars in Sudan generated forced migration on an unprecedented scale, creating the world's largest crisis of human displacement. The heaviest toll on the southerners took place during the second civil war, when an estimated 5 million people were forced to flee their homes. Many sought protection in refugee camps in Uganda, Chad, Ethiopia, and northern Kenya. Hundreds of thousands fled to Egypt, a large number of whom were subsequently repatriated by the United Nations High Commissioner for Refugees to Canada, Australia, and the United States. Countless more travelled to north Sudan, and to the capital city of Khartoum, in particular, where they were classified as internally displaced people.

The arduous process of repatriating exiles to South Sudan began in earnest with the referendum in 2010. However, resettlement has been heavily impeded by ongoing violence, both with Sudan in the north, and between groups competing for land, cattle, and resources within South Sudan. While a significant number of people who migrated to countries in the Global North have begun to return home, bringing with them badly needed education and technical skills, their long-term commitment to their desperately under-resourced homeland has been justifiably restrained.

Currently, a polygamous Dinka family unit will often consist of one wife and family in a northern locality (e.g., Omaha, USA), a second wife and family in a neighboring country (e.g. Kenya), while the husband resides in South Sudan, where he is preparing for the eventual homecoming of the entire family. Given this distributed existence, Dinka families often appear to exist in a constant state of mobility. While in the past they would have pursued the seasonal rotation between several cattle camps and villages, their mobility occasioned by economic necessity and familial rites and activities, today they seem to follow a similar pattern of circumnavigation; the main difference being that the world has effectively been gathered into their social and economic rangelands.

Discussion Topics

- In what ways do conditions of war affect musical practices? Do some research on music in other parts of the world which are affected by conflict.

- In other cultures, marital or relationship problems are dealt with in other media and contexts. What advantages do you think song might have as a medium for expressing these kinds of issues?

- What are the differences between a cassette and an mp3, and how do these differences affect the ways in which they are used and circulate?

Further Listening

Music of the Sudan: The Role of Song and Dance in Dinka Society, Album One: War Songs and Hymns (FW04301, Smithsonian Folkways, Washington, DC, 1976).

Music of the Sudan: The Role of Song and Dance in Dinka Society, Album Two: Women's Dance Songs (FW04302, Smithsonian Folkways, Washington, DC, 1976). *Music of the*

Sudan: The Role of Song and Dance in Dinka Society, Album Three: Burial Hymns and War Songs (FW04303, Smithsonian Folkways, Washington, DC, 1976).

>   Three albums containing a rich selection of 1976 recordings made by Francis Mading Deng. Extensive liner notes include English translations of song lyrics.

Recommended Reading

Deng, Francis Mading (1972) *The Dinka of the Sudan*. New York: Holt, Rinehart, & Winston.

>   Francis Mading Deng was the son of a Dinka chief, and undertook postgraduate studies in law at Yale and in London. The author of many books on Sudanese and Dinka history, culture, and politics, he is also a leading Sudanese diplomat and statesman.

Deng, Francis Mading (1973) *The Dinka and their Songs*. Oxford: Oxford University Press.

>   A detailed overview of Dinka song practices by a cultural insider, introducing cattle songs, hymns, and more songs dealing with relations between men and women, including some songs composed by women.

Deng, Francis Mading (1978) *Africans of Two Worlds*. New Haven, NJ: Yale University Press.

>   Extracts from 11 interviews with Dinka chiefs, recorded in 1972 and 1973, with commentaries.

Eggers, Dave (2006) *What is the What?* London: Hamish Hamilton Ltd.

>   A novel based on the real-life story of Valentino Achak Deng, a Dinka refugee who escaped Sudan as a child. It describes his journey through the refugee camps of Ethiopia and Kenya to the United States, and the hardships of his new life.

Lienhardt Godfrey (1961) *Divinity and Experience, the Religion of the Dinka*. Oxford: Oxford University Press.

>   A classic study of religion by a British anthropologist, based on long-term fieldwork among the Dinka in the early twentieth century.

Ryle, John (1982) "Warriors of the White Nile, The Dinka." In *Peoples of the World*. Amsterdam: Time-Life Books.

>   An accessible photographic introduction to the Dinka.

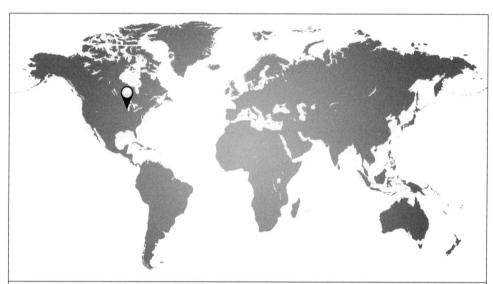

Location: Lake Meadow Shopping Center, Southside Chicago, USA

Strange Routes: "Dancing Girl": Flows, Formats, and Fortune in Music

Sung by Terry Callier; recorded by Cadet Records, 1972

Chapter twelve

Strange Routes: "Dancing Girl"

Flows, Formats, and Fortune in Music

Caspar Melville

Summary

In this chapter, I will tell the story of how one record—Terry Callier's *What Color is Love*, recorded in Chicago in 1972, bought in a second-hand record shop in California in 1989—came to be in my hands as I sit in Central London, England, in 2014. It is a story that suggests the importance of movement in culture. We often assume a close relationship between culture and place, and imagine that cultural expression articulates the essence of a particular people or society. But such a view produces a very static notion of how culture works. What if we take another tack and focus instead on how culture moves: how cultural products produced in one context can acquire new meanings in other contexts far removed in space or time. If we supplement our image of cultural "roots" with a notion of "routes," we can focus on exploring the journeys culture makes, and pay attention to the processes of **hybridity** that create new forms of culture. Through mixing different traditions a new image of how culture and music circulate emerges.

This chapter also aims to show how movement through time and space can also be evoked through music. I focus on just one of the album's tracks, one that best exemplifies the distinctiveness of Callier's sound, the unusually long opening track "Dancing Girl." With words and music by Callier, this song traces its own journey through the history of black American music, referencing, in miniature, Afro-American musical styles from New Orleans jazz to gospel and electrified soul, providing an almost cinematic tour of black life in the 1970s.

KEY WORDS
- diaspora
- musical referencing
- race
- recording formats
- studio mixing

Why this Piece?

Music is intangible by its very nature, yet we tend to speak about it as if it were something material, something solid. Something made from—composed of—pieces. As in this book's title, we conventionally use the word "piece" metaphorically, to identify a particular instance of music—a song, a symphony, a jingle—but much of our experience of music actually comes via a more or less physical form, a "piece" of music such as a CD, a digital file, a cassette tape, or a vinyl record.

I hold one such piece of music in my hand. It is flat, less than an eighth of an inch thick, about 12 inches square: a grooved black plastic disc in a cardboard sleeve. When I hold it, it is mute. But I can, if I want, take the disc from the sleeve, put it on a rotating table, place a needle attached to an arm onto its grooves, and it will reveal itself as sound, organized in a special way: a way that I love. This record is more than 40 years old, although I have had it for only 23 of those years. I know where it was made but I do not know what journeys it took in its first 17 years of life. I do know that it has travelled tens of thousands of miles with me. Records can have value for any listener, but they take on a particular importance for those who work as DJs (disc jockeys), for whom records (at least until the development of digital **mixing** devices) were the primary tools of the trade. As the property of a sometime DJ, this record has travelled with me numerous times in my record box to gigs in London, New York, Plymouth, and San Francisco.

Let me describe this piece of music: it is an LP (long player,) also known as an album, called *What Color is Love*, a collection of seven songs by the African-American singer-songwriter Terry Callier, released in 1972 by the Chicago label

FIGURE 12.1 **Cover image from Terry Callier's** *What Color is Love*

Cadet Records (a subsidiary of Chess Records). On the front is a photograph shot by the renowned photographer Joel Brodsky: a beautiful naked woman with coffee-colored skin sits curled up on an armchair (artfully arranged so as to conceal her modesty), gazing mournfully into the middle distance, smoking a cigarette from which she is too melancholy to flick the accreted ash. The sleeve of my record is somewhat time worn with a faint stain (coffee?), and the corners are crumpled, revealing the fact that it has passed through many hands and been much played. A sticker on the top says "Logos," identifying the shop, in Santa Cruz, California, where I bought it, and revealing that it cost me $5.

Attending to the "strange routes" that culture travels (the title of this chapter is a deliberate echo of Billy Holiday's anti-lynching song "Strange Fruit") reveals how virulent and promiscuous art and culture can be, how little they respect the boundaries assumed to separate people into discrete races, ethnicities, or nations. Music, as the least tangible and most plastic of arts, is particularly well suited to travel, to be shared and in that sharing to be blended and remixed into new forms. The journey made by this record echoes similar journeys made across what the critical theorist Paul Gilroy has termed the Black Atlantic, the pathways criss-crossing the Atlantic Ocean that link Africa, Europe, and the New World, a 400-year circulatory system that saw a huge trade in products and riches from "old world" to new; including, of course, the trade in human beings we call the "Atlantic Slave Trade."

Against a model that views human populations as distinct and separate, which trades on notions of culture as pure or authentic and in need of defence from "contamination," a model that imagines culture as the unalloyed expression of some kind of essence (a perspective known as "essentialism"), the music of the Black Atlantic, of which Terry Callier's album is one small part, represents the counter-vailing importance of mobility and mixing which is often called "hybridity." In this view, culture stands not as a symbol of ethnic or national purity but as a symbol of cooperation, collaboration, and sympathy across lines of race and nation.

This record is just one instance of a vast phenomenon: the surprising ways in which popular art produced in one context can, through the unanticipated flows of global cultural transmission, find value, meaning, and new audiences in very different times and places. In particular, it materializes a link between the cultural and racial politics of 1970s' America and that of Britain's post-colonial cities of the late twentieth century.

But this story also leaves room for the strangeness, the un-anticipatable operation of fortune or serendipity. Chance played a part in dictating why this particular record was made, bought, and then discarded, and in the late flourishing of Terry Callier's musical career long after he himself had given up. There is even a cameo role for an earthquake, without which Callier's record might never have come into my hands.

Musical Features

TIMED LISTENING GUIDE

0:01   *Introduction*: Acoustic guitar plays a repeated pattern, with hand chimes accompaniment

0:18   *Vocal*: Terry Callier sings the opening refrain over guitar with background percussion embellishment

0:41   *Strings*: Including harp, introduced, quietly at first, into the background, remaining behind vocal; guitar and percussion in the mix. At 1:18, an organ enters; prominent and sweeping strings

1:56   *End of Part 1*: Background falls away and we return to acoustic guitar, playing solo at a slow tempo

2:18   *Transition—Welcome to the Twilight Zone*: Strings enter behind the guitar, joined by electric piano (but drop out by 2:30 when voice comes in), then a mournful trumpet, played in an almost New Orleans style, announcing a new phase. Callier's vocals are high in the mix, tempo slow and elegiac

3:14   *Part 2—Meanwhile in the Ghetto*: Acoustic guitar kicks into a higher tempo playing a funky riff. Tenor sax sails in behind the vocal, played in the **bebop** style of Charlie Parker as Callier sings of "Bird playing in his room." The pattern of the sung vocal echoes Charlie Parker's bebop experiments with rhythm, tune, and tempo. The musical background with drums, walking bass, and keyboard fills, connotes the feel of a jazz club. The vocals are again at the front of the mix; Callier's voice strong but also near breaking, charged with pain

4:03   *. . . just a little further down the road*: An insistent horn riff announces another change of pace, the tempo increases as the scene moves from Bird's hotel room out onto the streets

        Background fills with horns, strings, drums, and bass; sense of anguish and drama accentuated with horns, strings, and cymbals higher in the mix. More sleazy piano sound

4:43   *Boogie, bop or boogaloo?*: As Callier imagines a prostitute's encounter with a customer, equating black musical styles with sex, the band emerges playing a kind of sleazy jazz with bass and trap drums prominent in the mix

5:10   *Here Comes the Funk*: A cymbal cascade brings the section to an end; as it dies away a new funky bass ostinato emerges before a strong backbeat on the drums kicks off an insistent up-tempo funk rhythm, but with the addition of folk-style acoustic guitar. Callier sings in a **scat** style that does away with words

        The piece builds as horns, strings, and the whole ensemble join in a crescendo that rises and falls several times in euphoric waves before falling apart in cymbal cascades and increasingly pained vocal exhortations

7:33   *All Fall Down*: Out of the cymbal and snare cascade emerges the same acoustic guitar riff as in the introduction. "I saw a dream last night"

        Sweeping strings, glockenspiel, and electric piano to close

What Color is Love was the second album in a series of three that Callier recorded for Cadet Records. All three were produced, arranged, and conducted by the producer/arranger Charles Stepney who developed a distinctive sound that combined soul, **"psychedelic"** rock and sweeping strings associated with Western classical music. Stepney's fusion of these different genres was ahead of its time, and not universally admired. Soul and rock fans were wary of the use of orchestration, which they feared might gentrify music that relied on a gritty feel, while the mainstream pop and classical audience found the soulful and psychedelic elements alien. Callier's Stepney-produced albums were critically acclaimed but they failed to sell. Yet Stepney's sound would go on to have a huge influence on popular music, providing inspiration for the **disco** explosion of the late 1970s.

For Callier's albums, Stepney designed a soundscape that married Callier's soulful voice and acoustic guitar with the driving rhythms of **R&B** and a lush orchestration usually associated with romantic ballads. The lyrics, all written by Callier, combine personal themes of love and loneliness with the hot political themes of the day, such as the need for racial justice, and the ethics of war. In addressing racial justice and the Vietnam war, Callier was working within the "protest soul" tradition that was typical of this era in black American music, exemplified by Marvin Gaye's 1971 LP *What's Going On*. But Callier imported a distinctly "folk" element into his sound that was unusual for black music of the period. He drew on tropes made familiar in the folk tradition of Woody Guthrie and Pete Seeger—drifters, trains, the virtues of the "ordinary Joe" (the title of one of Callier's songs)—and his pleas for social justice were pitched in terms that were not confined to America's black population. In the context of America's racial segregation of the period, this mixing of "black" and "white" forms of musical expression was politically significant but also commercially risky.

FIGURE 12.2 **Lake Meadow Shopping Center, Southside Chicago, 1973**
John H. White/EPA. Licensed under the Creative Commons

So what does it sound like? The first thing to note is the wide range of sound textures achieved through the use of a very big band. Its core comprised some 30 veteran Chicago session men who had played on hundreds of blues, jazz, and soul records released during the golden age of the city's record industry; many of them were accomplished jazz soloists and band leaders in their own right. This core band was supplemented with the string section of the Chicago Philharmonic Orchestra, frequent collaborators with Stepney. Behind Callier's distinctive vocals and acoustic guitar, always front and center in the mix, sits a funk band comprising two electric bass guitars, electric guitar, drum kit, electric piano, congas, bongos, and a variety of other percussion instruments; a horn section comprising trumpet, alto and tenor sax, flute and French horns; and a large string section comprising violins, violas, cellos, and a harp. The recording, involving the labor of so many people over several days in the state-of-the-art RCA studios in downtown Chicago, represented a significant investment by Cadet.

"Dancing Girl" is densely textured and passes through a variety of moods swings and tonal changes, but it is relatively simple in form. Using a limited range of melodic materials and simple alternating harmonies underpinned by a consistent rhythmic pulse, it gains its force from the way the elements of voice, guitar, percussion, drums, strings, and horns are brought in and out of the mix. It is testament to Charles Stepney's great skill with a multi-track recording desk. Although there is some evidence of overdubbing and a few subtle effects, the overall feel is of a live recording; studio trickery is at a minimum and the entire ensemble sounds like it is playing together in real time.

"Dancing Girl" is framed at the beginning and end by a dream sequence. Over a backdrop of acoustic guitar line and tinkling hand chimes, Callier paints the image of the dancing girl, "a vision in amber lace," who moves with "such rhythm and grace." He enjoins the listener to follow her to "a quiet place, somewhere between time and space," a place where "we shall be free." The girl embodies a kind of utopia, the possibility that art—surely what the girl symbolizes? —might offer comfort or salvation.

But salvation from what? The music is about to tell us. As the delicate mood of the opening section begins to break down we realize that the music is not leading us to a place of freedom, or not yet at least. In place of the beguiling dancing girl, we get a nightmarish vision of existential despair. Callier's voice drops a register: "Each of us is born alone," he sings over a plangent trumpet, "Well, welcome to the Twilight Zone." This carries a double meaning. It references both the popular American science fiction program *The Twilight Zone*, and conjures the liminal, twilight world of the American ghetto. The melancholy trumpet line is played by veteran jazz trumpeter Art Hoyle, who also played with the avant garde Sun Ra Arkestra, providing a sonic link to the jazz past. The nightmarish quality of the passage is underscored by the loss of meaning, even music loses it power: "Things we cannot see appear, singing songs we cannot hear."

We come to the first of two almost cinematic vignettes of black life in America: "Meanwhile in the ghetto dust and gloom . . . and Bird is playing in his room."

We are transported to a run-down hotel where a great artist struggles alone with his demons. Callier imagines the great jazz alto saxophonist Charlie "YardBird" Parker practicing in his room, as Don Myrick's alto plays in a style that evokes Bird's canonical bebop jazz. Lyrics and musical form combine in a plea to Parker, a notorious heroin addict, to set aside the drugs. Callier's vocal lines echo Parker's trademark melodic runs and repetitions: "all those, all those notes, all those notes, can't take the pain away/man you'll surely come to harm/with that needle on up in your arm/and dope can never turn the night to day."

Then another transition, as the virtual camera pulls back from the room and sweeps: "just a little further down the road . . . baby sister walks these streets at night." The music becomes funkier, more menacing and tougher, as we travel in space and time from Bird's bebop hotel of the 1940s to the "blaxploitation" streets of 1970s America where Afro-American woman are forced into prostitution by poverty and drug addiction: "well the wind blow heavy/and the children need new shoes." Callier's tone combines compassion for the addict and the hooker with a strong sense of social anger. In this passage, he draws a remarkable analogy between sexual services and musical styles: "tell her what you want to do," he cajoles the listener, now cast in the role of the client, "boogie, bop, or boogaloo." In this scenario, Callier is acting as the pimp; clearly, these musical terms are standing in for sexual positions that can be purchased from the streetwalker. But they also refer to the ancient racist equation between blackness and unbridled sexuality, historically a source of anxiety for white America. They can also be read to suggest the link between fear and desire that lies behind racism, where the "other" is assumed to have innate almost animal-like physical characteristics—strength, grace, musicality, sexual magnetism—for which they are both feared and desired." In this reading, black music serves as something both forbidden and exotic, a commodity to be sampled by culture tourists from the better side of town, like the white New Yorkers of the 1920s and 1930s venturing uptown to Harlem's nightclubs in search of dance music and forbidden thrills before jumping back in their limos and returning to the safety of the white city downtown.

In another twist of mood, the song moves beyond these tightly drawn vignettes, beyond language itself. The music takes another step toward electrified funk, punctuated with horn stabs reminiscent of the funk sound made popular by James Brown. Callier eschews lyrics and breaks into a form of vocalese, as if language were no longer adequate to express the emotion of lives squandered in the American ghetto. The music combines influences from across the spectrum of jazz, from the bebop sounds of the 1940s to the late 1960s experiments in **"free jazz"** of saxophonists John Coltrane and Ornette Coleman.

The track swirls to a crescendo, until itself breaking down again, the bass line stutters, the cymbals fizz to a kind of musical whiteout. Out from under emerges once again the solo acoustic guitar, and the voice of the opening dream sequence. We are back in Callier's dream, following the dancing girl. Now we have been shown the degradations of the ghetto—addiction, prostitution, racism—we can see why we might need to go beyond time and space, to find a place of safety and unity. We can feel what it might be like to be free.

BIOGRAPHY

Terry Callier, who died in 2012, was born in Northside in Chicago in 1945. He grew up in a city rich with black musical traditions (a cradle of jazz in the 1920s and 1930s and the Blues in the 1940s and 1950s) and thick with music-making. Callier, schooled in popular song and jazz by his musical mother, started his career singing in local doo-wop groups. He gradually developed a distinctive style that merged the traditions of Afro-American popular music—R&B, soul and jazz—with American folk, the music of Pete Seeger and Woody Guthrie which played such an important part in the counterculture in the 1960s.

After an audition at Chicago's legendary Chess Records when he was just 18, Callier's first single "Look at Me Now" was released on that label's more experimental imprint, Cadet, in 1962. Although this was as a fairly conventional upbeat soul record, even then the distinct timbre of Callier's voice suggested a contrast to the rougher textures of the soul vocal tradition and a deeper connection to folk traditions than was usual in Afro-American popular music. Cadet offered Callier a place on tour with Etta James and Muddy Waters, but his mother insisted he stayed home to study for his exams.

His first studio album, *The New Folk Sound of Terry Callier*, was released in 1968 (it had been recorded several years earlier but his producer had disappeared into the Mexican desert with the tapes). Tracks such as "900 Miles (from Home)" and "I'm a Drifter" mark a connection to American folk tradition, suggesting a deep investment in the lives of the disempowered and transient, particularly the hobo, which he shared with the folk troubadours.

FIGURE 12.3 **Terry Callier performing in Stockholm, late 1990**

Photograph by Johan Palmgren

He released a series of albums for Cadet in the early 1970s and two for Electra records in at the end of the decade. Although always well reviewed, none of Callier's albums was commercially successful. In the early 1980s he retired from music, taking a job as a computer programmer at the University of Chicago in order to support his daughter.

[Some of this information is derived from an interview I conducted with Callier for a British jazz magazine, *Jazid*, in 2002.]

Social Context

Tryin' Times, America in the 1970s

In his song writing, Terry Callier cut across the "color line" that demarked American music. He drew consciously on both black and white traditions in his music, jointly claiming both jazz saxophonist John Coltrane and country and western singer Hank Williams as influences. Although he fits within the tradition of radical black musicians, like the politically outspoken singers Gil Scott Heron and Eugene McDaniels, Callier's tone was less confrontational, more akin to the dignified non-violence of Martin Luther King. Callier's challenge to the ideology of racial superiority, and the continuation of racialized inequality, gained power from the simple and unpretentious way in which it was delivered. Posing a deceptively simple question such as "What color is love?," with the obvious answer that love knows no color, effectively undermines arguments about ethnic or racial purity or who is entitled to love whom. Against a backdrop of racial segregation and deep lying anxieties around racial mixing, Callier projected a hybrid of "white" and "black" musical styles, a socially conscious music aimed at healing America's racial rifts. This made his music original, but it also made it hard to market. Was he a soul man, a jazz man, a folk singer?

The world into which Callier released *What Color is Love* was marked by social and economic crisis and racial strife. Just as it was released, the catastrophic OPEC embargo led to rocketing oil prices that shook the economies and confidence of the Western democracies, America in particular. The preceding decade in America had seen a series of bloody political catastrophes including the assassination of President John F. Kennedy in 1963, and then his younger brother Senator Bobby Kennedy in 1968. The escalating conflict in Vietnam, "children fighting their father's war," as Callier puts it in "Ho Tsee Mee (Song of the Sun)" from the same album, was rapidly losing public support as images of the conflict were beamed directly into American living rooms on evening TV news reports. Racial conflict had boiled over in the late 1960s following the assassination of Malcolm X in 1965 and civil rights leader Martin Luther King in 1968. American cities became the scenes of violent confrontation between black youth and police throughout the late 1960s, often in response to police brutality. Full-scale riots in Watts, California, in 1965 and Detroit, Michigan, in 1967, were echoed in hundreds of other towns following King's assassination. In 1968, Callier's hometown of Chicago was the scene of some of the worst violence as the police force attempted to suppress anti-Vietnam demonstrations. Callier's music of the early 1970s, even the love songs, is thick with the sense of injustice and the melancholy of the politics of this period.

Popular music in America had long been a racially divided industry, reflecting the racial segregation that held sway since slavery was abolished. In the south, black people were forbidden from sharing amenities with whites, but even in the supposedly more enlightened northern cities the races lived largely separate lives with different neighborhoods, facilities, and entertainments. Race mixing in music, although in practice common, was still controversial. At some musical venues, and not just in the south, black band members had to use a separate entrance. Even jazz stars such as Duke Ellington and Miles Davis, who were widely feted by the white intelligentsia, found themselves subject to discrimination and police brutality.

The popular music charts had been divided along racial lines since the 1930s; black music sales were counted separately in the Billboard chart. Initially the market for black music was called "race records" then, as the music changed, "rhythm and blues," then "R&B" and, by 1972, "soul." Whatever the name, the effect was to keep black music quarantined in its own ghetto, even as it supplied the inspiration for many of the major innovations in mainstream popular music.

This racial distinction carried over into the companies that recorded and released the music. Record labels generally considered themselves to be suppliers to one or the other racial group, rarely both. Most major labels focused on bankable stars, and that meant predominately white artistes who would sell in white suburbia and were acceptable to advertisers and sponsors on commercial radio (no matter that they might be playing music that was clearly black in origin). The much smaller and poorer black market was catered for either by specialist divisions within major labels, or by a handful of independents such as the Vee Jay label in Gary, Indiana. Those who, like Callier, refused to recognize the clear demarcations on which the market depended were far more likely to suffer than succeed. Despite critical acclaim, Callier's hybrid music could not find a market. By the 1980s, a frustrated Callier quit music altogether, and did not touch a guitar for five years. And that could have been the end of his story. But it wasn't.

2-tone: London in the 1980s

The London of the 1980s is separated from 1970s' Chicago by a decade and 4000 miles, but they had important things in common. Britain in the 1980s was experiencing unprecedentedly high levels of social upheaval and political ferment; an unpopular war was being fought, racial tensions were high, and musicians of the period channeled their feelings about these things into song. A socially conservative government under Prime Minister Margaret Thatcher, elected in 1979, instituted sweeping and contentious changes, including the widespread privatization of public services and, although it hardly compares to the protracted quagmire of Vietnam, the futile armed conflict with Argentina over the tiny Falkland Islands in 1982 was unpopular and divisive.

Unlike America, the majority of the black British population came to Britain as voluntary migrants, most from the former British colonies in the Caribbean (Jamaica, Trinidad, Barbados, St Lucia) during the 1950s and 1960s. Although they were the descendants of Africans transported to the New World as slaves, often by British merchant slave ships, they were officially British citizens—since everyone living under British imperial rule had the right to a passport—and had come to the "mother country" seeking employment and a better life. The majority settled in the major cities, including London and Birmingham. In many places, to their great surprise and outrage, rather than being greeted as fellow citizens, these migrants were met with hostility and racism.

In 1968 Conservative politician Enoch Powell made a famous speech in which he foresaw race-mixing leading to "rivers of blood." Many, including some trades unions, supported his position. The government responded by increasingly tightening immigration controls. Tensions rose throughout the 1970s, exacerbated by economic crisis and the decline of British manufacturing. Unemployment soared in the early 1980s and explicitly racist politics were on the rise. The National Front,

FIGURE 12.4
Poster for the Rock Against Racism carnival, London, 1978, which featured both reggae and punk bands

a neo-fascist party dedicated to "keeping Britain White," gained some popular support, and a new youth subculture, the skinheads, emerged. They somehow managed the precarious psychological feat of loving Jamaican music while violently attacking black people. Racially motivated street violence became commonplace.

By the 1980s, when the "second generation," the British-born children of Caribbean migrants, were reaching adulthood, a sense of widespread dissatisfaction at discrimination, police brutality, and inequality created a mood of militancy among black British youth. This mood found an appropriate soundtrack initially in the rebellious sounds of Jamaican roots reggae, Bob Marley in particular, which then inspired a new British scene—2 Tone—where racially mixed bands such as The Specials blended Jamaican ska with punk into a distinctively multiracial British genre.

In 1981, and again in 1985, British cities with significant black populations exploded into violence, as young people, most but not all black, resisted what they saw as deliberately targeted police brutality. Through such insurrections and associated community activism—including the Rock Against Racism campaign and the Anti-Nazi league which both realized the political power of popular culture—new multicultural alliances emerged. These alliances were secured and deepened through music.

As Britain's manufacturing industries, docks, shipbuilding, steel, and mining, suffered serious decline, new possibilities for sociality and creativity were emerging among the ruins of London's former industrial might. The once thriving warehouses and factories of London's defunct port in the east of the capital, now stood dormant. Young people, black and white, recognized the new opportunities the space offered. A multicultural generation of entrepreneurs and hustlers exploited these possibilities to create a new nighttime economy for the capital. Empty warehouses, considered redundant and therefore not well guarded, were taken over. A sound system was set up, DJs would supply the records, flyers were rapidly printed and distributed, a simple bar could be stocked with a trip to the cash and carry. These were the makings of the all-night dance parties that became known as "warehouse parties." Scores of such parties were held all over London between 1985 and 1990, in old warehouses, factories, cinemas, docks, even temporarily empty offices.

What was distinctive about these warehouse parties was the composition of the crowd and the music. London nightlife up until that point had been relatively restrictive: clubs required local authority licenses, which in turn required good relations with the police. Commercial clubs employed aggressive bouncers and an informal kind of racial apartheid operated. Young black men trying to get into the mainstream venues in the West End often found themselves excluded because they were assumed to be troublemakers. An informal network of clubs and parties existed in London neighborhoods with a high concentration of Caribbean migrants: Brixton in the south, Tottenham in the north, Ealing in the west. These semi-hidden zones of black sociability resounded primarily to Jamaican reggae and ska. Meanwhile clubs uptown (with the exception of a few specialist soul nights) favored a playlist of established chart hits or commercial disco.

FIGURE 12.5 Flyer for clubs organized by Shake and Fingerpop, a group of promoters and DJs from West London led by DJ Norman Jay (MBE), named after a track by American R&B artist Junior Walker

The warehouse parties, for the first time, brought these constituencies together in a new kind of space that was beyond surveillance by police, and outside the usual zones of turf warfare that stratified youth culture. Here the crowd could decide its own music policy. The result was club nights that were remarkable for the racial mix of the audience, who came from across London to congregate in out of the way or abandoned areas such as the old docks in Southwark, or the abandoned warehouses in Paddington Basin. And what music was deemed appropriate for this new social formation? Although influenced both by reggae and by the new sounds of American hip hop, the primary musical resources were black American soul-jazz and funk from the early 1970s. This music, both socially conscious and attuned to the dance floor, was long forgotten in America. It was also almost entirely unknown to the new audience in the UK.

Within this new scene, the role of DJ as curator and aficionado—the person who finds and selects unknown music on behalf of the dancing crowd—took on special importance. Because this music was old and in many cases out of print, the so-called "Rare Groove" scene stood outside the usual circuits of the music industry. These vinyl records were hard to find and the only place they could be heard was at a party or on an illegal pirate radio station.

Prominent within this scene were three powerful narrative themes. The first was a close association with black politics and social life, a determinedly social realist outlook that narrated the stories of black suffering in America. An emblematic example is Marlena Shaw's "Woman of the Ghetto," addressed to American politicians: "You may have been to one ghetto, but have you lived there at all?" Crucially, although the song has a dark subject, it has a driving funk rhythm designed for the dance floor. This social realist aesthetic was reinforced with an underlying identification with Africa, as the Afrocentric politics of Afro-American radicalism infiltrated the music. The idea of Africa functioned as a powerful critique of the West and a political idea that another way was possible for those who suffered at the hands of white supremacy. It also ensured that the crime of slavery was kept alive in popular memory, as a reminder of a wrong not yet righted. A third

PRIMARY SOURCE

In 1991 Eddie Pillar, the head of the London-based record label Acid Jazz, wanted to re-release one of Terry Callier's lesser known singles, "I Just Can't See Myself (Without You)," which had become popular in his own club. Pillar, a canny entrepreneur, wanted to capitalize on Callier's status in the UK but he needed Callier's permission to re-release. On making some enquiries, it became clear that no one knew where he was. Cadet thought he might have moved to LA, but no one could say for sure. Pillar persevered, calling US Directory Enquiries until he finally turned up an entry for Terence Orlando Callier, at an address in a Chicago suburb. When Pillar called, the girl who answered the phone said there was no Terry at that address and hung up. He called again the next day, and the next, with the same result. But Pillar kept plugging away and eventually the exasperated teenager handed the phone to her father, who said, "This is Terry. My daughter says if I don't speak to you you'll keep calling forever." Pillar explained what he wanted and invited a very skeptical Callier to London to perform.

Later that year Callier travelled to London with his daughter and played a gig at the famed jazz venue known as The 100 Club on Oxford Street. It was full to capacity and afterwards an emotional Callier expressed his great surprise that the members of the audience were able to sing along to every word of every song, even the nine-minute long "Dancing Girl." Thus was Callier's career, long failed, and forgotten in the land of his birth, revived. Over the next two decades Callier toured the UK frequently (initially keeping his university job and touring during holidays). He recorded five studio albums for a variety of UK labels (including the ultra-hip Talkin' Loud), and released a slew of singles, some of which were collaborations with the most progressive of new artists such as Massive Attack, 4Hero, and Beth Orton. His 1998 album *Timepeace* won a United Nations award.

FIGURE 12.6
Acid jazz re-release of
"I Just Can't See Myself"

Formats

TECHNOLOGY

The history of music, as the popular music academic Simon Frith has argued, is itself partly a history of the technology of storage and recall. With the development of sound recording and storage—Edison's aluminium disks, Berliner's wax cylinders, and then, ingeniously the Shellac discs made from ground-up Indonesian bugs—music became easier to store and to transport, and to buy and sell. Cheaper and more capacious methods of storage—the magnetic tape cassette, the CD, and now the immaterial digital file and the limitless virtual shelves of the Cloud—have greatly accelerated the mobility of music, but this movement of music via networks of sharing, and social relationships did not start with the internet. Music has always moved. The ability to render sound as a thing, to capture it, and then sell it, created the conditions of the global music market. But it also freed music from its embeddedness in particular places, peoples, and communities.

The proliferation of the internet, and in particular the activity of music fans who upload their favorite tracks to YouTube to be listened to for free, means that a moment's search will turn up all the tracks from *What Color is Love*, and dozens of other recordings. Combined views for all the different video versions of "Dancing Girl" add up to several hundred thousand, which means that far more people have heard the song now than ever did when it was first released. An anomalous effect of the digitization of culture of which YouTube is such a huge part has been to revive interest in older musical formats. According to the music industry monitoring group IFPI sales of vinyl records in the US rose by 32 per cent in 2013, an unexpected recovery for a format that was supposed to have been made redundant by new digital formats. The internet appears to be helping to revive these "analog" technologies, serving as an information and sales delivery network for vintage forms of culture. You can even pick up your own copy of the original pressing of *What Color Is Love* from the auction site eBay for around $100. Culture is in constant motion as new technologies open up new possibilities and new mixes give rise to new kinds of popular art.

narrative was a strong sense that music would be able to create a new kind of meaning beyond race; that music and dance could offer not only a sanctuary from the everyday violence of racial hatred, but also a point of connection and a motivation for a new form of sociopolitical solidarity: a soundtrack for freedom played out in a community of dancing bodies.

In this music, social realism, black radical politics, and Afrocentric yearning sat on top of music that was geared around dance. It was an ideology of movement that argued that occupying space and dancing to this soundtrack of Afro-American politics was an act of political resistance in itself. And although most of the music was made by black Americans, for and about black people and the black experience, still the producers of the parties, DJs, promoters, and the crowd were racially mixed. Whatever lessons the music had to teach could, as critical theorist Paul Gilroy insists, be taught and learned by anyone who cared to listen and dance.

It should not be hard to see how Terry Callier's music, deliberately crossing color lines, infused with a strong belief in the power of music to heal, could fit so well into such a musical mix. His sophisticated jazzy tempo changes were something of a challenge to the dancer, yet Callier's music was widely circulated among this crowd, swapped on mix tapes, played on the illegal pirate radio stations that held the scene together, and valued by the musical aficionados who came out of the "Rare Groove" scene with a passion for what had previously been discarded. It was on a mix tape made by one of these record collectors that I first heard "Dancing Girl," and by the late 1980s, unbeknownst to Callier himself, "Dancing Girl" had become one of the best loved anthems of the London warehouse party scene. Callier was a star in London, although he did not know it.

Coda: On Serendipity

It was perhaps not entirely by chance that Callier's music had found an audience in Britain in the 1980s and 1990s: the common threads of social and political life gave his music special resonance. But blind chance, or serendipity (if you want to give it a positive spin), does also play a part in how culture moves. For example, I would not have my copy of *What Color is Love*, and could not have written this chapter, without the entirely unanticipated shifting of tectonic plates in northern California, in 1989. If an earthquake measuring 6.9 on the Richter Scale had not rippled along the San Andreas Fault, then Logos, the venerable book and record emporium in Santa Cruz would not have had to close its damaged store and open its storage warehouse as a temporary retail outlet. If it had not had to open its warehouse, it is quite possible that the thousands of records contained in there would not have been put out for sale all at once, and a vinyl-hungry British student might not have been able to wander in one day, and the next day and the next, and rifle through the acres of records to finally alight on an only slightly scratched and well-thumbed original pressing of Terry Callier's *What Color is Love* LP from 1972 for which he paid $5. Thus it is that social forces, personal taste, fortune, and the implacable inevitabilities of catastrophe combined to bring me something I feel like I was meant to have and wouldn't want to be without.

Discussion Topics

- Listen to "Dancing Girl" and pay attention to how it makes you feel. What in the music gives you clues to its emotional mood?

- "Dancing Girl" refers to other kinds of music, for example, the bebop of saxophonist Charlie Parker. Can you think of other examples of music that makes these kinds of reference? Is there a difference between referencing and copying?

- What does it mean to call some music "black" music? Where might "blackness" lie in music? In the sound? In who produces it? In who consumes it? Should race matter in music?

Further Listening

Terry Callier. *The Best of Terry Callier on Cadet* (Charly Records).
Compiled by British DJ Kevin Beadle, this collection brings together the best tracks from all three of Terry Callier's Cadet albums of the early 1970s, including "Dancing Girl," "Alley Wind Song," and "You're Going To Miss Your Candyman."

Woody Guthrie. *The Asch Recordings*, Vols 1–4 (Smithsonian/Folkways).
Perhaps the most important collection of songs in the America's folk tradition from the hugely prolific Woody Guthrie, a big influence on Bob Dylan and Terry Callier.

Charlie Parker. *The Best of Charlie Parker: 20th Century Masters—The Millennium Collection* (Verve).
A good introduction to the music of the alto saxophonist who is widely acknowledged as the outstanding genuises of jazz improvisation. This includes many of his best loved tracks recorded with big and small bands as well as several from his famed (and famously controversial) sessions with strings.

Various 6 *Norman Jay MBE Presents Good Times* (Resist Music).
Part 6 in a long-running compilation series from the godfather of the London "Rare Groove" scene DJ Norman Jay, featuring a signature mix of music from the rare R&B of Archie Bell & the Drells and Lena Horn to the contemporary club music of Bugz in the Attic and DJ Spinna.

Terry Callier. *Total Recall* (Mr Bongo).
On the album from 2003, Terry Callier tracks are remixed by many of the UKs top producers including Groove Armada, Zero 7, and Bluey from Incognito, suggesting his influence lives on for a new generation.

Recommended Reading

Gilroy, Paul (1993) *The Black Atlantic: Modernity and Doubles Consciousness*. London: Verso.
In this hugely influential book, cultural theorist Paul Gilroy argues that the music and culture of the Black Atlantic, which originates in the Atlantic Slave Trade, amounts to a "counterculture" to modernity and carries vital messages that are critical of racism and capitalism and promote the values of freedom and solidarity in a way that is not racially exclusive.

Frith, Simon (1996) *Performing Rites*. Oxford: Oxford University Press.
A sparkling summary of ways of thinking about popular music from the leading popular music scholar. In Chapter 6, Frith explicitly explores the relationship between music and race.

Melville, Caspar and David Hesmondhalgh (2001) "Urban Breakbeat Culture: Repercussions of hip hop in the United Kingdom." In Tony Mitchell, ed. *Global Noise: Rap and Hip Hop Outside the USA*. Middletown, CT: Wesleyan University Press.
This essay analyzes the intimate relationship between American and British Black Atlantic music—which took root in the 1980s around soul and funk and then mutated as hip hop and house—stimulated the evolution of new musical genres in the UK such as acid house and trip hop.

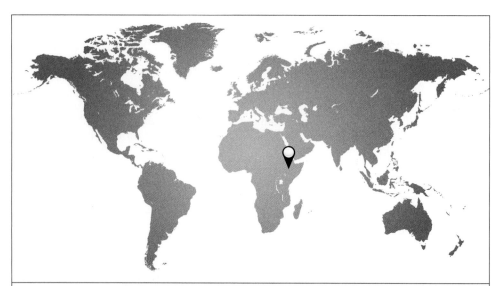

Location: Addis Ababa, Ethiopia

"Tezeta" (Nostalgia): Memory and Loss in Ethiopia and the Diaspora

Performed by Asnaqetch Werqu (voice and *krar*); recorded by Asnaqetch Werqu 1974, PH 215, Philips-Ethiopia; re-released in 2004 by Buda Musique, France

Chapter thirteen
"Tezeta" (Nostalgia)

Memory and Loss in Ethiopia and the Diaspora

Ilana Webster-Kogen

Summary

In an imagined **canon** of Ethiopian songs, the undisputed top position goes to "Tezeta," a song that evokes feelings of sadness and affection for country, friends, and relations. The song's performance practice has changed over time as Ethiopian musicians moved from the countryside to the city, and eventually abroad. Until the 1970s, rural *Azmari*s (folk-poets) performed "Tezeta" on local stringed instruments. In the 1970s, it emerged as the preeminent **Ethiojazz** standard performed on bass guitars and saxophones by Ethiojazz artists. Today "Tezeta" remains a favorite at home while earning special status across the Ethiopian diaspora among migrants who preserve and experiment with it, sampling it in rap songs and adapting the main themes into local languages and musical vernaculars. The song evokes potent nostalgia for the homeland through a lovesick lament in which Ethiopia is subtly personified. Close analysis and mapping of the multitude of "Tezeta" recordings and adaptations explains how trends in Ethiopian music follow the changes in identity and affiliation wrought by 40 years of migratory upheaval.

> **KEY WORDS**
> - bards
> - diaspora
> - migration
> - nostalgia
> - repertoire

Why this Piece?

"I don't understand how you can work on music. When I listen to music, it makes me sad. It's not a good thing." Connecting his troubles in life to his ambivalent feelings towards Ethiopian culture, my friend Abdulmalik was clearly translating the feeling of *tezeta*, or lovelorn nostalgia, one of the most widespread musical concepts in Ethiopia. When he listens to music, he thinks of his family and his country, and he feels sorrow that he has to spend his life working abroad where he has none of the comforts of family.

One of the hardest tasks of cultural translation is learning to understand not only the sounds we hear when we listen to music, but the meaning those sounds have for the people who create them. To Abdulmalik, who grew up Muslim in a mixed-faith family, not all music is equal: Qur'anic recitation would not be classified as music at all, and certain kinds of popular music would be considered immoral. But in our conversation, Abdulmalik refers to one specific style of music: folk songs from Ethiopia, played on a variety of local and Western instruments, in Ethiopian pentatonic modes. By far the most famous of these songs is "Tezeta," and I have heard more versions of it than of any other Ethiopian song.

The first time I heard "Tezeta" I could not have predicted that it would become a crucial song in my work on Ethiopian migrants. At the time, in 2006, I was in my friend's car in New York City, and he was playing a version from the CD series *Ethiopiques*. The version he played featured a brass solo, played on Western instruments, and I recognized many of the musical elements from studying jazz. That version had only a few lines of lyrics, however, and I have often thought there was more emotional resonance in the acoustic versions with long vocal solos, as in the version featured in this chapter. Since 2006, I have heard about a dozen versions in the Ethiojazz style, recorded in Addis Ababa by famous singers from the "Swinging Addis" era before 1974, so named for the vibrant jazz scene and flamboyant clothing that resembled contemporary "Swinging London." I have heard folk versions played by rural *Azmaris* on farms in Ethiopia's northern region, and in ethnographic recordings in university libraries. I have heard recorded versions during set breaks during concerts in Paris, and live versions at Ethiopian restaurants in Tel Aviv, and I have talked about the feeling of *tezeta* with Abulmalik in Abu Dhabi, capital of the United Arab Emirates, where about 100,000 Ethiopians live and work to send money home. Over the years, I have heard Ethiopians across the diaspora summarizing their experience of missing a life that might not even be quite as they remember it through the lens of this potent song.

Musical Features

TIMED LISTENING GUIDE

(quaver = approx. 75)

0.01	Modal introduction. The **krar** comes in alone played by Asnaqetch Werqu, improvising in a minor modal tonality
0.11–0.36	Exposition of the melody. The *krar* gradually settles into the meter that can be understood as a slow 6/8 (around 75bpm). It introduces the basic melodic pattern in one five-**measure** cycle, which will be repeated in different ways almost 20 times. Every verse begins with an ascending major 3rd on top of a semitone
0.38–0.46	First section of vocal cycle: ascent. Asnaqetch Werqu begins to sing, introducing the vocal pattern. In each vocal cycle, the first two measures (and lines of lyrics) are identical melodically, ending on a semitone ascent
0.48–0.57	Second section of vocal cycle: descent/resolution. The lyrics in the third and fourth measures of the cycle both mention *tezeta* (nostalgia/heartsickness). These two measures are melodically identical, descending to resolve on the tonic

0.57–1.02	Final section of vocal cycle: humming. To complete the vocal cycle, the fifth measure is alternately hummed or sung without words. Again, she begins by ascending in semitones and major thirds, and descending to the tonic
1.02–1.26	Recapitulation of the five-measure vocal cycle. Asnaqetch Werqu repeats the vocal cycle, accompanied by the *krar*: two measures ascending, two measures descending and resolving, one measure humming
1.26–1.51	Dropping an octave. Voice sings the descending melodic line for two measures, an octave lower. When Asnaqetch Werqu varies her vocal patterns, or veers from a typical five-note cycle, she fills in the pattern to accommodate. To complete the five-measure cycle after dropping an octave, she sings two descending measures and hums the fifth measure as usual
1.51–2.37	Recapitulation. The five-measure cycle (two measures ending on ascent, two measures ending on descent, fifth measure humming or singing without words) repeats twice
2.37–3.25	Unusual cycles. Werqu changes the formula for the next two vocal cycles: she ends on ascent for the first two measures as usual, and descends on the third, humming measures four and five. For the next cycle, she drops her voice an octave for two measures, and then completes the cycle as usual (two measures ending on descent/resolution, and the last humming)
3.28–4.06	Instrumental interlude. Five-measure cycle followed by an instrumental interlude with only a *krar*. The melodic interlude lasts for one cycle, but we notice here that the measures are less staggered. Werqu plays basically in a 6/8 meter throughout this piece, but she delays or staggers notes frequently when she is singing, which she doesn't do as much when the *krar* plays solo
4.07–4.59	Extra measure added to the cycle. Werqu adds an extra measure to the end of the second cycle here, creating a six-measure cycle
5.00–5.22	Final lyrical vocal cycle and fade-out (three ascending lines). To complete her lyrics, and returning to the word *tezeta*, Werqu sings lyrics in all five of this verse's lines instead of humming the fifth or singing it without words
5.22–5.44	All-humming cycle followed by fade-out. As the song fades out, Werqu hums the last cycle

"Tezeta" originated as a folk song that can be played on either of the main melodic stringed instruments of northern Ethiopia. The most common *Azmari* instrument is the **massenqo**, a one-stringed spike fiddle that is played upright. Perhaps since the *massenqo* only has one string, and the *Azmari* plays the scale with all five fingers, sometimes using the thumb for ornamentation, the Ethiopian pentatonic modal system developed as a method of arranging one's hand around the fingerboard to create new melodies. There are four main modes: *tezeta*, *batti*, *ambassel*, and *anchihoy*, each of which is named after a classic folk song or a town in northern Ethiopia.

Ethiopia is divided into nine main regions, and a different ethnic group of the same name dominates each region: Amhara, Oromia, Tigray, Afar, Harari, Gambela, Somali, Benishangul-Gumaz, and the Southern Nations. The music of these regions varies dramatically, with some regions sharing musical styles with Ethiopia's neighbors (Somalia, Eritrea, Sudan, South Sudan, and Kenya).

FIGURE 13.1 **Asnaqetch Werqu**
Courtesy of Buda Musique

The regions to the east and south have rich musical traditions, often connected to religious lifecycle events.

However, few of the musical styles of these regions are known to the global music market; the music that is exported to the rest of the world comes from the northern regions of Amhara and Tigray, and from the Gurage population areas surrounding the capital, Addis Ababa. The traditional music in this chapter, performed by *Azmari*s, comes from Amhara and Addis Ababa, and is played primarily on the *massenqo*.

In the example given in this chapter, however, the musician Asnaqetch Werqu (1935–2011; see Figure 13.1) plays not the ubiquitous *Azmari massenqo*, but the pleasant *krar*, a six-stringed lyre similar to those found in Sudan and Uganda (see Figure 13.2). The version she plays in this recording is in a minor mode, a variant of the usually major *tezeta* mode. The melodic contour, which gradually descends to the tonic at the end of each vocal line, is mirrored by the lyrics that explain the bittersweet experience of memory.

"Tezeta" can be performed in a city or the countryside, outdoors or inside an *Azmari-bet*, a music house where *Azmari*s improvise lyrics that mock their patrons. This method of improvisation comes from a centuries' old literary tradition called "*sem-enna-werq*," or "wax and gold." Taken from the custom of casting gold in

FIGURE 13.2 **Bowl lyre (*krar*)**

Photography by Christopher White.
Courtesy of the University of Oregon
Museum of Natural and Cultural History

wax, which is then peeled away to reveal the gold, Ethiopian writers use turns of phrase and double meaning to make statements with deeper, sometimes emotional or controversial meaning. Amharic literature and poetry display this technique, and Ethiopians are proud of their longstanding literary tradition. *Azmari*s use the same technique, making seemingly harmless jokes that often cut to deeper critiques of power dynamics and human relations. "Wax and gold" is on full display in virtually every version of "Tezeta" in which an *Azmari* sings that he or she is lovelorn. When they hear a song about an individual, listeners often interpret the song as carrying a double meaning, often assuming that the singer is voicing a political critique, dreaming wistfully of a lost, better time. Since Ethiopia has been under the control of a contested leadership for several decades, and does not enjoy a free press, this longing for better times must be hidden within the "wax" layer of dreaming of a lost lover.

Talking to Ethiopian musicians about songs like "Tezeta" reveals some fixed conventions of musical performance as well as some distinctions between music played inside Ethiopia and music presented to the world. First, while their discussions of "Tezeta" often pay attention to the melody and meter, it is very rare to hear any discussion of **harmony** in Ethiopian music. While both *Azmari* music and its 1970s' descendant Ethiojazz are often polyphonic in texture, different voices are rarely conceptualized as harmonizing with one another. Heterophony and imitative polyphony are common textures: an *Azmari* might play a version of "Tezeta" on the ***washint*** flute in which he plays a highly ornamented melody, and then repeats the identical melody vocally. With the absence of discussion about

TECHNOLOGY

Massenqo versus Synthesizer

The *krar* and *massenqo* are the most important secular stringed instruments in Ethiopia, but they are not necessarily those played most frequently today. If you go to an *Azmari-bet* in Addis Ababa, the *Azmari* will be playing the *massenqo*, and maybe a percussion accompaniment. However, in Eskesta dance videos, and in musical establishments across the Ethiopian diaspora, the **synthesizer** and the drum machine frequently supplement the *massenqo* as a main instrument.

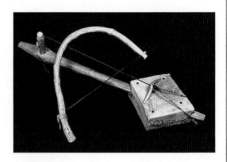

FIGURE 13.3 Massenqo

Photograph by Jack Liu. Courtesy University of the Oregon Museum of Natural and Cultural History

This change has been controversial for a number of reasons. There are arguments of virtuosity—that a synthesizer is programmed to play certain notes, and lacks the capability to demonstrate mastery of the modes. Perhaps more controversially, the widespread use of synthesizers has also prompted the rise of auto-tune, which is looked on with distaste among traditionalists everywhere. Some musicians reject the drum machine and synth on aesthetic grounds, claiming that they play too loudly and drown out the voices of the *Azmari* and/or the *massenqo*. And traditionalists lament the general consolidation of performance styles into a narrower repertoire that does not require as much training.

However, the drum machine has been immensely helpful in certain contexts. In the *Azmari-bet* in Tel Aviv where I did fieldwork in 2009, there often was no dancer on hand to lead the audience in Eskesta dancing. The atmosphere in the club is electrified when the whole audience gets on its feet, so the musicians want people dancing as much as possible. The drum machine promoted audience participation because people felt confident that they could follow the beat when there was a drum machine, but not when they were just following the *massenqo*. In Eskesta videos, the synthesizer is loud, just as its accusers say—but this aesthetic means that the music will be loud enough to create the right ambience for group dancing. A *massenqo* on its own can be very quiet, and a synthesizer offers the kind of amplification and scaling that dance music requires to get the audience really excited.

harmony, musicians tend to emphasize melody as the most important element of most northern Ethiopian musical styles. In *Azmari* performance, the melody is often subordinate to the provocative improvised lyrics, but the solo voice is always played up. In Ethiojazz, by contrast, the key distinguishing characteristic for foreigners who buy the *Ethiopiques* albums is the modal, dissonant sound of the brass melodic instruments.

Discussion of rhythm in Ethiopian music, however, yields far less consensus from musicians and experts. A great deal of the *Azmari* and Ethiojazz repertoire is performed in 6/8, which some musicians will describe as triple meter, and others as a **compound meter** (or duple). Songs in the Ethiojazz style were often rendered in 4/4 to fit with popular music conventions in the 1970s and 1980s. However, it is rare that a musician will describe the **pulse** in such technical terms; it is understood that musicians should be able to switch easily from 6/8 to 4/4, and that they should be able to give it a pulse that sounds like either duple or triple. Perhaps the greatest point of contention in the terminology of Ethiopian music is the importance of rhythm. Readers will certainly be aware that stereotypes circulate of Africa being the "continent of rhythm," and people often generalize that sub-Saharan African music focuses on rhythm above all other elements. Reacting against these stereotypes, Ethiopian music scholars such as Ashenafi Kebede have carefully distanced Ethiopia from the "rest of Africa" and tried to "elevate" Ethiopian music by downplaying the rhythmic aspects of the music. But since much of the music discussed in this chapter exists in part as an accompaniment to dance (particularly Eskesta, the iconic Ethiopian shoulder dance), it makes little sense to downplay the element that most directly influences the embodied aspect of the music for audiences. Perhaps the de-emphasizing over the years of Ethiopian rhythm is connected to the Ethiopian exceptionalist discourse that we will examine later.

Social Context

Ethiopia claims a longstanding literary tradition, but "Tezeta" cannot be traced back to any individual writer. Folk music was performed until recently only in rural areas, where an *Azmari* would sing in the fields and roam the countryside in search of patronage. We can still find *Azmari*s playing in the farmlands of northwestern Ethiopia, but many of them have moved to cities, and in Addis Ababa the *Azmari-bet* is a cornerstone of urban nightlife (see Figure 13.4). In this oral culture, an *Azmari* will choose a mode, and improvise lyrics within that mode, usually mocking the visitors who shower him with money while female dancers dance Eskesta, an important component to any musical performance. Dancers usually wear white robes (even/especially in the diaspora), and women will often wear their hair in intricate braids. Female dancers can dance individually, or in groups of five or more, with or without male dancers. Female dancers also circulate collecting tips, wearing their tips in a headband. The dancer is responsible for getting the audiences on their feet at an *Azmari-bet*, and members of the audience often dance along, clap, or ululate.

Werqu is a rare example of a female *Azmari*. Historically, the *Azmari* profession was hereditary, with fathers teaching their sons before they left home for apprenticeship. Today, musicians still train with their parents, while others train in the church or brass bands, or travel to Addis Ababa to study at the Yared School of Music. Werqu was self-trained, and the first female *Azmari* to rise to national fame. She also worked as an actress in Addis Ababa during Haile Selassie's reign until 1974.

FIGURE 13.4 **CD Cover Showing Interior of an *Azmari-bet***
Courtesy of Buda Musique

Going to an *Azmari-bet* in Addis Ababa is unique because audiences get to see a whole lineup of different musicians in a night, but the conventions of performance are similar anywhere in the world. Many Ethiopian restaurants offer live music and dance. Patrons tend to come with groups of friends or family members, and the *Azmari* circulates around the room to sing to individuals. The lyrics can get quite raucous, and the mood is kept light with free-flowing beer or *tejj*, Ethiopian honey wine. During set breaks, while dancers rest and *Azmari*s switch places, patrons can usually expect a CD of classic songs, and "Tezeta" is frequently on the set list.

"Tezeta" takes on different meanings for residents of Ethiopia and members of the diaspora. As Ethiopia's population is scattered across the world, living in Toronto and London, Washington, DC, and Tel Aviv, "Tezeta" is much more than

PRIMARY SOURCE

Cultural Adaptations in the Diaspora

The biggest Ethiopian diaspora populations live in Washington, DC, and Tel Aviv, each with over 100,000 Ethiopian migrants. The "DC Ethiopians" are often prosperous, consisting of elites who fled Addis Ababa before the military dictatorship took over in 1974. Many of these people were able to take their assets with them, and have integrated comfortably into American life. Ethiopian-Israelis, on the other hand, have had a much harder time integrating. Most of these migrants, who are now permanently settled in Israel, come from Gondar in northwestern Ethiopia. This population, sometimes known as Beta Israel (formerly Falasha), comprises most of Ethiopia's Jews. They look back on life in Ethiopia with a combination of fondness and sadness.

Other Ethiopian diasporas face a different set of challenges. Workers in the Persian Gulf (in Abu Dhabi, Dubai, Doha, Riyadh, and Jeddah) are often abroad temporarily, working in a family's home or as a security guard and sending money home. These labor migrants do not expect to become citizens, and they do not have strong social networks in place for communal support. In other cities, such as London, Rome, and Toronto, groups of Ethiopians and Eritreans—often considered enemies at home because of their war in the 1990s and the ongoing border dispute—mix together over food and entertainment. Many of these migrants are refugees or asylum seekers and they establish social networks through Ethiopian restaurants. These restaurants encapsulate many of the tensions at play when Ethiopians and Eritreans come together as migrants.

One of my favorite Ethiopian restaurants in the diaspora is located near Termini station in Rome, in a small neighborhood with a lot of Ethiopian shops and businesses. Its name is written in Amharic and Italian. It caters primarily to Ethiopian customers, but the name, "Kilimangiaro," makes it recognizably African to tourists and Italians. Of course, Mount Kilimanjaro is not located in Ethiopia, but in Tanzania, next to the Kenyan border. And yet, Ethiopians and Eritreans don't mind the name, because it brings to mind an image of East Africa that is more easily identifiable to most non-Ethiopian/Eritrean customers. The restaurant serves Ethiopian food, but it attracts "foreign" customers by conjuring images that are perhaps more accessible to outsiders.

FIGURE 13.5 **Ethiopian food**
Photograph by Jim Hickson

FIGURE 13.6 **Ristorante Kilimangiaro**
Photograph by Jim Hickson

The idea of Ethiopian migrants translating Ethiopian culture on behalf of potential consumers happens frequently in popular music. Indeed, while "Tezeta" remains the most widely known song in the Ethiopian diaspora, in the past few years, several female musicians across the Ethiopian diaspora have adapted the feeling of *tezeta* into a set of modern pop songs in musicians' adopted local language. If we look at Washington, DC, or Tel Aviv, or the emerging Ethiopian diaspora in Harlem, we see a set of songs being released called "Home" that often pair with songs about failed relationships, thereby translating the concept of *tezeta* for local audiences in much the same way that "Kilimangiaro" restaurant makes itself accessible to tourists in Rome.

The first singer to put out songs from the genre is Cabra Casay, who lives in Israel and performs as the main singer in the popular multi-ethnic band The Idan Raichel Project. She was born in Gedaref, a Sudanese refugee camp, and moved to Israel as a child, making her first trip to Ethiopia in 2006. From this trip came the song "Habayta," which means "Home" in Hebrew, and in which she sings about how both going out to Ethiopia and returning to Israel is going home for her. At the same time, she performs songs about breaking up with her boyfriend, such as "Milim Yafot Me-eileh" which means "Nicer Words than These." In this song, she explains that she will return to her boyfriend eventually, but that she has no good answer for him about why they can't be together.

Also in 2006, Tigist Shibabew, whose sister Gigi is one of Ethiopia's most popular singers, released a soul-funk album called "Bole2Harlem," named after her journey from Addis Ababa's Bole airport to the African American neighborhood in New York City. This album, named after the band of the same name, also contains a song called "Home," but this one is sung in Amharic. In the chorus, Tigist repeats the word "home" 12 times, and sings the rest of the words in Amharic. The album also has a song called "Quralew," which is a cognate of the word "love," and this song is also performed in a soul-funk style rarely found in Ethiopia. Sadly, this was to be the last of her albums, as Tigist Shibabew died in a tragic accident in 2008.

Still another female diaspora singer put out a set of songs about home and love. Wayna Wondowssen, who grew up in Washington, DC, released a song called "Home"

FIGURE 13.7 **Wayna Wondowssen**
Photograph courtesy of Wayna Wondowssen

on her 2008 album *Higher Ground*. The album name is a clear tribute to the gospel influence that we can hear in her voice. As in the "Bole2Harlem" version, Wayna sings a chorus where she repeats the word "home" multiple times. And as with the other singers, she has a song about a breakup on this album, called "My love." This song is a poignant story about domestic violence, with the narrator leaving an abusive relationship with her husband.

In all three diaspora communities, we find examples of young female singers who adapt to local musical styles and release songs in local languages about failed relationships and nostalgia for their homeland. These singers have taken a cue from "Tezeta" to sing about their personal lives alongside their migrant status, which gives us a modern, localized set of repertoires where migrants can access the same set of feelings about Ethiopia in whichever part of the diaspora they find themselves.

a song about lost love; it takes on personal meaning for immigrants about missing their home. Ethiopia's vibrant diaspora has adapted the classic song in two interesting ways: "Tezeta" itself has been sampled in rap songs—most notably, in Chicago rapper Common's song "The Game" (2004). Second, female singers who have no plans to move back to Ethiopia anytime soon have captured the idea of *tezeta* in songs that they call, in their many new local languages, "Home" (see Primary Source box).

Adapting "Tezeta" through rap and fusion is not the only strategy at musicians' disposal for making it attractive to wide audiences. In the 1970s, when the popular style of Ethiojazz was going strong, now legendary musicians such as Mahmoud Ahmed and Alemayehu Eshete recorded Ethiojazz versions of "Tezeta" that were recognizably similar to the rural folk versions played on *massenqo* and *krar*, or the *washint*. The Ethiojazz versions were performed on Western instruments, with heavy emphasis on brass instruments including saxophone and trumpet. These musicians still played within *Qignit*, the name for the Ethiopian modal system, but they incorporated musical elements from other modes such as the **tritone**, a dissonant interval in Western music theory.

The musicians from the classic Ethiojazz period in the 1970s are some of Ethiopia's most famous musicians abroad. Mahmoud Ahmed, the "shoeshine boy," is a reigning icon from the period, as is Getatchew Mekurya, who performs his saxophone abroad in colorful dress. Alemayehu Eshete, the "Ethiopian James Brown" is beloved abroad for his American soul-style dress and high kicks and grunts in concerts. More recently, a vibrant recording industry has sprung up in the Unites States, and female musicians such as Aster Aweke, who has travelled back and forth from Los Angeles for decades (see Biography Box), and Gigi (Ejigayehu Shibabew), who collaborates frequently with jazz musicians in New York, appeal to Ethiopians in the diaspora and back home.

The youngest generation of musicians, however, demonstrates the continuing importance of wax and gold. The undisputed king of Ethiopian popular music is Teddy Afro, and as his name suggests, he performs a reggae-influenced style: the diminutive "Teddy" can be pronounced more easily by fans in North America than

FIGURE 13.8 **St George's Cathedral**
Photograph by Ilana Webster-Kogen

his given name, Tewodros, while "Afro" suggests a global/Afrodiasporic aesthetic. In 2008 he was arrested on hit-and-run charges, and he was incarcerated for over a year, although the evidence against him was thin. Musicians live in particular risk in Ethiopia, since they are at the mercy of a government that limits free speech. Just as *Azmari*s have historically had to pay homage to their patrons in exchange for food and shelter, today musicians have to tread carefully in case they run afoul of the authorities. In such cases, nostalgia for the past is a code for hope for a better life.

When Ethiopians talk about nostalgia for the past, they are referring to a past that is imagined to be different and superior to the present. Ethiopians often highlight the features of Ethiopia that have made it distinct through history. First and foremost is its powerful and ancient church, the Ethiopian Orthodox Church, whose rock-hewn churches draw tourists to Lalibela, and whose nineteenth-century cathedrals dot the skyline of Addis Ababa.

During Lent, services move outdoors, where musicians play the *beganna*, a 10-stringed "harp" that sits a meter high (a religious counterpart to the *krar*). The Ethiopian Orthodox branch of Christianity is powerful and historic: adopted in the fourth century, the Ethiopian church is the second oldest in the world, a fact that Ethiopian Christians frequently remind visitors. Even in Jerusalem, the Ethiopian imprint sits quietly behind the scenes: Ethiopian monks live quite out of sight in a monastery directly above the Church of the Holy Sepulcher. Ethiopians

Aster Aweke

Ethiopian music might not have the enormous audiences around the world that some South African or West African musicians achieve, but two musicians have successfully broken through to the "world music" market. Teddy Afro and Aster Aweke (both mentioned in this chapter) regularly tour around Africa and Europe. Aster Aweke in particular has a devoted following across the USA, Scandinavia, and Israel, all of which she tours regularly. Her life story follows a trajectory that is symbolic for many Ethiopians, since she came of age during the coup d'état that unseated the Emperor. Likewise, her musical style has developed in tandem with the developmental changes in Ethiopia within the past few decades.

Aster Aweke was born in northern Ethiopia in the late 1950s, and she was trained in the theatrical tradition in Addis Ababa. Many musicians of this era trained in the Church, the national theatre, or the Imperial Guards' band, so her pathway into the music industry was typical in this sense. Like many other musicians of her era, Aster left Ethiopia in the 1970s, and moved to Washington, DC, and then to Los Angeles. In more recent years she has resettled in Ethiopia, travelling back and forth frequently.

FIGURE 13.9 **Aster Aweke, Amsterdam, 21 May 1994**

Photograph by Frans Schellekens. Courtesy of Getty Images

Aster has recorded multiple versions of "Tezeta," each style enacting a dynamic tension within Ethiopian musical circles about tradition and change. She has recorded ballad versions—she is best known for love songs—and more up-tempo versions, some with Ethiojazz instrumentation and others with drum machines and synthesizers. Her earlier albums of the late 1980s and early 1990s were heavily influenced by soul music, while the later albums (including her latest 2013 album) draw much more from the music that accompanies Eskesta dancing.

For Ethiopians at home and abroad, Aster embodies success for Ethiopia. She went abroad but she was still connected to the homeland; she has a prestigious reputation among non-Ethiopians, and she has popularized the high-pitched female Ethiopian vocal style around the world. While other beloved musicians have earned success abroad by fusing their own style with blues or jazz singing styles, Aster's vocal repertoire includes Ethiopian-style ululation rather than jazz-style vibrato, and her lyrics are nearly always in Amharic. While most Ethiopians who earn an international reputation do so by incorporating Afrodiasporic musical elements, Aster is the best known Ethiopian musician abroad whose style remains recognizably and unmistakably Ethiopian.

are proud of their ancient Church tradition, believing that it connects them to a long-lasting literary civilization.

This distinguished religious history goes hand in hand with Ethiopia's equally dignified political and literary history. The Ethiopian Church's texts are written in Ge'ez, a south Semitic language that preceded Amharic and Tigrinya. Like Amharic, Ge'ez is written in Fidal, or Ethiopic script. The tradition of wax and gold is represented in fiction and proverbs, while the literary mechanism of subversion dates back to the fourteenth-century text that is the founding document of Ethiopian civilization, the *Kebra Negast*. This epic, often depicted artistically in Ethiopian restaurants, tells the story of Menilek, the prince who stole the Ark of the Convenant from his father Solomon (his mother was the Queen of Sheba, who, according to the Hebrew Bible, visited the King's Temple in Jerusalem), thus transferring religious authority symbolically to Ethiopia.

The third prong in Ethiopia's proud history is the history of independence and empire. Ethiopia was never colonized during the European expansion of the nineteenth century, and apart from Liberia, it was the only nation in Africa to remain independent (apart from a brief Italian occupation around World War II). The symbol of Ethiopia's independence in the twentieth century was Emperor Haile Selassie, who was crowned in 1930, inspiring the birth of the Rastafari religious movement in Jamaica. Haile Selassie was revered as a dignitary, and a portrait of his address to the League of Nations in 1936 is mounted on the walls of St George's Cathedral in Addis Ababa, where he was crowned.

The glorification of the past in Ethiopia contrasts starkly with the difficulties of life today. Ethiopia is a center for economic development, but much of the country's population lives in poverty, and the appearance of national unity in the foundation epics is not borne out by the separatist battles on the country's borders. Eritrea successfully seceded from Ethiopia in 1991/1993, and the Oromo in the south (constituting Ethiopia's largest ethnic group) aim to do likewise. And many of the qualities that bring Ethiopians pride about their past contribute to the country's problems today. First, the impulse towards national autonomy that drove Ethiopian (and Eritrean) soldiers to defeat the Italians at the Battle of Adwa (1896) has also triggered a desire for ethnic independence among the groups mentioned earlier, destabilizing the nation. Second, since European powers did not extend their mercantile trade routes into Ethiopia, Ethiopia's infrastructure is still developing, with even the capital city Addis Ababa lacking street lamps on main roads. Meanwhile, Ethiopia shares a number of health problems with many other countries in sub-Saharan Africa, such as the devastation wrought by HIV/AIDS, and high mortality rates among infants and mothers.

In a sense, the abiding popularity of "Tezeta" helps Ethiopians to navigate the present and to idealize the past while recognizing its shortcomings. Just as singers of "Tezeta" do not sing about trying to win back the lost lover, Ethiopians remember that Haile Selassie was deposed and expelled from Ethiopia, in part, because much of the population did not support him. Likewise, the power of the Church occludes the statistic that the country is 34 per cent Muslim, that Pentecostalism is on the rise among people who want to experience religion first hand instead of mediated through monks, and that the small Jewish population has emigrated following years of laws limiting their rights. "Tezeta" encourages Ethiopians to appreciate their past while still being mindful that it makes little sense to spend one's whole life there.

Discussion Topics

- How has the song "Tezeta" changed stylistically over time? Listen to Aster Aweke's version (https://www.youtube.com/watch?v=TVvIwhxEIZ0) and compare it with the version on the *krar*:

  - Describe the vocal style.
  - How does the Western instrumentation affect the performance?
  - Compare the tonality in the two versions.
  - What makes Aster Aweke's version sound Ethiopian?

- How does Ethiopian history—including Christianity, Empire, and independence—affect the way we interpret the two versions of the song?

Further Listening

Mahmoud Ahmed. Volume 7: *Ere Mela Mela* (Re-issue) (Buda Musique, 1999).

Tilahoun Gessesse. Volume 17: *Tilahun Gessesse*. (Buda Musique, 2004).
  Highlights in the Buda Records series *Ethiopiques*. It currently has 28 discs available, and releases several new ones each year. The series editor, Francis Falceto, has been committed to releasing classic, contemporary, and regionally marginal material, so there is a wonderful variety. A whole disc is devoted to different versions of "Tezeta."

Various Artists. *The Very Best of Ethiopiques*. (Buda Musique, 2007).

Various Artists. Volume 2: *Tetchawet! Urban Azmaris of the 90s*. (Buda Musique, 1998).

Various Artists. Volume 10: *Tezeta: Ethiopian Blues and Ballads*. (Buda Musique, 2002).

Recommended Reading

Falceto, Francis (2001) *Abyssinie Swing: A Pictorial History of Modern Ethiopian Music*. Addis Ababa: Shama Books.
> Francis Falceto presents images of the vibrant Ethiopian music scene in the 1970s, before musicians fled the Mengistu regime.

Kebede, Ashenafi (1977) "The Bowl-Lyre of Northeast Africa. *Krar*: The devil's instrument." *Ethnomusicology* 21(3): 379–395.
> Ashenafi Kebede was the most prominent scholar of Ethiopian music in the twentieth century, as well as a composer. In this early descriptive work, he explains the morphology and performance practice of the *krar*, as well as the historical taboos around certain instruments.

Levine, Donald (1965) *Wax and Gold: Tradition and Innovation in Ethiopian Culture*. Chicago: University of Chicago Press.
> This classic work explains the function of wax and gold in Ethiopian society, arguing that it lays the foundation for many of Ethiopia's cultural idiosyncrasies.

Parfitt, Tudor and Emanuela Trevisan Semi (eds.) (1999) *The Beta Israel in Ethiopia and Israel: Studies on Ethiopian Jews*. Richmond: Curzon.
> This volume is one of the first interdisciplinary that looks at an Ethiopian diaspora population. Including over a dozen contributing authors, the compilation gives a thorough explanation of Ethiopian life in Israel, which is the second largest diaspora in the world (behind the USA). Most of the chapters are dedicated to the integration problems that Ethiopians have encountered after migration.

Powne, Michael (1968) *Ethiopian Music: An Introduction*. New York: Oxford University Press.
> Still the only book to describe every instrument and musical mode in detail, this somewhat dated work surveys the religious and traditional music of northern Ethiopia and Addis Ababa.

Shelemay, Kay Kaufmann (1986) *Music, Ritual, and Falasha History*. East Lansing, MI: Michigan State University Press.
> Shelemay's musical analysis of Ethiopian liturgy is an extraordinary work in that her conclusions transformed the scholarly understanding of the divergence of Ethiopian Judaism from Christianity. Through her rigorous approach to analyzing religious music, she demonstrates the function of music as an important historical tool.

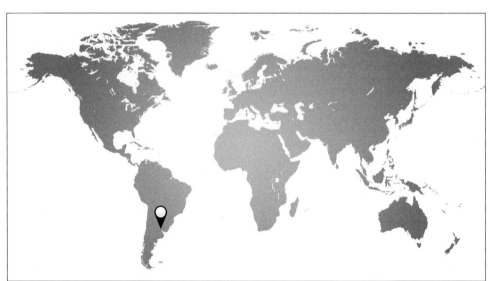

Location: Argentina/Bolivia

"El Alto de La Paz" (The End of the Truce): Digital Cumbia, Circulation of Music, and Music of Circulation

Produced by Mati Zundel (laptop), featuring MC Boogat (rap); released on the album *Amazónico Gravitante* (Waxploitation/ZZK Records, 2011)

Chapter fourteen

"El Alto de La Paz" (The End of the Truce)

Digital Cumbia, Circulation of Music, and Music of Circulation[1]

Geoffrey Baker

Summary

Argentinean producer Mati Zundel began writing "El Alto de La Paz" on his laptop while travelling through Bolivia on an extended Latin American road trip. He emailed a demo version of the track to MC Boogat in Montreal in Canada; Boogat recorded rapped vocals over the top and emailed it back to Zundel, who was now at a beach in Ecuador. The principal musical elements of the song—**cumbia, reggaeton,** and rap—are Afro-diasporic genres with roots in the Caribbean that circulate throughout the Americas and reveal the

KEY WORDS
- digital technologies
- fusion
- global circulation
- internet
- migration

movements of people and culture. As Zundel travelled across the continent, his musical style began to change: he picked up new musical knowledge, re-evaluated his home culture, and learned to speak to audiences in other countries. Through travel, he gradually reconstituted himself and his music as Latin American.

Zundel's song emerged from Buenos Aires's electronic music underground, yet this "local" scene was substantially created by the transnational movements of foreign intermediaries and Argentinean musicians, and by social media activity and the distribution of recordings. It may therefore be characterized as a "culture of circulation." Transnational exchanges have long been associated with the legitimation of Latin American popular musics, and digital cumbia is no exception, illustrating how circulation may boost cultural value. "El Alto de La Paz" is a song that speaks of multiple forms and layers of circulation, and how they can constitute a song, a singer, and a scene.

Why this Piece?

The origin myth of digital cumbia begins with the first Festicumex (festival of experimental cumbias), organized by the Dutch conceptual artist Dick el Demasiado.

---

1 This chapter draws on research for the project "Music, Digitization, Mediation: Towards Interdisciplinary Music Studies," funded by a European Research Council Advanced Grant.

The festival took place in Honduras in 1996—or, to be more precise, it didn't. There was a website for the event, multiple bands, a compilation CD, and even a book about the scene—but the whole thing was an elaborate hoax by the mischievous Dutchman. The festival only existed on the internet; the bands were invented; the music on the CD was all by him; the book, which he sent to journalists and sociologists, was also by him (under a pseudonym), and also part of the prank. This really is an origin myth. However, Dick el Demasiado was so taken by his own joke that he created a real Festicumex in Buenos Aires in 2003, putting together several bands to play the music that he had written for the fake festival, and this catalyzed the emergence of a digital cumbia scene in the Argentinean capital.

Festicumex caught my attention for two reasons: it was a prescient joke about internet crazes and virtual scenes in the digital age, and it showed Buenos Aires's digital cumbia scene as founded on an act (or illusion) of transnational circulation. The scene that appealed to Dick el Demasiado did not yet exist, so he projected the idea of it internationally and it eventually came into being. Nearly a decade later, Mati Zundel, part of a wave of Argentinean digital cumbia artists inspired by the 2003 Festicumex, released the song "El Alto de La Paz," featuring Montreal-based MC Boogat. Started on a laptop and finished by email while Zundel was backpacking across South America, this song resonated with me because it exemplified the continued centrality of flows and movements in the genre, which may be characterized as a "culture of circulation."

Musical Features

TIMED LISTENING GUIDE

0:00	Reggaeton rhythm on bass and snare drums, cumbia on *güiro*. La Paz street sounds (low in the mix). From 0:08 damped off-beat rhythm guitar chords characteristic of cumbia
0:14	Rap starts—lots of **reverb**
0:25	Chorus, based on the following short phrase:

	Whole chorus repeated twice. The **parallel** 5ths and drawn out words at the end give it an edgy feel. This is reinforced by gunshot sounds at the start of the chorus, and deep, distorted synthesizer sounds, an element of rock music
0:52	Rap resumes. More sounds added into the mix, for instance synthesized brass interjections based on chorus fragment
1.19	*Güiro* rhythm doubles in speed
1:21	Synthesizer chords characteristic of electronic dance music
1:32	Chorus (as at 0:25)
1.58	Rap resumes, over sci-fi shooting noises. More sounds added to mix

2.25	*Güiro* rhythm doubles in speed
2:38—2.51	Chorus
	Build up characteristic of **EDM** (bass drops out, crescendo of sound effects)
3.05	Final rap section—ends at 3:15. Gradually other sounds drop out. By 3:30 only percussive sounds left
3.44	La Paz street sounds

TECHNOLOGY

"El Alto de la Paz" was produced on a Sony Vaio VGN 320 laptop with a microphone and headphones, using the software Ableton Live and Reason.

What distinguishes Latin America's digital popular musics is perhaps not their circulatory nature, given the region's long history of cultural exchange, but rather the intensification of circulation afforded by new technologies, particularly the internet, and the increasing difficulty in identifying a point of origin, however imaginary. These musics are ever more clearly *of* or *about* circulation as much as *in* circulation. For example, moombahton, a mixture of reggaeton and Dutch house that has left its mark on Latin digital fusions, is often said to come from and reside in the internet rather than a particular geographical location. According to legend, the genre was born when a DJ, Dave Nada, slowed down the track "Moombah" at a Latin music party in Washington, DC, in 2009, yet unlike with most genres, the sound took

FIGURE 14.1 **Mati Zundel's Home Studio**

Photograph by Mati Zundel

hold internationally *before* establishing itself in any one place. The genre coalesced on the internet as producers around the world uploaded their tracks to Soundcloud. The producer Diplo claimed: "It was global from the beginning. [Unlike] something like dubstep that was centered in London, and then moved to Canada, and Australia . . . Moombahton . . . just happened everywhere." Tribal (or 3Ball) originated in Monterrey, Mexico, yet it is emblematic of the way that new musics are increasingly born out of internet surfing and downloading and then live and circulate online. As music flows across the web, the location of producers is often unimportant, even unknown. Many Latin digital fusions could come from anywhere and go anywhere; geographical distinctions become less and less important to the musics' social lives.

Digital cumbia is such a culture of circulation, one that is arguably more coherent on the internet than in the offline world. It has no single source, emerging from different points in Latin America in the early 2000s, and its central nodes are Facebook, Soundcloud groups, and blogs (e.g., The New Cumbia Makers and Nu Cumbia Experience). Producers contribute music from all around the world, with minimal attention paid to origin and Latin America granted no special status. Such internet groups are perhaps the central manifestation of this genre that can be surprisingly elusive on the streets of a Latin American city. If more traditional forms of cumbia are the soundtrack to countless large dances every weekend, digital cumbia primarily inhabits digital spaces.

"El Alto de La Paz" is a fusion of several regional and international genres, produced on a computer. The most prominent elements are cumbia (a popular dance form originally from Colombia but found throughout Latin America), reggaeton (again, popular throughout Latin America and the Caribbean, although most closely associated with Puerto Rico), and rap. The 2/4 cumbia rhythm (at its simplest, a crotchet and two quavers) is heard on the *güiro* (a scraped percussion instrument) and **cowbell**, and the 4/4 reggaeton rhythm, with its characteristic 3+3+2 pattern, is heard on the bass and snare drums. All the lyrics except the chorus are rapped. The track also displays characteristic features of rock (such as **distortion** in the synthesizer sound) and electronic dance music (EDM), such as the synthesizer chords from 1.21–1.32, the build-up from 2.38–2.51, and the percussion-only intro and outro, which helps DJs to mix the song with others. These elements, drawn from sound libraries or Zundel's own recordings, are layered on top of other, less prominent sounds and effects using music software, creating a rhythmically and timbrally dense texture.

The chorus's lyrics are a rallying cry against longstanding social injustices in Bolivia, dating back to the Spanish conquest in the sixteenth century:

I came to burn the white flag
To raise up a guerrilla army from the mountains
To unmask the false friend
And stop the truce.

FIGURE 14.2 **Boogat**

Photograph by Guillaume Simoneau

In his "hymn to the urban guerrilla," Boogat draws on rap's association with social and political protest in Latin America. From Argentina to Mexico, as well as in immigrant communities in North America, rappers have used their art to denounce racism, marginalization, inequality, corruption, and other social and economic ills. Boogat declares that in Bolivia, the poor have been both mistreated and written out of history:

> For so long they stole our bread
> That sad history that is always forgotten.

"El Alto de La Paz" is a play on words, combining the names of the two cities where it originated (El Alto and La Paz) with the meaning "the end of the truce" —in other words, the time for action has come:

> If the mouth is a pistol, the word is a bullet
> The sentence is a cartridge to fire at the meddler
> A sound that kills you without even asking for money
> My art is sharp, raw like ceviche.

However fierce Boogat's words, the struggle that he celebrates is a mental one— "knowledge is a great weapon" —and his aim is utopian:

> Taking control to change our role
> Another world is possible and that is our goal.

Social Context: Cultures of Circulation

"Cultures of circulation" is a phrase coined by Benjamin Lee and Edward LiPuma in order to focus attention on the role of circulation in constituting objects, subjects, and social totalities. Rather than thinking about circulation as transmission, the process between production and consumption, or the movement of already defined objects and people, scholars in cultural studies and the social sciences increasingly recognize its dynamic, performative character, and its active role in *making* those objects and people (and the social groups to which they belong)—hence cultures *of* rather than simply *in* circulation.

Transnational circulation has played a role in Argentinean popular music since the sixteenth century. **Tango** merged the cultures of successive waves of Spanish colonists, African slaves, and European immigrants, and its transformation from a disdained music of the urban underclass into a symbol of national identity depended on a long-distance round trip just before World War I to Paris and London, where it was enthusiastically adopted by local elites and provoked "tangomania." Tango's history illustrates how value may be generated by the movements of a cultural form. In more recent decades, the two most widely consumed genres of popular music in Argentina have been rock and cumbia, genres of North American and Colombian origin respectively. Yet cumbia itself grew out of the continuous movement of people, ideas, and sounds through Colombia's Caribbean coast, and so too may be considered a culture of circulation.

Today, the circulation of cumbia throughout the Americas contributes to producing the region as a transnational social totality, the imagined community of *el pueblo latinoamericano* (the Latin American people). One musician described cumbia as "the spinal cord of the Americas," a nice illustration of the constitution of the hemisphere as a metaphorical body through the circulation of music. Another labeled it "the empress of the Americas," imagining the region as a single state under the rule of a rhythm.

Since the turn of the millennium, Buenos Aires has emerged as a regional hub of international EDM and new digital fusions, though in a continuation of Argentina's transnational musical history, electro-tango was consolidated as a genre above all by Gotan Project, a trio of Paris-based musicians of whom only one was Argentinean. The city's digital cumbia scene, meanwhile, shows the fruits of a Dutchman's playful ventures, a decade on from the 2003 Festicumex. At its heart lies ZZK Records, founded in 2008 to bring together laptop producers mixing cumbia and other Latin American genres with styles such as hip hop, **dancehall**, techno, and dub. In 2012, Mati Zundel, a ZZK artist, released the album *Amazónico Gravitante*, featuring the song "El Alto de La Paz."

Mati Zundel wrote "El Alto de La Paz" while on an extended road trip across South America. He spoke of the energy and renewal that he derives from travel: "the rhythm of the streets inspires me," he told me, "and I try to make music that calls out for movement." Zundel checked into a cheap hotel room in La Paz, the Bolivian capital, opened his laptop, and produced the track in a single night, so taken by the sounds of the city that he even incorporated the cries of bus conductors

PRIMARY SOURCE

Mati Zundel's music has been called psychedelic cumbia. His beats fuse rhythms from diverse parts of South America, and increasingly reflect the musical influences of a man who has been on the move the last few years—in body and spirit. Since the release of his *Neobailongo* EP, he has traveled rural Latin America with a backpack and a microphone, picking up indigenous rhythms and native chants from Bolivia to Ecuador and all through the Amazon interior.

MZ: Everything started in La Paz, Bolivia. It really surprised me how the last time I was there huayno [a traditional highland Andean genre] was what everyone was listening to, that was the street sound but this time it was all reggaeton. In La Paz and in the city of [El] Alto, reggaeton was everywhere so I put this track together thinking that really MC Boogat would be perfect for it. So I got to the Alto City Festival and before taking off for La Paz I sent the track to Boogat calling it "Alto de la Paz" (combining the names of the two cities into the hook!). Three months later while I was at a beach in Ecuador I got an email from Boogat; it was our track and it blew my mind what he'd done with it!

There are energetic songs that put you in the club, that were created in Buenos Aires, and there other tracks that are much more mellow, that were written out in the country. Getting to go to festivals and parties in the middle of Argentina, Bolivia, Peru, Ecuador, and Colombia I found other rhythms to use for dance music, with native instruments like the charango guitar and the bombo leguero drum.

EH: Where in Brazil is Marina Gasolina from? How did you end up collaborating with her?

MZ: You know I don't even know what part of Brazil Marina is from. I found her a cappella on the internet and downloaded it, and she ended up giving the go ahead to use her vocals for the record.

[This is an edited extract from an interview by Eve Hyman published on 11 May 2012 on the website World Hip Hop Market, at: http://worldhiphopmarket.com/ exclusive-interview-argentinian-musician-mati-zundel-and-hip-hop-leanings/.]

FIGURE 14.3 **World Hip Hop Market website**

FIGURE 14.4 Mati Zundel in La Paz
Image courtesy of Mati Zundel

that he had recorded in a busy street. He then collaborated by email with Boogat, a rapper in Canada, illustrating how digital technology facilitates circulatory practices.

This is a song about circulation in more ways than one, however. Its principal musical elements—reggaeton, rap, and cumbia—are Afro-diasporic genres that circulate throughout the Americas; with roots in Africa and the Caribbean, they speak of transnational flows of people and culture dating back to the era of slavery. Reggaeton, the newest of the three, has no single point of origin, but rather emerged from human and cultural movements between Puerto Rico, Jamaica, Panama, and the USA. It spread across the Americas in just a few years—Zundel was struck by its sudden appropriation of the urban soundscape in Bolivia—and its current ubiquity marks it out as the sound of contemporary, digitally enhanced cultural flows across the hemisphere. Furthermore, the elements of rock and EDM in the song reflect Argentina's openness to musical currents emanating from the global north.

The song's lyrics, meanwhile, draw on the ideology of Latin American new social movements, which are also transnational cultures of circulation; it is for this reason that a Montreal-based rapper of Mexican/Paraguayan parentage was able to write lyrics about Bolivian social realities for an Argentinean production in the first person. Interestingly, Zundel had named his song after the two cities that he was moving between, but Boogat read the words as meaning "the end of the truce." Circulation may produce ruptures and misunderstandings, yet these may be productive—in this case, converting Zundel's instrumental track into a protest song.

"El Alto de La Paz" evokes several distinct forms of transnational circulation, such as diaspora, cosmopolitanism, and migration, which have quite different meanings. In Buenos Aires, the higher social classes tend to be more mobile than the lower. Zundel's music emerges from a scene rooted in a chic neighborhood, Palermo, in which traveling is a sign of a successful, modern individual. The song's highly mobile genesis thus carries particular class connotations. Yet Zundel, a middle-class, cosmopolitan traveler, combined forces with Boogat, the son of migrants in Canada, and worked with musical styles rooted in the African diaspora and primarily associated with the urban poor. Their music and lyrics signal solidarity with the downtrodden, whose stasis is hinted at in lines such as:

> But enough already with the waiting in line
> And accepting a beating as our condition.

Poor people's transnational movements tend to be motivated by necessity more than desire. Cumbia has historically been regarded in Buenos Aires as "the music of the maid," often an economic migrant from the Argentinean provinces, Paraguay, or Bolivia. But Boogat suggests that the disadvantaged are no longer prepared to stand still or be moved around, and technological change and intensified circulation bring greater possibilities to organize resistance:

> This is going out to the people in important posts
> The technological revolution has come to f*ck you over.

Circulation may appear in restrictive as well as liberatory guise. When ZZK Records licensed all its music to Waxploitation, a label based in Los Angeles, all the samples on its albums had to be cleared in accordance with US intellectual property (IP) laws. ZZK had grown out of an underground scene in which producers had sampled freely and voraciously, with few concerns or formal permissions, since their ambitions were limited; but increasing the music's circulation overseas meant conforming to foreign IP norms. Clearing samples was a headache for artists like Zundel, who had to draw up retrospective contracts with musicians who had collaborated out of friendship and remove unidentifiable or unofficial samples. Like several other ZZK producers, he changed his production process considerably as a consequence, reducing **sampling** and increasing the role of live instruments. Transnational circulation thus imposed compromises and changes. Zundel even abandoned his artistic name, Lagartijeando, as it was considered unpronounceable by non-Latin audiences. Having already been influenced by his travels, Zundel's musical style was further constituted by its intended circulation. Here we see both territorialized (human) and deterritorialized (internet-based) movement shaping music.

Where is the Buenos Aires Underground?

ZZK Records emerged from a burgeoning underground digital cumbia scene. It began as a club night in 2006 and coalesced into a label two years later, and in 2012 it released the compilation album *Future Sounds of Buenos Aires* (FSOBA) in partnership with Waxploitation. This seems like a straightforward story: as ZZK put it in a press release, "FSOBA is an official presentation of the Buenos Aires electronic underground to the world."

Yet this neat division between local and global is disturbed by the fact that the Buenos Aires underground in question was catalyzed and consolidated by the circulation of foreign musicians through the city and their championing of Argentinean cumbia, which had hitherto attracted limited attention from local EDM producers. Two of its foundational figures were a Dutchman, Dick el Demasiado, and a North American DJ, Gavin Burnett aka Oro11. Burnett, who spent an extended period in Buenos Aires, helped to open the ears of local middle-class tastemakers to fusions of cumbia with hip hop, dub, and reggae, building on the foundations laid down by Festicumex. With Argentinean cumbia itself the result of the circulation of music and musicians from Colombia, Mexico, and Peru since the 1940s, the digital cumbia scene emerged from repeated waves of transnational circulation—a characteristic development in a port city.

In addition, Grant C. Dull, ZZK's cofounder and director, is also North American, and the label is rooted in his interests and previous experience. After an economic crisis in 2001, the Argentinean peso was devalued by up to 75 per cent; the country went from being one of the most expensive tourist destinations in South America to one of the cheapest, gaining a cool, edgy, Berlin-esque reputation in the process, which encouraged an influx of young, hip, culturally curious visitors from overseas, including Dull and Burnett. In 2004, Dull cofounded What's Up Buenos Aires (WUBA), an internet portal aimed at connecting foreign audiences with the Buenos Aires cultural scene. ZZK club nights, which he launched two years later, attracted a partly foreign clientele; they began in San Telmo and moved to Palermo, the two neighborhoods most frequented by foreign visitors. DJ and journalist Juan Data described ZZK as a "new underground scene that was still ignored by most locals but eagerly embraced by first-world expats living in Buenos Aires."

The neighborhood of Palermo was also strongly marked by globalization in the early 2000s, with an influx of international business outlets and the consolidation of a cosmopolitan "creative" class defined in part by its early and enthusiastic adoption of new technologies from the global north. This class formed ZZK's other key constituency. Both WUBA and ZZK thus emerged during a particular moment of intensified transnational circulation through Buenos Aires, and were produced and consumed by a mixture of hip tourists and local cosmopolitans; both enterprises revolved around promoting (or constructing) Buenos Aires as a fashionable, cutting-edge cultural destination. Digital cumbia is a product of this time and place, and hence far from a simply "local" scene; the Buenos Aires electronic underground and the world were thoroughly imbricated from the start.

FIGURE 14.5 **Cover image from Mati Zundel's** *Amazónico Gravitante*
Courtesy of Waxploitation Records

Indeed, the Buenos Aires underground that the compilation album invokes is in part an imagined locality that is constituted by its very naming and circulation on a US label. A number of the artists on the compilation either established their careers or currently live outside Buenos Aires: Frikstailers (from northern Argentina) are based in Mexico, Fauna and Super Guachín in the provincial city of Mendoza, and Chancha via Circuito and Mati Zundel live in small towns. At the time of writing, the scene in question is difficult to pin down in the city itself; it has few regular haunts, and ZZK is more active in Europe than Argentina. The Buenos Aires urban underground is largely immaterial at present: brought into being primarily through social media activity and the circulation of recordings, and coming most clearly into focus when evoked (or performed) by an album launch and press release for international consumption.

Music may be increasingly mobile and deterritorialized, yet authenticity is still linked to a considerable degree to place; ZZK's image thus demands located-ness.

Nevertheless, the local place in question—the Buenos Aires underground—is a discursive construction, formed and performed by its circulation on the global stage, illustrating how the global and the local are in a continuous process of mutual constitution. More clearly defined in its fluidity than its scarce fixed points, it is a characteristic culture of circulation.

The "future sound" of ZZK's music, meanwhile, has been shaped by the restrictions imposed by dealing with the transnational music industry. The laptop aesthetic characteristic of the label's early days has been somewhat displaced by the incorporation of more live instruments, in part a consequence of the requirement to abide by US IP norms and the economic importance of creating an appealing live show. ZZK's music may be the "Future Sounds of Buenos Aires," but during the label's eight years of existence, increasing transnational circulation has impacted on its aesthetics.

Circulation as Legitimation: the Señor Coconut Effect

Cumbia has been widely consumed in Argentina since the 1960s, but primarily by the "popular" (i.e. working and lower middle) classes. Except for a brief period in the early 1990s, the middle and upper classes tended to disdain what they considered to be "the music of the maid." Ten years on from the 2003 Festicumex, however, cumbia has become more widely accepted. Many musicians cite Festicumex as a catalyst for the change in attitude, though they also point to DJ Gavin Burnett. In both cases, a foreigner creating cumbia fusions helped to legitimize the genre among the middle and upper classes.

Digital cumbia is the latest example of a long history of legitimation of Latin American popular musics through circulation. Approval by European or North American elites played a key role in the local legitimation of Argentinean tango and Cuban *son*. It was only after they traveled overseas and back, or were endorsed by foreign visitors, that such popular musics of lower class origins were incorporated by the local middle and upper classes as a productive symbol of national identity. Cumbia, too, has taken on legitimacy via circulation through Europe—what I am tempted to call the Señor Coconut effect.

Yumber Vera Rojas has underlined how the emergence of middle-class "new cumbia" scenes across Latin America since the late 1990s was catalyzed by the interventions of foreign figures—primarily Richard Blair (Sidestepper, English) in Colombia and Uwe Schmidt (Señor Coconut, German) in Chile, alongside Dick el Demasiado and Grant Dull in Buenos Aires. Richard Blair recounts how he arrived in Colombia in the mid-1990s to find that tropical music was deeply unfashionable and there was virtually no interest in fusing the ubiquitous international musics (above all rock) with local traditions, as has become so commonplace today.

Juan Data argues that tastemakers in Argentina have tended to be more interested in foreign music, so without foreign intermediaries, new local styles struggle to achieve recognition. Also, foreigners usually have a more limited awareness of the

Mati Zundel was born in the small town of Dolores, 135 miles from Buenos Aires, in 1982. He grew up surrounded by cumbia—but he did not like it, and was drawn to rock and EDM instead. It was only when he went to Mexico in 2008 that he became aware of the importance of his local music. He began to appreciate music that reminded him of home, and found that Mexicans were less interested in hearing his European-style EDM than knowing what Argentinean music sounded like. A year in Mexico raised doubts about his musical direction.

Back in Argentina, he began to mix with artists from ZZK Records and eventually signed to the label himself. But in 2010 he took off again, this time on a year-long road trip through Bolivia, Peru, Ecuador, and Colombia. He researched and recorded local musical traditions and began to play Andean instruments. He also performed his laptop music en route and discovered that Andean audiences were less receptive to his hard-edged EDM than those in Buenos Aires. If he wanted to play music across the Americas, he needed a style that was more approachable for people in other countries. The more he travelled, the more he adopted acoustic, folkloric elements and moved towards an overtly Latin American sound. On the move, his music was inflected by new influences and audience responses, and he saw his local culture through new eyes. As he traveled, Zundel and his music were remade as Latin American.

FIGURE 14.6 **Mati Zundel**

Photograph by Mark van der Aa

negative associations (such as tackiness) attached to tropical music by the local middle and upper classes, and can thus approach this music with less of the cultural baggage that accompanies it at home. Juan Data reads DJ Gavin Burnett's intervention in this way:

> Gavin didn't have any of the negative preconceptions towards cumbia that all the young hip urban kids his age in Buenos Aires had . . . We are talking about the snobbiest capital of a country that proudly considers itself the most European . . . of the Southern Cone, where urban kids grow up listening exclusively to whatever is cool in the Anglo-speaking half of the world and looking down on local traditional dance rhythms produced in neighbor countries.

Data thus puts a positive spin on the decontextualizing capacity of circulation, which is often read negatively. In his account, foreign intermediaries appear as open minded, not hampered by ignorance, allowing the creation of new meanings—ones that may liberate or elevate the music in question.

In histories of Buenos Aires's digital cumbia scene, several important figures are either foreigners or Argentineans who lived overseas, and the music has often taken a circuitous route to acceptance. In some cases, the music circulated overseas and arrived back again in cosmopolitan hands; ZZK's El Remolón, for example, cited Señor Coconut as a key inspiration. In others, as with Mati Zundel, travelling and seeing their own culture from outside was a catalyst for starting to appreciate cumbia. Miss Bolivia, who collaborated on Zundel's track "Bronca" on *Amazónico Gravitante*, only embraced cumbia after a spell living in New York. El Mayonesa, a ZZK collaborator who spent periods in Spain and Estonia, is another case in point: "living far away, I started to like it from a distance, I started to feel my Argentinean-ness." As members of the middle class, these musicians had grown up surrounded by negative attitudes to cumbia, which they broadly shared, and valorization came only after some form of circulation.

Transnational circulation may participate in the creation of cultural value, but it may also delegitimize a musical form, and may even do both simultaneously for different constituencies. If a musical form receives approval from foreign tastemakers and audiences, its stock may well rise; but if it is considered to be *designed* for transnational circulation, tailored to overseas rather than domestic tastes, it may be criticized locally as excessively calculated and therefore lacking authenticity. While cultural importation by figures such as Richard Blair, Uwe Schmidt, and Dick el Demasiado has been widely praised, genres like electro-tango and digital cumbia have sometimes been tagged more negatively as "music for export." Circulation thus brings into play judgments and debates about value and authenticity; for some, it validates musical quality, for others, it evokes self-exoticization or marketing.

Coda

After the release of *Amazónico Gravitante*, Mati Zundel licensed a track for an Aerolíneas Argentinas advertisement, which enabled him to quit his job and go travelling again, this time mainly to Brazil, though he also returned to Bolivia to see how audiences reacted to "El Alto de La Paz." In Brazil, he generally left his laptop in his hotel room and went out with just a guitar so that he could interact with local musicians more easily. New technologies had allowed him to engage in long-distance collaborations while recording *Amazónico Gravitante*, but translating the album into live performance was a challenge; he and Boogat—living at opposite ends of the Americas—have never performed "El Alto de La Paz" live. This experience encouraged him to work with more traditional resources on his Brazilian trip. As with his Andean journey, he found that a lot of his music did not convince local audiences, and he was already thinking about what might work better on a future visit. Mati Zundel's music was on the move again.

Discussion Topics

- Do you think that such new ways of working via the internet are likely to strengthen or weaken Latin America's musical culture?

- Can you think of another genre that has gained symbolic value through external validation?

Further Listening

Future Sounds of Buenos Aires (ZZK Records, 2012).

Recommended Reading

Fernández L'Hoeste, Héctor D., and Pablo Vila (2013) *Cumbia!: Scenes of a Migrant Latin American Music Genre.* Durham, NC: Duke University Press.
> A collection of essays looking at particular manifestations of cumbia through different disciplinary lenses. They highlight how intersecting forms of identity—such as nation, region, class, race, ethnicity, and gender—are negotiated through interaction with the music.

Lee, Benjamin and Edward LiPuma (2002) "Cultures of Circulation: The imaginations of modernity." *Public Culture* 14(1): 191–213.
> This article argues that circulation is a cultural process created by the interactions between specific types of circulating form and the interpretive communities built around them.

Tsing, Anna (2000) "The Global Situation." *Cultural Anthropology* 15(3): 327–360.
> Tsing proposes that globalization's ability to "excite and inspire" should not cause us to shy away from its critical study, but should serve as a source of critical reflection.

Wade, Peter (2004) "Globalization and Appropriation in Latin American Popular Music." *Latin American Research Review* 39(1): 273–284.
Review article introducing and appraising recent scholarship in the field.

Glossary

A cappella   Solo or group singing without instruments.

Anhemitonic   Without semitones; a scale or mode in which the distance between all steps is a tone or more.

Atuel   South Sudanese Dinka clapping sticks.

Azmari   Ethiopian folk-poets; formerly itinerant rural bards, today they more commonly perform in urban music houses (*Azmari bet*), accompanying themselves on the *massenqo* fiddle. Their improvised lyrics may make veiled critiques of power holders.

Balafon   Wooden xylophone used in Mande music.

Baqsy   A term widespread across Central Asia, used to refer to bards (singers of epic tales) or ritual healers who may undertake shamanic-style spiritual journeys enabled by their music.

Bar mitzvah   Jewish coming-of-age ceremony.

Bàtá   Yorùbá drum ensemble comprising at least three drums: the *ìyáàlù* (mother drum), *the omele abo* (female accompanying drum) and the *omele akọ* (male accompanying drum). The *ìyáàlù* can "talk" by imitating the rhythms of speech, and three small *omele akọ* may be tied together to emulate the three tones of Yorùbá speech.

Batería   Musical ensemble used in Capoeira Angola, composed of eight instruments: three *berimbau* musical bows, and a percussion section consisting of two *pandeiro* tambourines, one *agogô* bell, one *reco reco* bamboo scraper and an *atabaque* foot drum.

Bebop   Style of jazz developed in the early to mid-1940s, based on smaller ensembles that shifted the focus away from the intricate arrangements of the large swing bands to improvisation and group interaction.

Biwa   Japanese short-necked fretted lute, with four or five strings, played with a large plectrum, often used to accompany narrative storytelling.

Büwi   Muslim female ritual specialists among the Uyghurs of East Turkestan.

Cadence   A melodic or harmonic pattern that closes a musical phrase.

Call-and-response   Alternating, sometimes overlapping, phrases usually sung by a solo and group.

Candomblé   West African religion brought to Brazil by people who had been enslaved.

Canon   Body of musical works considered most representative or important and influential within a given genre.

Capoeira Angola   A Brazilian art form developed by African slaves, it combines physical play, characterized by kicks, escapes, head butts, and sweeps, with music.

Chant   Speech with rhythmic or melodic regularities, a heightened or stylized form of speech, often repetitive, often associated with religious practice.

Changdan   Korean metrical pattern, literally "long-short."

Chord   A set of three or more pitches sounded simultaneously to create a harmonic effect.

Coda   From Western classical music. A passage that extends and then closes a piece of music.

Compound metre   Meter in which the pulse is subdivided into threes.

Cowbell   Metal bell with clapper used for cattle but also as a percussion instrument.

Cumbia   Popular dance form originally from Colombia but found throughout Latin America.

Dalang   Balinese puppeteer, singer and storyteller; a man of knowledge and skill, who may also serve as a priest (*manku dalang*) with the power to call on the gods and conduct purificatory rituals.

Dancehall   A genre of Jamaican popular music that originated in the late 1970s.

Devadāsī   Indian tradition of female temple dancers and musicians, who were stigmatized and marginalized in the early twentieth century.

Dhikr   Meditative practice associated with Muslim Sufi orders, involving the repeated chanting of the names of God or phrases from the Qur'an accompanied by ritualized body movements and rhythmic breathing.

Diatonic   Term used to describe scales, melody, harmony, and styles based on the pitches derived from the heptatonic (seven-note) Western scale.

Disco   Genre of dance music that developed among alternative communities in New York City and Philadelphia during the late 1960s. The disco sound features soaring vocals over a steady four beat, and a lush synthesized orchestral mix.

Dissonance   Term used in the harmonic theory of the Western art music tradition to describe a combination of tones that sounds harsh or unpleasant, and hence unstable, producing tension that demands an onward motion to a stable chord.

Distortion   In music, literally any change made to a waveform; effects produced in studio recording to imitate feedback or excessive gain from an amp; they are integral to the rock guitar sound, and important in other genres such as electric blues and jazz fusion.

Dizi   Chinese transverse bamboo flute.

Djembe   Skin-covered goblet drum, tuned with ropes and played with the hands.

Dombyra   Small, long-necked, fretted, plucked lute, with two strings made of gut or nylon, found in parts of Central Asia including Kazakhstan, used to play instrumental pieces, or accompany bardic singing.

Duple metre   Meter in which the main pulse is grouped into twos.

Dutar   Long-necked, fretted, plucked lute, related to the dombra, with two strings made of silk nylon, played by Central Asian peoples including Uyghurs, used to accompany singing.

EDM   Electronic dance music. A variety of dance music genres created and used by DJs for nightclubs and other dance environments. Although the use of synthesizers and electronic dance music dates back much earlier, the genre grew in popularity from the 1990s.

Ethiojazz   1970s popular Ethiopian genre, based in the capital Addis Ababa, which set traditional *Azmari* songs to a brass-heavy jazz accompaniment. More recently popularized in the West by the *Ethiopiques* series from Buda Records.

Flageoletto   Technique for producing harmonics on a stringed instrument, by bowing near the bridge and lightly fingering the strings.

Free jazz   Approach to jazz music developed in the 1950s and 1960s, usually considered experimental and avant garde; free jazz musicians attempted to change or break down the established conventions of jazz.

Fuke   One of the sects of Japanese Zen Buddhism.

Gaikyoku   "Foreign" or "disorderly" pieces in traditional Japanese music, i.e., secular entertainment pieces.

Gamelan   Ensemble from Bali or Java in Indonesia, whose instruments are mostly made of bronze: gongs, rows of small gong kettles, and instruments with metal keys in rows like xylophones.

Gendér wayang   A small quartet of bronze metallophones, used in Bali to accompany the shadow play (*wayang kulit*).

Glissando   A slide from one pitch to another.

Grace note   A very short note played to decorate a principal note.

Griot   West African hereditary bards in the Mande cultural world.

Groove   Musicking in synchrony, rhythmic entrainment, equivalent to "swing" or "flow."

Güiro   A Latin American scraped percussion instrument, consisting of an open-ended, hollow gourd with notches cut in one side.

Harmony   The simultaneous combining of pitches to create musical interest.

Heptatonic scale   A scale of seven pitches.

Heterophonic   Two or more musicians perform the same melody simultaneously, each ornamenting or otherwise interpreting it in a slightly different way.

Hōgaku   Japanese national music.

Honkyoku   Lit. "original" pieces in the Japanese *shakuhachi* repertoire, derived from the repertoire of *komusō* Buddhist monks during the Edo period (1603–1867).

Hybridity   Literally "mixing" between separate races or cultures; a term associated with post-colonial discourse and critiques of cultural imperialism.

Improvisation   Musical creativity in the course of performance.

ICH   Intangible Cultural Heritage, as recognized by UNESCO: "traditions or living expressions inherited from our ancestors and passed on to our descendants, such as oral traditions, performing arts, social practices, rituals, festive events, knowledge and practices."

Interlocking parts   Where musicians sound individual notes or small motifs alternately, to create a combined mono- or polyphonic texture, they are said to interlock or hocket. The texture resulting is called interlocking.

Jelimuso   Female *griot/s* (hereditary bards) of the West African Mande cultural world.

Kayagŭm   Korean 12-string half-tube plucked zither supported by 12 movable bridges. The player plucks and flicks the strings with the right hand, and presses down the strings to the left of the movable bridges with the left hand.

Klezmer   Jewish musical tradition that developed in Eastern Europe, now global. Best known for the dance tunes and instrumental display pieces for weddings and other celebrations.

Kora   West African 21-string harp, made from a large calabash and covered with cow skin, with a long hardwood neck. The strings run in two parallel ranks, held in place by notches on a bridge.

Koto   Japanese zither, with 13 strings strung over 13 moveable bridges.

Krar   Five- or six-stringed bowl-shaped lyre from Eritrea and Ethiopia, often decorated with beads or colored thread. The instrument is tuned to a pentatonic scale, and can be bowed, plucked, or strummed.

Küi   A genre of programmatic music found among nomadic peoples of Central Asia, in which a story is depicted solely by means of instrumental sound.

Ladainha   Song or "litany" that introduces play in Capoeira Angola. It often has a prayer-like or reflective quality, and is sung as a solo.

Lor   Small southern Sudanese Dinka drum.

Linear   A term used to describe the progression of music in time, often applied to melody, as opposed to simultaneously sounded "vertical" harmony.

Maqām   System of melodic modes used in Arabic music; literally "place," or "position"; defines the pitches, patterns, and development of a piece of music, provides the basis for improvisation.

Massenqo   Single-stringed, Ethiopian spike fiddle, often played by *Azmari* bards.

Measure   Equivalent to metrical unit, or bar.

Melisma   A singing style in which one syllable is sung to several different pitches in succession (as opposed to syllabic singing, where there is one pitch per syllable).

Melody/melodic   Succession of tones that form a single musical entity; a combination of pitch and rhythm.

Meri/Kari   Terms given to notes with a particular sound quality on the *shakuhachi*, produced by altering the angle of the head in relation to the instrument.

Metallophone   Any musical instrument consisting of tuned metal bars that are struck to make sound.

Meter (UK **metre**)   The consistent grouping of pulse beats into larger metrical units.

Microtone   Interval smaller than a semitone.

Minor   A variant of the Western diatonic scale, with a flattened 3rd degree, often considered to sound sad.

Mixing   Audio mixing is a creative process in which multiple recorded sounds are combined into one or more channels. In the process, the source signal's level, frequency content, dynamics, and panoramic position are manipulated, and effects such as reverb may be added.

Mode   A scale combined with specific melodic characteristics, such as strong and weak scale-degrees, melodic motifs, characteristic ornaments etc., and often having aesthetic or extra-musical associations.

Motif   A recurring melodic fragment or succession of notes.

Muezzin   The person who gives the call to prayer in Muslim societies.

Muraiki   Aesthetic effect in *shakuhachi* music, achieved by blowing a diffuse air stream to create a loud breathy sound.

Musiqa   Arabic term; derives from the same root as the English "music" but is more narrowly defined, usually implying instrumental music and not normally used with reference to Islamic sounded practices.

Musique concrète   Electro-acoustic music based on the manipulation of recorded sounds (natural or manmade, including musical sounds) as well as sounds purely electronically produced. A branch of Western contemporary music composition developed from the 1940s onwards, particularly associated with the French composer Pierre Schaeffer.

Notation   A system for representing musical sound through written symbols, spoken or sung syllables, gestures, etc.

Nuclear note   A pitch or pitches that are given more prominence in a scale, and to which a melody often returns, e.g., a tonic in the Western diatonic scale.

Nyama   An esoteric force or power contained within Mande cultural expressions.

Onomatopoeia   In linguistics, this term refers to a word that phonetically imitates, resembles, or suggests the source of the sound that it describes. It is also sometimes used in music to denote sound mimesis.

Oral transmission   Where musical knowledge, repertoire and practices are passed between generations without reliance on notation.

Òrìṣà (Orixá)   West African deities that derive from natural forces, historical figures, or craft lineages. Their worship is central to Yorùbá *bàtá* ritual drumming that summons the *òrìṣà* into the bodies of devotees. They are also referenced in songs within the Brazilian Capoeira Angola tradition.

Ornamentation   Musical embellishments that are not necessary to carry the overall line of the melody but serve instead to decorate or "ornament" the line.

Oud   Six-stringed, short-necked, fretless, pear-shaped lute, widely played across the Middle East.

Parallel (motion)   Where the movement of a melodic line is replicated at a certain interval above or below.

P'ansori   A Korean genre of musical storytelling performed by a vocalist and a drummer playing the *puk* barrel drum.

Pentatonic scale   A scale of five pitches.

Pitch   The quality of a sound that is described as "high" or "low," depending on the frequency of vibration that causes the sound (the "high/low" metaphor is not universal cross-culturally). Sounds of stable pitch can be arranged in order of "height" to form a scale.

Polyphony   Music that simultaneously combines several melodic lines; two or more different melodies sung or played simultaneously.

Psalm   Liturgical texts, gathered in the Hebrew bible, on themes of praising God, kingship, and laments; their sung performance is an important part of Jewish and Christian worship.

Psychedelic soul   A sub-genre of soul music, which mixes the characteristics of soul with psychedelic rock. It came to prominence in the late 1960s and continued into the 1970s, playing a major role in the development of funk music and disco.

Puk   Korean barrel drum.

Pulse   A regular beat, which may be grouped into larger units (bars or measures) to form the basis of musical meter.

Qasida   Poetic form found widespread across the Islamic world.

Qobyz   Kazakh two-stringed horsehair fiddle, hollowed out from a single piece of wood, with an open resonator, and a lower extension covered with camel skin.

R&B   Rhythm and blues, a genre of popular African-American music that originated in the 1940s. Term originally used by record companies to describe recordings marketed predominantly to urban African-Americans.

Rāga   Melodic mode in Indian classical music, and the basis for improvisation, literally "passion" or "delight." A rāga is not only a scale configuration but also possesses unique aesthetic qualities that might include strong and weak scale degrees, melodic motifs, or characteristic ornaments on particular scale-degrees.

Recitative   A style of vocal delivery usually associated with Western opera that is closer to the rhythms of ordinary speech, and distinguished from the more melodic "aria."

Reggaeton   Dance form popular throughout Latin America and the Caribbean, closely associated with Puerto Rico.

Requiem   Mass for the Dead: a ritual in the Christian tradition offered for the repose of a soul; associated musical compositions in the Western classical tradition.

Reverb   A popular recording effect used to digitally simulate a natural echo chamber, where a large number of acoustic reflections build up and then decay.

Rhythm   The temporal dimension of music in general: the organization of events successively in time; a specific pattern or sequence of durations and accents.

Ryū   School or guild; organized institutions of craftspeople or musicians in Japan.

Sama debate   Discussion within Islam on the religious acceptability of different types of musical practice.

Sampling The practice of taking a portion, or "sample," of one sound recording and reusing it in a new composition; most commonly associated with hip hop and electronic dance music.

Scale A consistent set of stable pitches arranged in ascending and/or descending order.

Scat Jazz vocal improvisation using wordless vocables.

Semitone A musical interval measured as 100 cents. The chromatic scale of 12 equal semitones to the octave is the basic pitch system for Western tonal music.

Shakuhachi Japanese end-blown flute, normally made of bamboo, used by the monks of the Fuke school of Zen Buddhism, and also in ensemble music and contemporary compositions.

Shamisen Three-stringed Japanese fretless lute, plucked with a large plectrum. Played in instrumental ensembles, to accompany various sung genres and drama.

Shofar Musical instrument of ancient origin, usually made of a ram's horn, used for Jewish religious purposes. Pitch is controlled by varying the player's embouchure. The *shofar* is blown as part of synagogue services on Rosh Hashanah and Yom Kippur.

Simple metre Meter in which the pulse is subdivided in twos.

Sléndro Five-note scale, used in gamelan music, in which the distances between the notes are slightly larger than a tone.

Sound mimesis The imitation of natural sounds, which might include animal or bird cries, wind or water; sometimes linked to shamanic ritual practices in which the mimetic sounds summon the spirits they imitate.

Sufism The mystical dimension of Islam; follower of an organized Sufi order formed around a master, who meet regularly to perform the spiritual practice of remembrance (*dhikr*).

Sumu Mande music parties, organized by women for women to mark lifecycle events.

Surrogate speech Where the melody and rhythm of spoken words are mimicked in instrumental music.

Syncopated "Off-beat" rhythmic stresses or accents, i.e. placement where they would not normally be expected to occur; fundamental to jazz and most forms of dance music.

Synthesizer An electronic instrument, usually played with a keyboard, which generates and modifies sounds electronically; it can imitate a variety of other musical instruments or generate new timbres.

Tāla Rhythmic mode, or meter, in Indian classical music, often indicated by a drum pattern or a sequence of hand gestures.

Tanso   Small Korean end-blown flute.

Tango   Globally popular dance form, closely associated with Argentina.

Texture   The way different "lines" or "voices" combine to create a total sound; closely related to the way performers interact during performance.

Timbre   Also known as tone color; the quality of a sound other than pitch or volume. Timbre is linked to the frequency spectrum of a sound, its attack and decay, and level of vibrato. Commonly used terms to describe timbre include: bright, dark, warm, harsh, or rich.

Tone   A pitched sound event occurring in a musical performance or composition, or in a musical system, often used interchangeably with "note" or "pitch." It can also refer to the interval of two semitones or the aesthetic quality of sound ("this violin has a beautiful tone"). "Speech tone" refers to pitched syllables found in tonal languages.

Tonic   The tonal center of a piece of music; the starting point of the scale.

Tritone   Musical interval composed of three adjacent whole tones.

T'ungso/t'ongso   Korean end-blown flute with a distinctively raspy timbre.

Variation   A compositional or improvisational technique where musical material is repeated in an altered form.

Vibrato   Regular, pulsating slight variations in pitch.

Vocables   Sung syllables that do not have any dictionary meaning, often described as "non-lexical vocables."

Washint   Ethiopian end-blown wooden flute, generally with four finger holes to play a pentatonic scale. Players often carry multiple flutes to fit different tunings.

Xiao/dongxiao   Chinese end-blown notched flute.

List of Contributors

Geoffrey Baker is Reader in Musicology and Ethnomusicology at Royal Holloway University of London. He specializes in music in Latin America, and he has published extensively on colonial Peru, including the award-winning book *Imposing Harmony: Music and Society in Colonial Cuzco* (Duke University Press, 2008). Geoffrey also works on contemporary urban music, and has published a book *Buena Vista in the Club: Rap, Reggaeton, and Revolution in Havana* (Duke University Press, 2011). He was co-investigator on the SOAS-based AHRC-funded project "Growing into Music."

Saida Daukeyeva has headed the Folklore Research Laboratory at the Kurmangazy Kazakh National Conservatory in Almaty, and is currently a Georg Forster Research Fellow (HERMES) at Humboldt University in Berlin. She holds a PhD in Ethnomusicology from SOAS, University of London. She is the author of *Philosophy of Music by Abu Nasr Muhammad al-Farabi* (Soros Foundation-Kazakhstan, 2002) and a co-editor of the textbook *Music of Central Asia* (Indiana University Press, 2015). Her research examines the construction of meaning, memory, place, and identity in Kazakh *qobyz* and *dombyra* performance and ritual practice.

Kiku Day is a postdoctoral fellow at the Interacting Minds Centre, Aarhus University in Denmark and a *jinashi shakuhachi* player in the Zensabō style. She obtained a Masters in Performance and Literature at Mills College, California, and her PhD in Ethnomusicology at SOAS, University of London. Her research focuses on the use of the *shakuhachi* today. Research topics have included the creative process during collaborations with composers, *shakuhachi* as represented on the internet, and meditation and *shakuhachi*.

Lucy Duran (PhD SOAS) is Senior Lecturer in African Music at SOAS, University of London. She has been researching Mande music in Mali, Gambia, and Senegal since 1977, with special reference to the *jelis* ("*griots*"), women singers, and the *kora*. She led the AHRC project "Growing into Music." She has also been music producer of more than 15 albums by leading Malian artists including Bassekou Kouyaté and Toumani Diabaté, with two Grammy nominations.

Nicholas Gray is Senior Lecturer in Ethnomusicology at SOAS, University of London, and author of *Improvisation and Composition in Balinese Gendér Wayang: Music of the Moving Shadows* (Ashgate, 2011). He is also a composer and performer, and studied *gendér wayang* for several years with I. Wayan Loceng in Sukawati, a village in south Bali famed for its shadow puppetry and the complexity of its *gendér* style.

Rachel Harris is Reader in the Music of China and Central Asia at SOAS, University of London. Her research interests include global musical flows, identity politics, and Islamic soundscapes. She is the author of two books on musical life in China's Xinjiang Uyghur Autonomous Region, and leader of the research project "Sounding Islam in China." She is actively engaged with outreach projects relating to Central Asian and Chinese music, including recordings, musical performance, and consultancy.

Angela Impey is Senior Lecturer in Ethnomusicology at SOAS, University of London. One strand of her research concerns the revival of the Jew's harp in southern Africa. She worked on the AHRC-funded project "Metre and Melody in Dinka Speech and Song" in South Sudan, and is currently co-investigator on an AHRC research project in west Namibia entitled "Future Pasts in an Apocalyptic Moment."

Zoë Marriage is Senior Lecturer in Development Studies at SOAS, University of London. She has researched extensively in countries affected by conflict in Africa and is the author of *Not Breaking the Rules, Not Playing the Game. International Assistance to Countries at War* (Hurst & Co., 2006). More recently Zoë has focused on the relationship between security and development in the Democratic Republic of Congo, and she is currently working on a political economy of capoeira, the Brazilian dance-fight-game.

Caspar Melville is Lecturer in Global Creative and Cultural Industries at SOAS University of London. His PhD research, undertaken at Goldsmiths College, London, explored the development of multi-racial club culture in London. He has previously worked as a music journalist and as editor of the magazine *New Humanist*. He is the author of *Taking Offence* (Seagull Books, 2012).

Rowan Pease completed her PhD on music of the ethnic Koreans living in China in 2001. She previously lived and worked in Hong Kong and China. She is editorial manager of *The China Quarterly* and has served for many years as a Senior Teaching Fellow for the Department of Music, SOAS, University of London. She has published several chapters on music of the Chinese Koreans and also on the Korean Wave in China. She is currently completing a project on music of the Cultural Revolution.

Amanda Villepastour is an ethnomusicologist in the School of Music, Cardiff University, Wales. Her research interests include music and linguistics, religion and gender in Africa and the Caribbean, with a specialization in Yorùbá music in Nigeria and the Cuban diaspora. She is the author of *Ancient Text Messages of the Yorùbá Bàtá Drum: Cracking the Code* (Ashgate, 2010) and editor of *"The Yorùbá God of Drumming: Transatlantic Perspectives on the Wood that Talks"* (University Press of Mississippi, 2015).

Ilana Webster-Kogen is Joe Loss Lecturer in Jewish Music at SOAS, University of London. Her work focuses on music across the Ethiopian diaspora, with emphasis on Afro-diasporic popular music in Tel Aviv. Her writing is published in *Ethnomusicology Forum*, the *Journal of African Cultural Studies*, and *African and Black Diaspora*.

Richard Widdess is Professor of Musicology at SOAS, University of London. His research focuses on music as a non-verbal expressive system, and in developing tools for analyzing musical structure and meaning. His regional interests focus on South Asia, particularly classical and religious music traditions of northern India and Nepal. His books include *Dāphā: Sacred Singing in a South Asian City* (Ashgate, 2014) and, with R. Sanyal *Dhrupad. Tradition and Performance in Indian Music* (Ashgate, 2004).

Abigail Wood, a graduate of Cambridge University, taught at SOAS for several years before moving to the University of Haifa to teach ethnomusicology. She has published widely on urban musics, including a recent book on Yiddish song in contemporary North America. Her current research focuses on sounds and music in the public sphere in Jerusalem's Old City.

Index

Page numbers in **bold** refer to figures.

eBooks
from Taylor & Francis

Helping you to choose the right eBooks for your Library

Add to your library's digital collection today with Taylor & Francis eBooks. We have over 50,000 eBooks in the Humanities, Social Sciences, Behavioural Sciences, Built Environment and Law, from leading imprints, including Routledge, Focal Press and Psychology Press.

Free Trials Available
We offer free trials to qualifying academic, corporate and government customers.

Choose from a range of subject packages or create your own!

Benefits for you
- Free MARC records
- COUNTER-compliant usage statistics
- Flexible purchase and pricing options
- All titles DRM-free.

Benefits for your user
- Off-site, anytime access via Athens or referring URL
- Print or copy pages or chapters
- Full content search
- Bookmark, highlight and annotate text
- Access to thousands of pages of quality research at the click of a button.

eCollections

Choose from over 30 subject eCollections, including:

Archaeology	Language Learning
Architecture	Law
Asian Studies	Literature
Business & Management	Media & Communication
Classical Studies	Middle East Studies
Construction	Music
Creative & Media Arts	Philosophy
Criminology & Criminal Justice	Planning
Economics	Politics
Education	Psychology & Mental Health
Energy	Religion
Engineering	Security
English Language & Linguistics	Social Work
Environment & Sustainability	Sociology
Geography	Sport
Health Studies	Theatre & Performance
History	Tourism, Hospitality & Events

For more information, pricing enquiries or to order a free trial, please contact your local sales team:
www.tandfebooks.com/page/sales

www.tandfebooks.com